A cat is...

# ...a masterpiece of design

A cat is perfectly designed to live and hunt in a three-dimensional world. It can clear five times its own height in a single jump. Its narrow chest enables a cat to move forward freely, silently, and accurately, placing one foot in front of the other. The cat's mobile backbone, in which each bone is loosely attached to the next, allows it to bend itself in half, rotating half of its back through a full 180 degrees relative to the other half—ideal for washing.

**In order to allow** the cat to run swiftly, its front legs are liberated from the shoulders by not having an attached collarbone. This "design feature"—often referred to as a floating shoulder—means that the legs are able to act as shock absorbers when a cat jumps down from a height.

# ...a sharp observer

A cat has beautiful, large eyes that give it incredible peripheral vision to detect both predator and prey. The eye's surface, the cornea, bulges out dramatically; this gives a wider angle of view and allows much more light to get in—about five times as much as gets into our eyes. The eye's internal cell structure is modified to enhance the vision of an animal that hunts primarily at dawn and dusk, when color vision is not a priority—and so a cat does not see all colors: the retina is sensitive only to blue and green, not to red. The eyes have a large number of cells that detect the slightest motion, and lenses that can resolve into sharp focus when needed. Superb binocular vision gives pinpoint accuracy when pouncing on prey.

**The pupil can dilate** to 90 percent of the eye area, allowing maximum light to enter and enhancing night vision. The pupil also dilates when a cat is frightened. In normal light, the pupil moves like the shutter on a camera, and it is capable of reducing to a narrow perpendicular slit in intense sunlight. The ability of the pupils to constrict or dilate so dramatically is far superior to even the most sophisticated of polarized sunglasses.

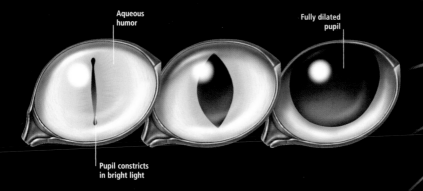

Aqueous humor

Fully dilated pupil

Pupil constricts in bright light

# ...a miniature panther

In both its anatomy and its behavior, the cat shares common characteristics with its larger feline relatives. All cats, large or small, must feed exclusively on vertebrate prey—they cannot survive without eating animal protein and fat. While some large cats, like the lion, have developed cooperative skills to capture large mammals, the domestic cat is a lone hunter, stalking and pouncing on prey. The domestic cat, in common with the leopard, patrols and defends its hunting territory. And just as the black panther is a black-coated variety of leopard, so black and other natural colors occur in the cat. However, in the case of the cat the range of these colors has been deliberately increased through selective breeding.

**All the domestic cat's** wild relations create and defend their own distinct territories. When cats from adjacent territories have chance encounters, injuries are avoided through displays of inten such as arched backs, bared teeth and bristled fur. They also stare eac other down, until one cat turns its head and breaks eye contact. It signals that it will withdraw, but an abrupt movement now provokes a lashing response from the victor. domestic cat disputes, this is whe the vanquished cat is bitten on its tail as it leaves the scene.

# ...an expert hunter

A cat has exemplary patience. Its favored hunting strategy is to scent a good hunting ground, sit, and wait. When prey appears, the cat pounces, pinning the prey with its forepaws. When hunting birds, a cat uses ground cover to stalk from, inching forward, freezing if it thinks it has been detected, until finally it sprints, leaps, springs, or pounces. If it is hungry, a cat kills its prey swiftly. A cat's canine teeth are perfectly formed to slip between the neck vertebrae of small rodents, killing instantly. After a successful hunt a cat may literally dance with delight, making high, curving, tension-relieving leaps in the air.

**When a cat catches sight of its prey,** it approaches stealthily, its belly close to the ground. When it is close enough to attempt a capture, it stops and awaits its opportunity. Its hind legs are spring-loaded in anticipation and, when "the moment" arises, they propel the cat toward the unfortunate victim, which is grasped with the forepaws.

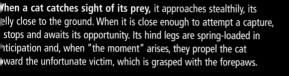

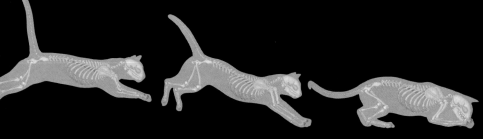

# ...a fastidious groomer

A cat spends 30 percent of its waking hours grooming itself or grooming other cats in its social group. Grooming does more than cleanse the hair of the remainders of a kill or remove skin parasites. It stimulates sebaceous gland secretions, necessary to maintain water-proofing. It cools the body through evaporation of saliva. Saliva accounts for one third of all daily body water loss. Whereas an indecisive person will scratch his or her head, an indecisive cat grooms itself.

**The cat's barbed tongue** is ideal for grooming its coat because the dead hair sticks to the tongue. However, swallowing this hair leads to hairballs, a problem that is worst in longhaired cats.

**When face-washing,** saliva is applied to the inside of a paw, which is then rubbed in a semi-circular motion on the face. More saliva is applied and the next part of the face is cleansed. This process is repeated with the other side of the face with the other paw.

**Kittens, like adult cats,** sleep for many hours of the day. In kittens, however, we know that there is a good reason for this: growth hormone is only released when the kitten is asleep.

# ...fond of sleeping

A cat spends almost twice as much time asleep as most other mammals—almost two thirds of its life. The amount of time it sleeps depends on how hungry it is. Warmth, security, and a full stomach induce sleep at almost any time. Most sleep—almost 75 percent— is light sleep. If a cat hears anything, there is increased electrical activity in the brain. The remaining 25 percent of sleep is deep sleep. Under partly or wholly closed eyelids, the eyes flicker rapidly, the paws flex, and the whiskers twitch. The brain is as active as when a cat is awake. Its dreams during deep sleep are known only to itself.

# Cat
# Owner's
# Manual

DR. BRUCE FOGLE

A DK PUBLISHING BOOK

**Dorling Kindersley**
LONDON, NEW YORK, MUNICH,
MELBOURNE, and DELHI

For Dorling Kindersley
Managing Editor **Deirdre Headon**
Managing Art Editor **Lee Griffiths**
Senior Art Editor **Wendy Bartlet**
Senior Editors **Heather Jones, Amber Tokeley, Simon Tuite**
DTP Designer **Louise Waller**
Production Manager **Lauren Britton**
Production Controller **Mandy Inness**
Picture Librarian **Hayley Smith**
Picture Researcher **Anna Grapes**
Jacket Designer **Nathalie Godwin**
US Editors **Christine Heilman, Margaret Parrish**

Produced for Dorling Kindersley by
**Sands Publishing Solutions LLP**
4 Jenner Way, Eccles, Aylesford,
Kent ME20 7SQ, United Kingdom

The *Cat Owner's Manual* provides general information on a wide range of animal health and veterinary topics. The book is not a substitute for advice from a qualified veterinary practitioner. You are advised always to consult your veterinary surgeon or other appropriate expert if you have specific questions in relation to your pet's health. Before administering any medicine or any treatment to your pet, you should ensure that you always read and follow the instructions contained in the information leaflet. The naming of any organization, product, or alternative therapy in this book does not imply endorsement by the publisher and the omission of any such names does not indicate disapproval. The publisher regrets it cannot accept any responsibility for acts or omissions based on the information in this book.

First American Edition, 2003
04  05  06  07   10 9 8 7 6 5 4 3

First published in the United States by
DK Publishing, Inc.
375 Hudson Street, New York, New York 10014
Copyright © 2003 Dorling Kindersley Limited, London
Text copyright © 2003 Bruce Fogle

Library of Congress Cataloging-in-Publication Data

Fogle, Bruce.
   Cat owner's manual / Bruce Fogle.
   p. cm.
   ISBN 0-7894-9320-9 (alk paper)
   1. Cats. I. Title.

SF447 .F62 2003
636.8'0887--dc21
                                        2002041145

Color reproduction by Colourscan
Printed and bound in Slovakia by Tlaciarne BB

For our complete product line visit
**www.dk.com**

# Contents

## Introduction  19

C H A P T E R   O N E
## Cat design 20

C H A P T E R   T W O
## Breeds 48

C H A P T E R   T H R E E
# Behavior 130

C H A P T E R   F O U R
# Living with your cat 162

C H A P T E R   F I V E
# Health concerns 208

# Introduction

The cat is incredible. In North America and Europe there are now more pet cats than pet dogs—over 175 million of them. But there are also more unowned or feral cats than owned felines. The domestic cat remains a self-sufficient, independent species and our least understood domestic animal. Our lack of understanding is simple: the way a cat thinks is dramatically different from the way we think. It is true that we've selectively bred cats to be at ease in human company, that we've enhanced the "kitten" in adult cats, but the domestic cat is the world's most successful feline because it has the genetic plasticity to adapt to the environment of the world's most successful primate, us. Most of the information in this book concentrates on the relationship we have with our cats and they have with us. From my perspective as a practicing vet, that relationship is at its most intense emotionally when a cat is unwell. It is up to us to ensure their physical and emotional well-being.

DR. BRUCE FOGLE
DVM, MRCVS

# CHAPTER ONE

# Cat design

Watch a cat stalk prey and the sophistication of feline design is obvious. Internally, the skeleton, muscles, nerves, and joints are designed for sudden bursts of energy, its digestive system is specialized to cope only with animal sources of nutrition, and its body wastes are adapted for use in communication with other cats. Its brain gives it the ability to learn throughout life, and its sensory abilities are outstanding. Its exquisite balance is adapted for climbing and living in a three-dimensional world. Its ability to hear and smell evolved to help it capture small mammals such as mice. Its design makes it almost the perfect carnivore.

# Origins

- Domestic cats first appeared 6,000 years ago
- Temperamental changes helped ensure successful cohabitation
- Popularity in Egypt made the cat an exportable product

Like other domestic animals, the cat is self-domesticated: it chose to live in close proximity to people because it was in its interests to do so. In order to infiltrate human settlements, the cat's ancestors underwent both physical and behavioral changes, creating the most successful ever of all the species of cat: the domestic cat.

### The birthplace of the domestic cat

Although the history of the cat is best documented in ancient Egypt, this was not necessarily its first domestic home. A cat's tooth from 9000 BC was found in Jericho, Israel. Wildcats did not inhabit Cyprus, so feline remains from before 5000 BC found on the

**This wall painting,** from c. 1290–1180 BC, was found at Beni Hasan, Egypt. It is the first artwork to show a cat in a domestic setting, crouching under a chair.

Mediterranean island suggest that cats were taken there, perhaps even as pets.

The earliest remains in Egypt to show affection between cats and people date from before 4000 BC. At a burial ground in Mostagedda, Middle Egypt, a man was buried with a gazelle and a small cat; Egyptologists believe that the gazelle was meant as his funerary meal and that the cat was his pet.

Egypt's first permanent human settlements, along the fertile floodplains of the Nile River, appeared around 4000 BC. With their granaries and silos, the settlements offered rodents and edible waste, as well as shelter and safety from larger predators, to any cat able and willing to take advantage of them.

Two small cats, the African wildcat (*Felis silvestris lybica*) and the jungle cat (*Felis chaus*), lived in this region. The less fearful African wildcat may have entered this new environment in search of prey.

A minor genetic mutation, perhaps involving the hormonal control of emotions, created a cat with a unique survival advantage: an ability to live and breed in human settlements.

### Adapt and survive

Environmental pressures meant that the wildcat underwent character changes. Placidity became an asset, since only the most placid and least fearful cats could survive in close proximity to so many people and animals.

**In its natural environment,** the African wildcat faces fierce competition for mates, prey, and territory. The domestic cat's origins may be found in a slight genetic mutation—reduced fear—in one family of wildcat.

There were also physical changes. Since camouflage was no longer needed, coat pattern and color mutations that would not have survived in the wild were perpetuated in the settlement cats. The gastrointestinal system changed to cope with a more varied diet; the domestic cat's intestines are longer than the wildcat's. The brain became almost 30 percent smaller because the cat was no longer so dependent upon its senses for survival.

## The road to success

Cats were appreciated as vermin-killers, but they also served another purpose. Rats and mice were devastating pests, but poisonous snakes were lethal, so wildcats were tolerated or even openly welcomed for their willingness to hunt cobras and vipers as well as rodents. The cat became increasingly popular because of its doubly protective role.

The absorption of the domesticated cat into Egyptian society seems to have been complete by about 2000 BC. The ancient Egyptians developed a deep respect and understanding of cats and

their behavior, and in time the cat became a prominent symbol in religion and superstition, its image being used on a huge variety of objects.

The domestic cat was now exportable: at first, only stories and images of the domestic cat were carried around the Mediterranean, but these reports were soon followed by the cats themselves.

### Hybrid theories

Among the many mummified feline remains found at Beni Hasan, Egypt, are several large skeletons of the marsh-dwelling jungle cat *Felis chaus*. This has led some to speculate that the domestic cat is in fact an evolutionary hybrid of the African wildcat and the jungle cat. However, Professor Eric Hurley's genetic studies of the cat, which use minute examinations of gene sequences, suggest that the domestic cat is genetically far too similar to the African wildcat to be a hybrid with any other species, including the jungle cat.

**JUNGLE CAT (*FELIS CHAUS*)**

# Skin, coat, and hair

■ Skin and hair have important life-preserving functions
■ Environmental differences are reflected by a cat's coat
■ Skin is a cat's first line of defense

A cat's skin is its first line of defense, keeping harmful microorganisms from entering the body. Millions of nerve endings detect heat, cold, and pain, while a profusion of blood vessels helps a cat to regulate its body temperature.

### Coat structure

The surface of a cat's hair consists of overlapping cuticle cells that reflect light and help to give the coat its sheen. A dull coat may signify cuticle damage.

Cats have compound hair follicles: up to six primary (guard) hairs grow from each follicle, each surrounded by finer, secondary (down and awn) hairs. This provides efficient insulation. Each follicle has its own muscle, which can

make the primary hairs stand on end. Cats "raise their hackles" when alarmed or angry, but also to reduce heat loss.

Two types of hair are specialized for sensation. The whiskers (vibrissae) are thick, stiff hairs found on the head, throat, and forelegs. Other large, single hairs (tylotrichs) are scattered over the skin and act like short whiskers.

### Coats for climates

Northern-climate breeds have dense coats with insulating down. When cold, the hair erects, trapping a layer of air that will keep the cat warm. Conversely, cats living in hot climates shed their

**Northern-climate breeds** are densely coated, with a layer of insulating down. They also have a layer of fat under the skin for extra insulation.

coat of down hair. Blood vessels in the skin dilate, speeding the loss of body heat. Cats do not sweat, but they lick their fur to lose heat; the evaporating saliva carries away body heat.

Cats are equipped with great defenses against heat and cold, but they are still prone to heat prostration and frostbite. Like dogs, they die quickly if trapped inside a hot car. A cat's fur loses its insulating capacity when wet, so cats are most at risk from hypothermia in freezing, wet weather.

**Without the protection** of a coat, the sphynx is very vulnerable to excessive heat and cold.

## Natural flora and fauna

A cat's skin is colonized by microbes that are vital to the skin's health. Different areas of the skin have different microclimates; those that are often moist or wet, or have dense hair and sweat glands, are most attractive to microbes.

## Skin and hair problems

As a cat's first line of defense, coat and skin are prone to a variety of disorders. Coat problems are obvious because the hair becomes brittle, dry, lusterless, or it falls out. A flea allergy is overwhelmingly the most common skin complaint.

## Skin structure

A cat's skin has two strata: the epidermis and the basal area. Beneath these is the dermis.

Each hair follicle has an associated sebaceous gland that secretes sebum, an oily substance that helps to give hair its sheen. Specialized sebaceous glands around the anus and between the toes may produce

pheromones, or sex scents. Other specialized sebaceous glands on the chin and lips help mark objects.

Single sensory tylotrich hair

Primary hair carries coat coloring

Epidermis, made up of about 40 layers of dead cells

Basal area consists of four layers of living cells

Strong, elastic dermis

Capillary

Special sebaceous gland responds to nervous signals

Down hair (soft, wavy secondary hair)

Awn hair (fine secondary hair)

Smooth surface

Nerve carries signals from skin and hair

Hair follicle

Sebaceous gland secretes skin oil

# Bones and joints

- Cats are built for speed
- Three kinds of joint allow for superb flexibility
- Breeding programs have caused skeletal problems

The feline skeleton evolved for a lifestyle of speed and agility. A cat's slender but robust legs support a narrow rib cage and a highly supple spine. Its shoulder blades are unattached to the main skeleton, permitting superb flexibility at any speed. The entire structure is held together by strong but elastic ligaments.

The hard structure of the skeleton protects the internal organs, provides points of attachment for muscles, and acts as a system of levers and joints necessary for fluid movement.

### The structure and growth of bone

Bones grow continuously during kittenhood. The skull begins as separate bones, to permit birth, then fuses along suture lines. The long bones of the limbs and rib cage begin as hollow cartilage tubes; they calcify in infancy, becoming bone.

Bones increase in length by production of bone at the growth plates, or epiphyses, at their ends. Epiphyses are nourished by a rich supply of tiny arteries. Growth is also influenced by growth and sex hormones. Curiously, the latter seems to inhibit activity: cats neutered very early grow slightly longer leg bones.

If a bone breaks, bone cells produce new bone to bridge the gap.

### Joints

Cats have three different kinds of joints: fibrous, cartilaginous, and synovial. Each has a different level of flexibility and a different function.

• **Fibrous joints:** This type of joint has no flexibility at all. The mandible (jawbone), for example, is really made up of two bones with a fibrous joint at the midline. If a cat lands heavily on its jawbone in a fall, this joint may split;

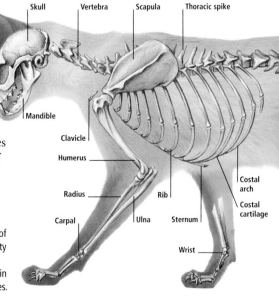

**The cat's skeleton** is a tiny replica of that of the big cats. The vertebrae give great mobility and the forelegs provide superb flexibility. The structure of the wrists allows dexterity in actions such as walking along narrow ledges.

Skull · Vertebra · Scapula · Thoracic spike · Mandible · Clavicle · Humerus · Radius · Rib · Carpal · Ulna · Sternum · Costal arch · Costal cartilage · Wrist

so, although the cat may seem to have broken its jaw, it has, in fact, torn this fibrous joint.

• **Cartilaginous joints:** Some joints, like the thick discs between the spinal vertebrae, are made from tough cartilage. In cats, these are looser and more supple than similar joints in other species, providing a greater degree of flexibility in the torso. During infancy, the growth plates at the ends of the long bones are temporarily cartilaginous joints, and as such they are less sturdy and more prone to damage than in adulthood.

• **Synovial joints:** These are found where the most movement is needed, such as in the legs. They are hinged or ball-and-socket joints, with smooth, articulating cartilage on their contact surfaces, and are surrounded by a joint capsule filled with lubricating synovial fluid. These joints may suffer from excess production of synovial fluid or inflammation due to arthritis or synovitis through injury, disease, or allergy.

## Retractable claws

Claws grow from the last bone of the toe and are anchored by tendons. They consist of modified skin: an outer cuticle of hard protein (keratin) protects the dermis, or quick. Cats' claws are kept sheathed for protection on the move. At rest, ligaments naturally sheath the claws. A cat exposes its claws by contracting digital flexor muscles in its legs, pulling taut the flexor tendons under the paw.

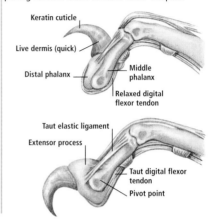

Keratin cuticle

Live dermis (quick)

Distal phalanx

Middle phalanx

Relaxed digital flexor tendon

Taut elastic ligament

Extensor process

Taut digital flexor tendon

Pivot point

## Ligaments

The tough bands that hold bones together, ligaments, are important in all joints, but vital in synovial joints, which are inherently unstable. The hip joint, in particular, is prone to dislocation.

## Skeletal variations and problems

Environmental pressures create natural variations in the cat's skeleton. In hot climates, cats are naturally small, with a higher surface-area-to-weight ratio, which helps cooling. Cats in cold climates have larger, heavier skeletons.

In the wild, severe skeletal anomalies disappear, usually because lethal problems are associated with them.

In recent times, active selection for breed standards has led to more dramatic skeletal variations. This has perpetuated the most considerable, and worrisome, skeletal problems.

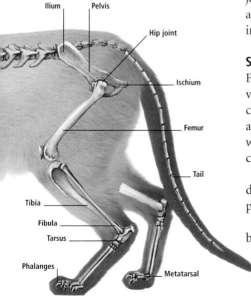

Ilium

Pelvis

Hip joint

Ischium

Femur

Tail

Tibia

Fibula

Tarsus

Phalanges

Metatarsal

# Muscles

■ Fast-acting, flexible muscles ensure graceful movements
■ Cats are good sprinters, but poor endurance athletes
■ The righting reflex allows cats to handle falls from a great height

The cat's balletic grace is due to both its skeleton and its highly flexible muscles, which are divided into three basic types. One is cardiac muscle, found only in the heart. The involuntary muscle that controls the other internal organs is called smooth, or non-striated, because this is how it appears under the microscope. The rest of the body's muscles are called striated, or striped, and are controlled at will in all conscious or instinctive movement.

## Muscle cells

Each individual muscle is made up of many muscle fibers held together by connective tissue. Muscle tissue consists of three different types of muscle cells.

• **Fast-twitch fatiguing cells:** A cat's muscles consist mostly of these cells, which work quickly but also tire quickly. They give a cat its speed and the ability to leap several times its own length, but use up all its energy in an instant.
• **Fast-twitch fatigue-resistant cells:** Cats are poor endurance athletes. This is because they have relatively few fast-twitch fatigue-resistant cells, which work quickly but tire more slowly.
• **Slow-twitch cells:** These cells work and tire slowly and produce slow, sustainable contractions. They are called into play during hunting activities: they enable the cat to move almost imperceptibly slowly and stealthily, or wait for long periods in a ready-to-spring position.

**Striped muscles** are symmetrical across the body and under the control of the nervous system *(see pp.32–3)*. Generally, striped muscles are arranged in opposing groups, performing opposing actions.

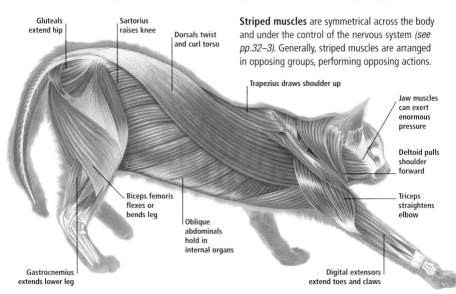

Gluteals
extend hip

Sartorius
raises knee

Dorsals twist
and curl torso

Trapezius draws shoulder up

Jaw muscles
can exert
enormous
pressure

Deltoid pulls
shoulder
forward

Biceps femoris
flexes or
bends leg

Oblique
abdominals
hold in
internal organs

Triceps
straightens
elbow

Gastrocnemius
extends lower leg

Digital extensors
extend toes and claws

## A floating shoulder

The cat's shoulder is a feat of muscle, in that the forelimb is connected to the rest of the body only by muscle. Unlike our collarbone, which connects the shoulder and breastbone, the cat's vestigial clavicle floats, anchored in place by muscle. The shoulder's freedom of movement effectively lengthens the cat's stride and enhances its range of motion.

## The feline gait

When a cat walks, most of its forward movement comes from its hind legs; its forelegs act like brakes when they hit the ground, almost negating the slight push forward they give on leaving it again.

The same is true when a cat trots. In this gait, the legs move in what is called contralateral fashion: the right front moves forward together with the left hind, and vice versa.

## Pounces and jumps

The cat's pliant muscles and flexible spine allow it to curl up, or to rotate its body by 180 degrees in midair. This flexibility also gives the cat a repertoire of graceful leaping movements suitable for different circumstances.

When pouncing, a cat springs with its hind legs, arches its back, and lands with its forepaws on its prize. Its refined wrist muscles allow it to rotate its wrists to grasp prey and to climb efficiently.

For a vertical jump, a cat judges the distance to be covered and calculates how much propulsive power from its hind leg muscles is needed.

This movement is different from the impromptu jumps a cat makes when chasing or being chased, and these, in turn, are different from the startle jump. In this, extensor muscles in all four legs activate simultaneously, and all the feet leave the ground at once, as if on springs.

## The righting reflex

The reflex that allows a cat to flip right-side-up depends on a flexible spine, resilient musculature, sharp sight, and an efficient hearing apparatus.

Vets have observed that falls from five to 10 floors are often fatal—cats reach 60 mph (100 km/h) after falling five floors, and the force of impact is too great to absorb. Curiously, falls from even greater heights sometimes cause little injury, because, once the cat has righted itself, it assumes the skydiver's free-fall position. The muscular relaxation, taken with the deceleration effected by outstretched limbs, lessens the impact and injury.

# The brain and endocrines

■ A cat's brain uses a fifth of the blood pumped by the heart
■ Hormones regulate bodily functions and feline behavior
■ Not all cat behavior is instinctive—cats can learn

All the senses and the body's hormone-producing glands send information to the brain, which interprets it and instructs the body on how to respond via the nervous system. This demands a great deal of energy and, although the brain accounts for less than 1 percent of body weight, it receives 20 percent of the blood pumped by the heart.

## Body-function controls

Hormones produced in the brain control most of the body's daily functions.
• **Antidiuretic hormone:** Produced by the hypothalamus gland, this hormone (ADH) controls the concentration of both urine and oxytocin, which stimulates labor and milk release in female cats. The hypothalamus also produces CRH or corticotrophin-releasing hormone, which controls the release of ACTH *(see below)*.
• **Adrenocorticotrophic hormone (ACTH):** This hormone stimulates the adrenal gland to produce cortisol in response to stress or danger.
• **Growth hormones:** The pituitary gland secretes the hormones controlling the production of growth hormone.
• **Thyroid-stimulating hormone (TSH):** TSH initiates activity in the thyroid, which controls metabolic rate.

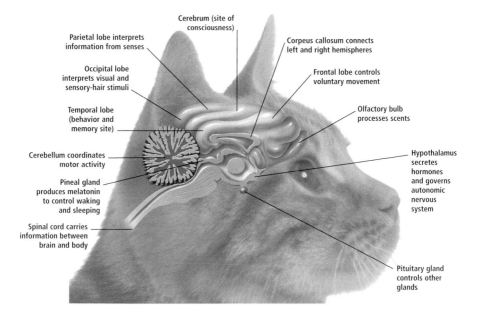

Cerebrum (site of consciousness)

Parietal lobe interprets information from senses

Occipital lobe interprets visual and sensory-hair stimuli

Temporal lobe (behavior and memory site)

Cerebellum coordinates motor activity

Pineal gland produces melatonin to control waking and sleeping

Spinal cord carries information between brain and body

Corpeus callosum connects left and right hemispheres

Frontal lobe controls voluntary movement

Olfactory bulb processes scents

Hypothalamus secretes hormones and governs autonomic nervous system

Pituitary gland controls other glands

## The adrenal glands

The adrenal glands lie adjacent to each kidney, and consist of an encapsulating cortex and a central core (medulla). The cortex produces cortisol and other hormones, which are instrumental in controlling metabolic rate and determining the body's response to injury. The medulla produces epinephrine and norepinephrine, better known as adrenaline and noradrenaline. These hormones control the heart rate and blood-vessel dilation. The adrenals are vital components of the biofeedback circuit. This system controls the fight-or-flight response, and has the most direct effect on feline behavior. The biofeedback mechanism dictates the innate disposition, sociability, and tamability of the cat.

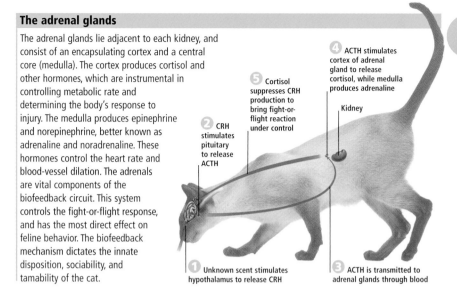

④ ACTH stimulates cortex of adrenal gland to release cortisol, while medulla produces adrenaline

⑤ Cortisol suppresses CRH production to bring fight-or-flight reaction under control

② CRH stimulates pituitary to release ACTH

Kidney

① Unknown scent stimulates hypothalamus to release CRH

③ ACTH is transmitted to adrenal glands through blood

• **Melanocyte-stimulating hormone (MSH):** This hormone stimulates the synthesis of melatonin, which is involved in triggering sleep cycles and controls the body's internal clock.

Production of sexual hormones, eggs, and sperm is controlled by follicle-stimulating hormone (FSH) in females and luteinizing hormone (LH) in males.

### The biological computer

The brain consists of billions of specialized cells (neurons), each with up to 10,000 connections to other cells. By seven weeks of age, messages move through a cat's brain at almost 240 mph (390 km/h). This rate tends to slow down with age.

Anatomically, the cat's brain is similar to that of other mammals. The cerebellum controls the muscles; the cerebrum governs learning, emotion, and behavior; and the brain stem connects to the nervous system. A network of cells called the limbic system is believed to integrate instinct and learning.

### Feline intelligence

Cats are born with instincts to mark and defend territory and hunt for sustenance, but must learn how to do these things.

By raising cats in our homes, we actively intervene in the development of their brains and behavior. A cat raised in a human home before seven weeks of age learns that humans are safe, while feral cats develop a valid suspicion of other animals and people, because cats are small and relatively defenseless against such adversaries.

Cats may appear unable to learn because they respond poorly to the social learning that we, as pack animals, use. Cats do not usually obey for praise, because esteem holds no survival advantage to a solo hunter, but they may respond to a food reward.

The clearest example of feline thought is the cat that fights against entering its carrier to go to the vet, but walks straight in for the return journey. Faced with two evils, the cat is quite capable of deciding which is the lesser.

# The nervous system

■ The spinal cord and the brain make up the central nervous system
■ Parts of the nervous system are under the cat's control
■ Cats rarely suffer from neurological problems

The nervous system works in close conjunction with the hormonal system to coordinate all of the cat's natural functions. The nervous system responds swiftly, accurately, and directly to events, both internal and external. Some areas of the nervous system are under the cat's voluntary control; others are controlled unconsciously.

Information travels through the nervous system in two directions: the sensory nerves tell the brain how a cat feels, and the motor nerves carry instructions for the body from the brain.

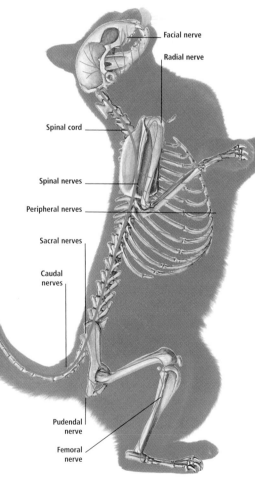

Facial nerve

Radial nerve

Spinal cord

Spinal nerves

Peripheral nerves

Sacral nerves

Caudal nerves

Pudendal nerve

Femoral nerve

### Central and peripheral
The nervous system is divided into two parts, central and peripheral. The former consists of the brain and the spinal cord—the command center and the superhighway for two-way transmission of impulses. The peripheral nervous system receives information about temperature, touch, and pain, and sends instructions to the muscles. It consists of the cranial nerves—responsible for the transmission of information from the senses—and the spinal, or peripheral, nerves, which link the extremities of the body to the central nervous system.

### Chemical messengers
The nervous system consists of nerve cells (neurons) and support cells that provide structure and produce myelin.

**The division of the nervous system** is for ease of understanding—it is not a physical split. Many nerve cells are partly in the central nervous system and partly in the peripheral nervous system.

## The myelin sheath

Myelin is a fatty, protective membrane that is found around the largest axons and increases the speed of communication along the nerves. Technically, a nerve fiber consists of an axon, its myelin sheathing, and the cell that makes the myelin. Myelin is produced by cells called oligodendrocytes in the central nervous system, and neurolemmocytes in the peripheral system. Few nerves have myelin sheathing at birth, but they are myelinated quickly and effectively.

A neuron's body is covered with branch-like structures (dendrites), which receive messages from other cells. Each cell also has a long, taillike structure (axon), which sends messages to other nerve cells or organs. All of these messages are carried by neurotransmitters, chemicals produced in the axons.

A cat's nervous system is constantly sending and receiving vast numbers of messages. Any cell commonly sends messages to thousands of other cells.

### Conscious control

Many functions of the nervous system are under the cat's control. When it sees prey, it readies its muscles to pounce. Sensory nerves carry messages to the brain, and motor nerves carry messages back to the muscles, stimulating them to work toward an accurate pounce.

### Unconscious control

Some activities, mostly those regulating heartbeat, breathing, and the digestive processes, are involuntary. They are controlled by the autonomic nervous system, which consists of two parts, sympathetic and parasympathetic. When a cat is at rest, the latter is in control: the pupils are relaxed, and the heart rate and breathing are slow and regular.

The sympathetic system takes over when a cat is stressed. It triggers the hypothalamus and the pituitary *(see p.30)* to stimulate the adrenal glands into the fight-or-flight response. Blood flows from internal organs into muscles, hair stands on end, the heart speeds up, and pupils dilate for better vision.

### Neurological problems

Neurological disorders are rare in cats. Viral infections (such as panleukopenia virus, rabies, and feline infectious peritonitis [FIP]), poisons, and a variety of parasites damage nerves. But traffic accidents are the most common causes of nerve damage. Presently, no intervention helps nerve cells regenerate.

**At times of stress,** the involuntary nervous system stimulates an instantaneous chain of events leading to a fight-or-flight response.

# Vision

- Cats are partly color-blind
- The cat's eyes are unable to focus sharply
- Low-light vision is a specialty

Most experts agree that cats are "color-blind." Tests have shown that the color-sensitive cone cells on cats' retinas are sensitive to blue and green, but not to red. In trials, cats are able to distinguish between green, blue, and yellow, but do not recognize red. In normal life, color appears meaningless to cats.

### Motion detection

Cats' eyes are more sensitive to movement than ours, with more motion-detecting rod cells in the retina. The high presence of rod cells also contributes to their ability to see in low-light conditions.

A cat sees the world in soft-focus—it cannot resolve detail sharply because the lens in its eye is large, to gather as much light as possible.

### Cats' eyes

A protective, clear cornea covers the eye's anterior fluid-filled chamber. Behind this is the three-part uvea: the colored iris, stabilizing ciliary body, and focusing lens. Behind the lens is the fluid-filled posterior chamber.

The retina lining the back of the eye "reads" the light, sending information down the optic nerve; behind it is the tapetum lucidum, a layer of specialized reflective tissue that allows the cat to make the most of available light.

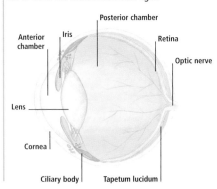

Posterior chamber

Anterior chamber

Iris

Retina

Optic nerve

Lens

Cornea

Ciliary body

Tapetum lucidum

The most spectacular modification in the cat's eye is the tapetum lucidum, a layer of reflective cells behind the retina. These mirrorlike cells bounce light back through the retina to give rods and cones a heightened ability to interpret information.

## Field of vision

Protruding eyes give cats a wider angle of vision than ours, and they also have superior peripheral vision; both are important to an animal that is both prey and predator.

Pupil becomes smaller in bright light

## The perfect eye

As is appropriate for such an opportunist hunter, a cat's eyes are designed to collect the maximum amount of light. The eye's surface, or cornea, is curved, and the lens is very large in comparison to the other dimensions of the eye.

**A cat's eyes shine green or gold** as light is reflected from layers of mirrorlike cells (tapetum lucidum) behind the retina. The cells improve the cat's night vision by reflecting back light.

In dim light, or when your cat is excited or scared, its pupils dilate to make the most of available light, while in bright conditions they can close completely to protect the retina, allowing light to pass through two narrow, longitudinal slits.

## Can cats see in the dark?

Contrary to popular belief, cats cannot see any better than humans in pitch darkness. However, they can see in one-sixth of the amount of light we need. Cats' pupils can dilate to as much as 90 percent of the eye area— enabling them to hunt for prey in the dawn light and at dusk.

**Like built-in sunglasses,** the muscles in the iris allow the pupil to change shape according to the available light. The pupil becomes oval in bright light.

# Hearing and balance

- Cats hear even the slightest of noises
- Cats can detect a far greater range of frequencies than humans
- Hearing is important for balance, too

Evolution has equipped the cat with excellent hearing, well adapted for hunting small rodents. A cat can detect the faintest high-pitched squeaks of a mouse or the rustle of tiny movements.

Noise consists of pressure waves traveling through the air. These are channeled through the ear, converted to electrical impulses, and carried to the brain, which interprets them.

Pressure in the inner ear is regulated by its connection to the back of the throat via the eustachian tube.

### Incredible range

More than a dozen muscles are used to control ear movement precisely. A cat can rotate its ears, independently if necessary, to listen for prey or danger. It can also hear frequencies as high as 65 kilohertz (kHz), a full octave and a half higher than our maximum of 20 kHz. Like humans, however, cats lose their ability to hear higher frequencies within their range with age.

### A balancing act

Cats are natural climbers and have a sensitive sense of balance. The organ of balance, the vestibular apparatus, is in the inner ear. Changes in direction or velocity register instantly in this organ, allowing the cat to compensate by changing its orientation.

## Funnel for sound

Sound travels down the ear canal and vibrates the eardrum, or tympanic membrane. In the middle ear, three bones called the ossicles transfer vibrations to the snail-shaped inner ear, or cochlea, and auditory nerve. The organ of balance, the vestibular apparatus, consists of fluid-filled chambers and canals, lined with sensitive hairs that pick up movements in the fluid and send signals to the brain.

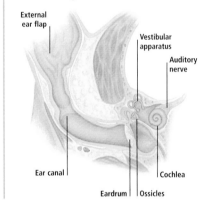

External ear flap

Vestibular apparatus

Auditory nerve

Ear canal

Cochlea

Eardrum    Ossicles

A DELICATE BALANCE

# Scent, taste, and touch

- The mouth and nose make a dynamic scenting duo
- A cat has up to 10 million taste buds on its tongue and throat
- The cat's body is touch-sensitive

Cats have twice as many smell-sensitive cells, or olfactory receptors, in their noses as humans do. Taste buds cover the tongue, while touch receptors are found all over a cat's body, but mostly in the paw pads and whiskers.

### Sense of smell

Cats use their sense of smell to scent prey or food, to detect danger, and to read the chemical messages left in urine or feces.

Odor molecules adhere to the sticky membranes that cover the curved bones (turbinates) inside the nasal chambers, while taste buds on the tongue detect the chemicals in foods.

In the roof of the mouth, cats have a vomeronasal, or Jacobson's, organ. When a cat uses this organ, its mouth opens in something between a grimace and a gape, called a flehmen. Assisted by the tongue, odors are "lapped" into the vomeronasal organ, and sent to the hypothalamus area of the brain by a different route than odors from the nose.

### Taste detection

The cat's tongue and part of the throat contain mounds of tissue, or papillae. An adult cat has about 250 papillae, each holding anything from 40 to 40,000 taste buds. Cats can detect sour, bitter, and salty tastes, but not sweet ones. Their taste buds are specialized to detect the amino acids of meat, but are less able

### Chemical receptors

Each taste bud on a cat's tongue has a taste hair that detects the chemicals in foods. Inside the nasal chambers, odor molecules adhere to the sticky membranes that cover the turbinate bones. Other chemical odor molecules are captured in the vomeronasal organ in the roof of the mouth.

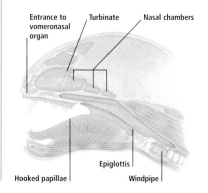

Entrance to vomeronasal organ | Turbinate | Nasal chambers

Epiglottis | Windpipe

Hooked papillae

than ours to detect the carbohydrate constituents of vegetable matter.

### Touch-sensitive whiskers

Kittens grow their highly mobile, touch-sensitive whiskers (vibrissae) while still in the womb. The vibrissae on the chin and upper lip are the longest and most abundant. They can be angled forward in greeting or backward out of the way when fighting or feeding. Whiskers above the eyes and on the cheeks warn of dangers to the eyes as a cat explores. Tip-to-tip, the facial whiskers indicate the smallest gap a cat can comfortably pass though. A sixth set of whiskers extends from the back of each foreleg.

# Breathing and circulation

- Different parts of the body need different amounts of blood
- Arteries carry oxygen, veins carry waste carbon dioxide
- Most cats are blood type A

The cat's lungs, heart, and circulatory system are designed for an animal of controlled actions, but with occasional sudden bursts of great energy.

### The respiratory system

Inhaled air passes through the nose's scenting apparatus, which is surrounded by the frontal sinuses. Here air is warmed, humidified, and filtered. Then it travels down the windpipe (trachea), and into the lungs through two bronchi. Each bronchus splits into many smaller bronchioles that end in tiny pockets called alveoli.

### The circulatory system

The body of a 12-lb (5-kg) cat contains about 12 fl oz (330 ml) of blood.

The muscular, elastic walls of arteries expand and contract as the heart pushes blood through them: this is the pulse. The thinner walls of the veins are more easily damaged; they have no pulse, and contain valves to ensure that the blood in them moves only one way, to the heart.

Different parts of the body need different amounts of blood. The brain is a small part of the body's weight, but takes 15 to 20 percent of its blood. Resting muscles get about twice this, but during pursuits or escapes, up to 90 percent of the blood can be diverted

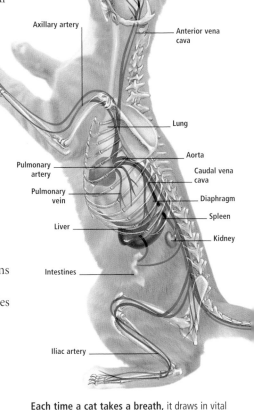

**Each time a cat takes a breath,** it draws in vital oxygen and exhales waste carbon dioxide. Every beat of its heart pumps these and other substances to and from the farthest reaches of the body.

into the muscles from other organs and even from the brain.

The amount of blood that each part of the body receives is controlled by nerves and hormones that cause small arteries to dilate in response to local activity, increasing the blood supply to that area.

## The role of arteries and veins

Arteries carry bright-red blood, rich in oxygen from the lungs and nutrients from the digestive system, from the heart to the body. Veins bring darker blood, laden with carbon dioxide and waste matter, back to the lungs, liver, and kidneys.

The exceptions to this are pulmonary arteries and veins. The former carry oxygen-depleted blood to the alveoli, where oxygen is absorbed from inhaled air. Pulmonary veins then return the refreshed blood to the heart, which pumps it out through arteries to the body. The oxygen diffuses into cells in exchange for carbon dioxide, and veins bring the depleted blood to the heart to be pumped to the lungs again.

## Blood composition

The bulk of blood volume is pale-yellow plasma. Another 30 to 45 percent is red blood cells, and the remainder is white cells and platelets.
• **Plasma:** The transportation portion of the blood carries nutrients from the digestive system and transports waste. Plasma levels are maintained by liquid absorbed along the large intestine.
• **Blood cells:** In kittens, the liver and spleen make blood cells; in adults, bone marrow produces them. Red cells carry oxygen through the arteries to the cells of the body. White blood cells *(see p.44)* defend the body against microbes and parasites, clear waste from injuries, detoxify substances released in allergic

### Blood problems

Some circulation problems have external causes. If a cat does not eat, there is too little water in the large intestines to maintain plasma levels, so water is drawn from elsewhere, causing dehydration.

In anemia, the level of red blood cells falls. Heavy flea infestation, injury, stomach ulcers, or tumors can cause temporary anemia. Illness can inhibit the bone marrow from producing new cells. Such nonregenerative anemia is often caused by feline leukemia virus (FeLV), kidney failure, nutritional deficiency, or poisoning.

Cats may develop diseases of the heart muscle (cardiomyopathy) or valves, or disruption of the heart's rate (arrhythmia). They can suffer blood clots (thromboembolisms) causing pain to the hind limbs.

reactions, and produce antibodies to fight infections.
• **Platelets:** These are responsible for clotting blood around wounds.

## Blood types

Cats have three blood types: A, B, and AB. Most cats are type A, but incidence of types varies geographically. Virtually all cats in Switzerland are type A, for example, but this drops to 97 percent in Britain and 85 percent in France. Many pedigree breeds are almost exclusively type A, but others show varying levels of type B. Type AB is extremely rare and not linked to breed.

# Consuming and eliminating

■ Meat is a vital part of a cat's diet
■ A cat's teeth and tongue are perfect tools for its carnivorous diet
■ The digestive system is adapted to eating little and often

The digestive system is responsible for breaking down food into molecules that can be absorbed into the bloodstream. It also acts as a barrier against harmful bacteria or other disease-causing agents that a cat may inadvertently ingest. Food is usually consumed, digested, utilized, and excreted within 24 hours.

### Ingestion and digestion

The cat's teeth tear meat, and its barbed tongue scrapes it from bones. Saliva binds and lubricates food for swallowing.

Food passes down the esophagus and into the stomach. The top of the stomach produces acid to break down fibers and an enzyme to break down protein. The stomach also secretes mucus to protect itself and the intestines against damage from these digestive juices. Muscle contractions mix food, which then passes into the duodenum.

The duodenum receives fat-dissolving bile from the gall bladder in the liver and enzymes from the pancreas. Along the length of the small intestine, digestion continues and nutrients are absorbed through the intestinal wall.

The blood carries these products to the liver, the largest internal organ. The

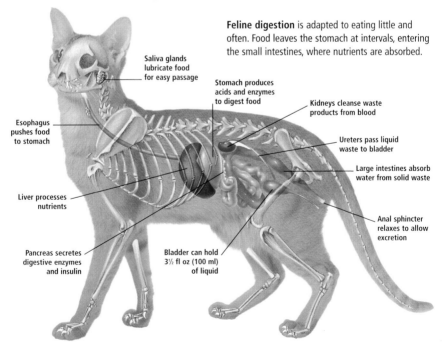

**Feline digestion** is adapted to eating little and often. Food leaves the stomach at intervals, entering the small intestines, where nutrients are absorbed.

Saliva glands lubricate food for easy passage

Stomach produces acids and enzymes to digest food

Kidneys cleanse waste products from blood

Esophagus pushes food to stomach

Ureters pass liquid waste to bladder

Large intestines absorb water from solid waste

Liver processes nutrients

Anal sphincter relaxes to allow excretion

Pancreas secretes digestive enzymes and insulin

Bladder can hold 3½ fl oz (100 ml) of liquid

## The cat's dentition

When kittens are born, 26 needle-sharp baby teeth are already in place. These are replaced by 30 permanent teeth during the first six months of life. The upper and lower incisors grasp the prey or food, the canines grip and kill, and the premolars and molars shear, cut, and chew meat. The cat has few molars, and the upper ones are almost vestigial because they are not vital in its mainly carnivorous natural diet.

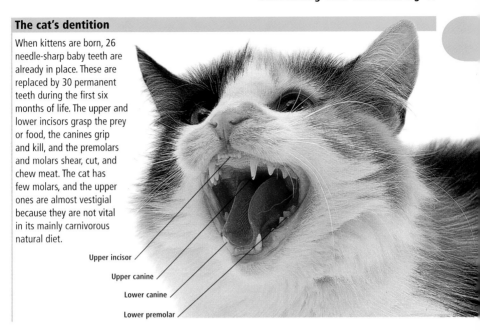

Upper incisor

Upper canine

Lower canine

Lower premolar

liver processes them into essential fatty acids and amino acids. Unlike the human or canine liver, the feline liver needs animal protein to manufacture the full complement of acids, so a cat will die if it does not eat meat. The liver also breaks down toxic substances.

### Waste disposal

After the nutrients are absorbed, waste enters the large intestine, or colon, where benign bacteria break it down. Water is absorbed through the colon wall, and mucus is secreted to lubricate the dry waste. When waste accumulates in the rectum, nerves signal that discharge is needed.

The blood carries waste from the liver to the kidneys, where tubules (nephrons) filter it out and excrete it as urine, of which cats produce 2 fl oz (60 ml) daily.

The kidneys also regulate blood pressure, maintain the chemical balance of the blood, activate vitamin D, and produce erythropoietin, a hormone that stimulates the production of red blood cells.

### Digestive hormones

The process of digestion is aided by hormones released by the thyroids, the parathyroids, and the pancreas.

The thyroid glands, one on each side of the windpipe, control the metabolic rate. An overactive thyroid, common in older cats, causes a voracious appetite, weight loss, and increased heart rate. An underactive thyroid is extremely rare in cats.

Next to each thyroid is a parathyroid gland, which produces a hormone needed to regulate calcium, important in muscle contraction, from bone.

Insulin, secreted in the pancreas, allows cells to absorb vital glucose from the blood. Overactive pituitary or adrenal glands release hormones that increase blood sugar, mimicking diabetes.

# Ensuring the future

- Puberty in cats occurs at five to nine months
- Unneutered males are always ready to mate
- Feline mating can be a noisy, aggressive affair

The cat's reproduction strategy is ideally suited to the lone hunter. Females come into season as daylight hours increase, ensuring births during the spring and summer, when food is most plentiful. Males are always ready to mate.

## The male system

Feline puberty usually occurs at five to nine months; from then on, a male cat's reproductive system is on standby, ready for use if the chance arises.

Luteinizing hormone (LH) from the pituitary gland stimulates the testes to make both sperm and the male hormone testosterone. Sperm production is best at slightly less than body heat, so testes are held in the scrotum outside the body. Sperm is stored in the epididymis at the base of the testes until needed, when it travels through the two spermatic cords to the prostate and bulbourethral glands. Here a sugar-rich transport medium, semen, is added.

### Neutering

In male cats, neutering is a minor operation. Under general anesthesia, the testicles are removed through a small incision in the scrotum. The spermatic cords and associated blood vessels are tied. This is usually done at about six months.

Neutering a female, or spaying, involves major abdominal surgery. The ovaries and uterus down to the cervix are removed. Spaying can be done before sexual maturity.

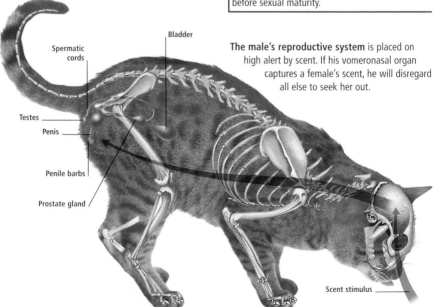

Bladder

Spermatic cords

Testes

Penis

Penile barbs

Prostate gland

Scent stimulus

**The male's reproductive system** is placed on high alert by scent. If his vomeronasal organ captures a female's scent, he will disregard all else to seek her out.

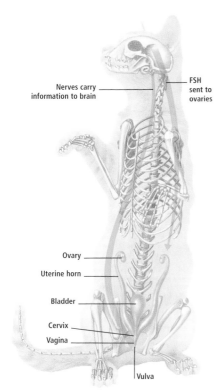

Nerves carry information to brain

FSH sent to ovaries

Ovary

Uterine horn

Bladder

Cervix

Vagina

Vulva

**The female's two ovaries,** which manufacture eggs and the hormone estrogen, are suspended from the roof of the abdomen, just behind the kidneys.

## Female hormones

Like most other domestic animals, the female cat is polyestrous, meaning she has many estrous periods, or seasons, throughout the year. But, unlike many other animal species that have estrous cycles all year round, cats are seasonally polyestrous: the female's reproductive cycle is most active as daylight hours increase, and then winds down as daylight hours decrease.

At the end of winter, increasing daylight hours stimulate her pituitary gland to produce follicle stimulating hormone (FSH). The FSH induces her ovaries to develop eggs and make the female hormone estrogen. The estrogen is released in the female's urine, acting as a calling card to any available males.

At puberty, which occurs at the same age as male puberty, the necessary eggs are waiting in the ovaries. In contrast to the reproductive systems of virtually all other mammals, however, the ovaries will not release these eggs until after mating has taken place.

## Feline mating

The female cat does not permit a male to mate with her until she is completely ready. When the male is allowed to mount her, he grasps the skin on her neck and mates immediately. A cat's penis is covered in hooklike barbs. As he withdraws, the barbs abrade the vulva, stimulating egg release.

Cats only release eggs after mating, but two or more matings are usually needed. Once the eggs have left the ovaries, a period of calm ensues, lasting from two days to two weeks, followed by another heat cycle if she does not conceive.

### Pregnancy and birth

Fertilization takes place in the uterine horns, and the fetuses are positioned in rows in each horn. Pregnancy lasts about 63 days.

Birth is usually uncomplicated, although some kittens may not live. Milk letdown occurs shortly after the birth, stimulated by suckling. The mother often leaves the birth nest a few days after the delivery, carrying her kittens one by one to a new, more odor-free, and thus, to her mind, safer den.

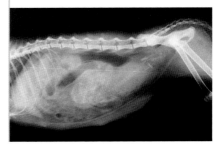

# Immunity

- The immune system defends the body from disease
- Sometimes the immune system misinterprets instructions
- Allergies and autoimmune diseases in cats are on the rise

The immune system protects against both internal dangers, such as cancer cells, and external pathogens, such as viruses and bacteria.

Under normal conditions, the immune system turns on and off as necessary. If it does not turn on properly, a cat is immune-suppressed. If it turns on at the wrong time or fails to turn off, a cat may develop allergy, asthma, or an auto-immune disease, in which the immune system attacks a vital part of the body.

### How the system works

Almost every part of the body, from the skin to the bone marrow, contains cells integral to a healthy immune system. A vital role is played by white blood cells, of which there are five main types.

- **Neutrophils:** The front-line "attack soldiers" of the immune system guard and protect against bacteria and fungi.
- **B-lymphocytes:** These cells produce antibodies—proteins that label and neutralize harmful microbes.
- **T-cells:** "Helper" T-cells prompt the B-lymphocytes' production of antibodies, while "suppressor" T-cells turn them off when a job is finished.
- **Memory T-cells:** These cells patrol the body, recognizing villains encountered in the past and mobilizing attack teams, including "natural killer" cells that attack and destroy viruses or tumor cells.
- **Macrophages:** These cells (literally "big eaters") are the final part of the system. They arrive and clean up the debris.

### Pain and stress

In the brain, chemicals called neuropeptides have a powerful effect on pain control, energy, and sense of well-being. Pain is part of the cat's defense system, prompting it to avoid continuing dangers. During a fight, a cat produces protective neuropeptides called endorphins that reduce the unpleasantness and intensity of pain. Chronic stress may trigger excesses or deficiencies in neuropeptides: pain and stress can therefore affect susceptibility to or speed of recovery from illness. Use only feline painkillers: drugs that work in dogs or humans can be lethal to cats.

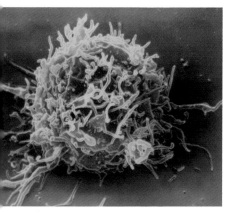

**T-cells are responsible** for stimulating or shutting down the production of antibodies, proteins that neutralize harmful microbes.

## An overactive immune system

Helper T-cells activate and deactivate parts of the immune system, but at times they misinterpret the instructions. They may respond when the cat's body is not being threatened by dangerous microbes, but is simply in contact with innocuous substances like flea saliva, house dust, or plant pollens. These substances can trigger an allergic reaction, which may appear as anything from itchy skin, watery eyes, or sneezing to vomiting or diarrhea.

If suppressor T-cells do not turn off effectively, the immune system remains in overdrive and may erroneously start attacking a specific part of the cat's own body—for example, the red blood cells. This self-destructive reaction is called autoimmune disease.

Vets are increasingly diagnosing both allergies and autoimmune diseases in cats. While this may be due in part to improved diagnostic methods, many vets feel that both these problems are on the increase. Corticosteroids are used to suppress an overactive immune system.

## An underactive immune system

A decline in the competence of a cat's immune system can be caused by old age or through infection with conditions such as feline immunodeficiency virus (FIV) or feline leukemia virus (FeLV). Affected cats are susceptible to cancers, infections, and autoimmune disorders.

## Cancer in cats

Cancer cells are renegades that trick the natural killer cells into regarding the cancer cells as "self" and not attacking them. After eluding the immune system, cancer cells multiply and spread to other parts of the body.

Some can produce chemicals that actively suppress a cat's immune system.

### Asthma and allergies

Feline allergic reactions to certain foods and chemicals are a relatively recent phenomenon.

When a cat inhales, swallows, or is otherwise in contact with any trigger substance, the immune system produces an antibody called immunoglobin E (IgE, *see right*). In allergic cats, IgE binds on to receptor sites on specialized immune cells called mast cells *(see below)*, located in the skin and the lining of the stomach, lungs, and upper airways.

Mast cell

Receptor site

Antibody IgE

These mast cells are like primed mines, filled with irritating chemicals, and the IgE causes the mast cells to literally explode, scattering irritating and inflammatory substances, such as histamine.

Antihistamine drugs neutralize the released histamine.

Irritating chemicals are released

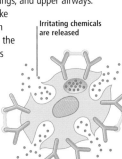

# Living with cats

- This is a mutually beneficial relationship
- Cats and humans adapt to each other
- Cats depend on us

Our relationship with cats is fairly recent and, on the whole, mutually beneficial. While cats were persecuted in medieval Europe and are still easy targets of abuse anywhere, joining human communities has been a successful evolutionary move for them, ensuring their spread across the world. However, living with humans has brought physical and psychological changes, and future risk.

## Wild to domestic

The anatomy of the domestic cat has changed slightly from its wildcat ancestor. As with all other domesticated species, the cat's brain is about one quarter smaller than that of the ancestral African wildcat. Areas of the brain vital for independent survival are simply not necessary when the home territory is relatively small and food readily available. Similarly, the intestines are shorter and the hormone-producing glands in the body are smaller. Domestic cats are also much noisier than their wildcat relatives.

These changes simply reflect the demands of the new environment in which the animal finds itself. The risk to the cat is that we may do as we have done with the dog and, through selective breeding, perpetuate shapes or sizes that would die out in the wild. Dwarfed cats with enlarged joints and shortened bones are already recognized as a breed (the munchkin), as are hairless cats (the sphynx).

## Influencing cat behavior

The cat's move into human environments was made a success by the development of individuals that were less fearful than their wildcat relatives. All cats are amenable to living with us

**Some evolutionary psychologists** claim that, due to their close proximity to humans, cats are developing softer voices.

**Not having to hunt** for their food has led, in part, to a reduction in the brain size of domestic cats.

### Changing voices?
Scientists have tried to determine whether cats' voices are changing due to their proximity to us. Some claim that there are evolutionary pressures toward a softer feline voice and the so-called "silent meow."

### Influencing genetics
We humans share 98.5 percent of our genes with the chimpanzee, but even 100 million years of separation have not been enough for genetic rearrangements. So it is with the cat. There will never be genetic changes as a result of domestication or selective breeding. We merely influence regulatory genes that switch other genes on and off.

if they are socialized early, but some are more affectionate than others. Although new breeds are promoted according to their allegedly enhanced sociability, the effectiveness of selective breeding in perpetuating this behavior trait has been neither proved nor disproved.

### The hypoallergenic cat
We can be allergic to a variety of animal danders (or dandruff), but cat dander is particularly irksome to many people. A protein called Fel D-1, found in cat saliva and shedding flakes of cat skin, is the culprit.

Technically, now that genetic manipulation is possible, it would not be difficult to discover the gene that controls production of Fel D-1 and modify this protein so that it is less likely to provoke an allergic response in people. However, this idea is fraught with moral and ethical considerations. We have serious decisions to make.

# CHAPTER TWO

# Breeds

Within the last 50 years, and continuing today, there
has been an explosion in the number of new breeds.
Some of these new breeds have been developed by
selectively breeding cats that evolved to survive in a
specific environment. In other instances, a chance
mutation has been perpetuated through careful
breeding following firm genetic principles. The most
recent intervention involves the planned breeding of
a wildcat species with the domestic cat, to produce a
unique coat color pattern. Many breed registries
prohibit such breeding, but the results are recognized
by other registries.

# Selective breeding

- Genetically and scientifically developed
- Different registries have different views
- Pedigree cats are still a minority

Cats have been in our homes for millennia, but only in the last century or so has selective breeding been actively pursued, borne out of the success of the first formal cat shows, held in the late 1800s, and the subsequent vogue in "purebred" cats. Registries soon formed to create standards and verify pedigrees.

## Modern registries

The role of breed registries is fraught with inconsistencies. It is hard to say what exactly a breed is—not all breeds are recognized by all registries, and a breed might be named one way in one registry and differently in another registry. The world's largest registry of pedigree cats is the Cat Fanciers' Association (CFA), founded in 1906. Its philosophy is purist, allowing, for example, only four Siamese colors. The most liberal of registries is The International Cat Association (TICA), founded in 1979 and based in North America. TICA accepts new breeds more

The Birman's pattern might naturally evolve in an isolated area, but it coincides neatly with other breed patterns. Some say it is a man-made breed.

rapidly than other major registries, even if only provisionally, thus encouraging experimentation. Britain's Governing Council of the Cat Fancy (GCCF) was formed in 1910. Its policies are staid, but less so than the CFA's, and its influence is worldwide. Most European countries have several registries, but at least one from each country belongs to the Fédération Internationale Féline (FIFé), founded in 1949. FIFé's policy is similar to that of Britain's GCCF: both organizations frown upon breeding for types associated with known defects, such as blue-eyed white cats, which have a high incidence of associated deafness.

The pointed kittens in this Oriental shorthair litter could be registered as Siamese by some associations and as "any other variety" Orientals by others.

## Old and new breeds

Cat breeds can be divided into two groups, which emerged chronologically. The first are those that appeared naturally in free-breeding (but possibly isolated) feline populations. Many of these are characterized by coat color or pattern, and genetically these are usually "recessives" that breed true, like the Abyssinian's ticked pattern, which is a recessive trait emphasized through selective breeding. Other breeds, like the Manx, feature distinctive mutations. Some breeds, such as the Maine coon and the Norwegian forest cat, developed naturally into types later recognized as breeds. Another feature defining these early breeds is coat length. The longhairs predate registries, but type and standards were very loose in those times.

**An island's** limited gene pool allowed bobbed tails to gain the prevalence that gave us Japanese bobtails.

## Genetic manipulation

More recently, breeds have been actively, and sometimes scientifically, developed; many have been created from scratch, with breeders using their new knowledge of genetics to create a palette of coat colors and patterns. This is the growth area in the cat world: more new breeds appeared in the 1900s than in the whole history of domestic cats preceding it. Some new breeds are simply longhaired versions of existing shorthairs, others are coat mutations. Meanwhile, examples of breeding away from natural type, such as the sphynx and munchkin, lead us to question whether the concept of breed standards inevitably leads to deviations towards potentially unhealthy extremes.

### Wider effects

Selective breeding has only a peripheral effect on the species as a whole. Pedigree cats make up less than 10 percent of the world cat population, even where they are popular. However, breed registries are of value for all cats, raising their profile as desirable and worthwhile animals.

**There is a tendency** to breed for temperament: the famously placid ragdoll is the most obvious example of this, but it is not alone.

# Color and coat patterns

■ Coat color was originally linked to camouflage
■ White cats are genetically colored
■ Different registries use different names for the same colors

The cat's original coat was of color-banded, or "agouti," hair. The first mutation to a single, non-agouti color (probably black) happened when the cat no longer needed its camouflage. Other mutations for red, white, and dilutions of solid colors contributed to the variety of colors that exists today.

### How hair color works

All colored hairs contain two components of melanin: eumelanin, which produces black and brown, and pheomelanin, producing red and yellow. All colors are based on the varying amount of these pigments in the shafts of each hair.

Cats with single-colored, non-agouti hair are called self or solid. Self coats

are recessive: the cat must carry two copies of the non-agouti gene in order to hide its true original tabby pattern.

### Standards for colors

Although there are only a few genes responsible for solid colors, breed associations complicate matters by giving the same color different names. Lilac is called lavender in some North American associations; chocolate Oriental shorthairs are called Havana in Britain and chestnut in North America; and chocolate Havana browns look closer to cinnamon and are called chestnut. Reds are often specified as red selfs, and in the Turkish Van, red-and-white is called auburn-and-white. Tortie-and-white cats are called calicos by some North American associations, most notably the CFA.

### Density of color

Some cats have vibrant self coats in black, chocolate, cinnamon, or sex-linked red. This is thanks to the dense gene (D), which is dominant and ensures that each hair is packed with pigment to give the richest color.

Other cats have lighter, "dilute" coats in blue, lilac, fawn, or sex-linked cream. These cats have two copies of the dilute gene (d), which is recessive and results in less pigment in each hair. The effect is a paler shade of a dense color.

**The dilute color gene** is most common in Eastern or Oriental breeds, such as this lilac-point Balinese.

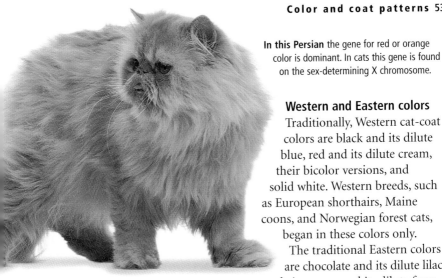

In this Persian the gene for red or orange color is dominant. In cats this gene is found on the sex-determining X chromosome.

## Western and Eastern colors

Traditionally, Western cat-coat colors are black and its dilute blue, red and its dilute cream, their bicolor versions, and solid white. Western breeds, such as European shorthairs, Maine coons, and Norwegian forest cats, began in these colors only.

The traditional Eastern colors are chocolate and its dilute lilac, and cinnamon and its dilute fawn. Some colors have been transposed from one group to another. In the UK, British shorthairs are accepted in Eastern colors; likewise Burmese are often bred in red and cream. Conservative cat associations, however, do not accept transposed colors in these breeds.

## Sex-linked red

In cats, the gene for red or orange color is located on the sex-determining X chromosome. In its dominant form (O), it makes the cat red; in its recessive form (o), it allows whatever other color the cat is carrying to show.

A male cat has only one copy of the gene, so if it carries one O it is red, and if it has one o it will be any other color.

The female cat can carry two copies of the gene. It will be red if it has two copies of O, or another color if it has two copies of o. Unlike males, a female cat can also be heterozygous (Oo). This combination gives it a mosaic pattern of red and black known as tortoiseshell. This combination interacts with all other color-controlling genes, producing torties in solid and dilute colors.

Black is the most common eumelanistic color. It often masks the genetic potential for other coat colors.

**The nose and ear tips** of white cats burn easily in the sun, so make sure they are protected.

## White cats

White is dominant over all other color genes, either as all-over white (W) or as the spotting gene (S) that gives us the bicolors. White hair contains no color-producing pigment at all.

Even if a white cat carries the W gene, which masks the expression of all other colors, it is genetically colored and it passes on its color potential to its offspring. A hint of a white cat's underlying color may show on the head of a newborn kitten.

## Bicolored cats

White-coated cats with patches of color are known as bicolored cats. They come in two types.

The standard bicolor is between one third and half white, with the white concentrated on the underparts and legs.

The Van pattern, originally associated with the Turkish Van but now also seen in other cats, consists of predominant white with solid or tortoiseshell patches restricted to the head and tail. One theory is that these cats carry two copies of the white spotting gene S, giving them a superabundance of white.

## Dominant pattern

All cats carry some form of the tabby gene, even those with self coats. The dominant agouti gene is called A, and any cat that inherits it from at least one parent will have a patterned coat. A cat that inherits the genetically recessive alternative to agouti (non-agouti, or a) from both parents will have a coat that appears solid but, when examined, may reveal tabby markings.

There are four basic types of tabby patterns. Though considerably different in appearance, they are variations of the same tabby gene.
• **Mackerel, or striped:** Narrow, parallel stripes run from the spine down the flanks to the belly.
• **Classic, or blotched:** Wide stripes form "oyster" swirls on the flanks, centered on a blotch.

**The wide stripes** forming swirls on the flanks of this cat are classic tabby markings.

• **Ticked, or Abyssinian:** Clear markings are restricted to the head, legs, and tail, while the body is softly flecked.
• **Spotted:** A spotted body, often combined with striped legs and tail.

## Subtle shading

Hair color is produced by pigment. The inhibitor gene (I) allows pigment to fill only the first part of the hair, producing subtle patterns that appear to change as a cat moves. In self cats, it creates a smoke, with a white undercoat. In agouti coats, degrees of shading give us shaded and silver colors and silver tabbies, which have appreciable colors, and tipped coats, merely "frosted" with color.

## Colorpoint patterns

The I gene is not the only gene to restrict color. Restriction of color to the extremities is called pointing. Pointed cats are light on their bodies and darker on their points, namely their ears, feet, tail, and nose. In male cats, hair is also darker on the scrotum.

**This Persian** is a good example of a standard bicolor—between one third and half its coat is white.

A heat-sensitive enzyme in the melanocytes, the cat's pigmenting cells, controls this pattern. Normal body temperature inhibits pigment production over most of the body, but the enzyme is activated and hair pigmented where skin temperature is lower. Because it is temperature-sensitive, kittens are born white, cats in cool countries have darker coats than those in warm parts of the world, and all cats' bodies darken markedly with age.

**The Siamese** shows the clearest form of pointing—an almost white body with dark extremities.

**Solid tortoiseshells** tend to have subtly mixed colors, while tortie-and-whites usually show large patches of black and red.

# Face shape and body form

- Defining factors for breeds
- Shape is linked to breed's origin
- Cats have a predetermined size range

Most cat breeds are defined by the shape of their bodies and faces and, at times, by physical features such as taillessness. A breed's personality traits are largely consistent with body shape: muscular breeds tend to be less lively than lean, long breeds. These differences tend to follow a west-to-east path, so a breed's type is often indicative of its origin.

## Cold-weather cats

The most compact cats evolved through natural selection in cold climates and are built to retain body heat. Breeds such as the British and American shorthairs have large, round heads; fairly short, broad muzzles; solid bodies with broad chests; sturdy legs and round paws; and short to medium-length, thick tails.

The original longhaired cats, the Persians, were also thick-set and muscular to withstand the harsh mountain winters of Turkey and Iran. Other robust longhairs evolved in cold climates from farm cats that lived partly outdoors. The moderately long faces of these cats make it easier to catch prey.

## Semiforeign breeds

A second group of cats has physical features somewhere between northern Europe's muscular cats and the more

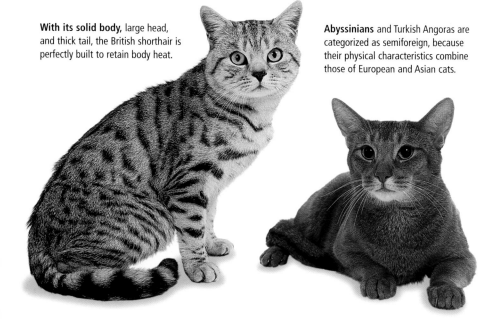

**With its solid body,** large head, and thick tail, the British shorthair is perfectly built to retain body heat.

**Abyssinians** and Turkish Angoras are categorized as semiforeign, because their physical characteristics combine those of European and Asian cats.

sinuous cats of Africa and Asia. These lean, muscular cats, like the Turkish Angora and Abyssinian, are called semiforeign. They have slanted eyes, moderately wedge-shaped heads, oval paws, and long, tapering tails.

## Oriental breeds

Most Oriental breeds evolved in warm climates. With their large ears, wedge-shaped heads, fine legs, slender bodies, and long, thin tails, these cats have developed maximum body surface area to rid themselves of excess heat. This conformation usually has oval, slanted eyes and is best seen in the Siamese.

Newer breeds have been created in the West to mimic Oriental style. The Oriental shorthair was created in the West after non-pointed shorthaired cats from southeast Asia died out from among the original Siamese imports.

## New departures in build

The possibility of breeding bigger or smaller cats intrigues many. However, the domestic cat seems to have a genetically predetermined size range, so when this has been tried the cats have reverted to normal size in the next generation. Only outcrossing to another species—a controversial move—might change this.

A few breeds are classified by a single anatomical feature, often arguably a malformation: the taillessness of the Manx is associated with potentially lethal medical conditions; other cats have extra toes. The single most striking change in cat build is the munchkin. This is a dwarfed breed: most of the bones in the body are normal, but the long bones of the legs are dramatically shortened.

The cat evolved to virtual perfection through thousands of years. Human interventions that threaten such inherent flawlessness seem particularly arrogant.

**The Siamese** is the ultimate example of the Oriental cat, with its slanted eyes, slender body, thin tail, and fine legs.

**Western breeds** like the Cornish and Devon rexes have been bred to look somewhat like Orientals.

# Eye color and shape

- All cats are born with blue eyes
- Blue-eyed white cats are often deaf
- The "natural" eye shape has been altered

BROWN

ORANGE

GOLD

Cats have unusually large eyes for the size of their heads. The ratio mirrors the proportions seen in most animals, including humans, during infancy; it triggers our willingness to care for young animals, and cats benefit from this.

**Adult cats' eyes** are coppery brown, orange, yellow, or green. Sometimes, they remain blue, as in kittenhood, due to coat-color genes.

## Eye color

Kittens are born with blue eyes. As they mature, the color becomes coppery brown, orange, yellow, or green. Only a few cats maintain blue eyes.

Although some breed standards do link the two, most eye colors are not governed by coat color. The only exception is blue eyes; they are caused by forms of albinism that lead to a lack of pigmentation in both the coat and the iris and occur in cats with a lot of white in their coats.

Siamese blue eyes have a different source and may be linked to poor three-dimensional vision rather than deafness. Early Siamese squinted to compensate, but breeding has removed the squint.

HAZEL

GREEN

GREEN

**Wildcats have hazel** or copper eyes, sometimes tending toward yellow or green. Green eyes are also common in random-bred cats.

BIRMAN BLUE

## Eye shape

Wildcats' eyes are oval and slightly slanted; breeds considered close to the "natural" cat currently have these eyes.

Generally speaking, old Western breeds, such as the Chartreux, have round, prominent eyes.

Some Eastern cats have round eyes, but almond-shaped slanted eyes are most common in foreign or Oriental breeds.

BLUE, SLANTED

BLUE

**Blue-eyed white cats** are often deaf. This is because the gene that causes the lack of pigment is linked to a gene that causes fluid to dry up in the hearing receptors in the cochlea.

# Breed profiles

- There are dozens of recognized breeds
- Individual cats have individual personalities
- Not all breeds are recognized by all registries

Pedigree cats originally came from random-bred populations and sometimes have an influence on them in return through accidental breedings.

### Breed descriptions

Each breed profile in this chapter includes a description of appearance and character. While appearances within a breed are consistent, personality traits can vary. Much depends on experience; even cats from the most genial of breeds can be made nervous by poor early socialization.

The breed histories outline the breed's ancestry and its route to acceptance by the registries. Some histories are easy to trace, others are less distinct: older breeds may be wrapped in myths, and the exact origins of even some of the newer breeds are unclear.

Salient information is grouped together in the Key Facts box of each profile. This provides details of origin, weight range, personality, and colors.

### International differences

Not all registries recognize the same breeds or the same colors and patterns in each breed. The same breed may even develop different looks in different countries, depending on the prevalent trends. Colors accepted by the main registry—GCCF for British cats, FIFé for mainland Europe, CFA for North America and Japan—are listed, as are (in *italic text*) additional colors that occur but are either not accepted or may be accepted in other registries, usually TICA.

**FAWN-POINT SIAMESE**

### The breed symbols

The details on personality given in the Key Facts offer a guide to tendencies across the given breeds. Individual cats may differ from the breed norm.

 Quiet     Vocal

 Self-contained     Gregarious

 Sedate     Active

#### GROOMING

 Little    Moderate     Daily

# Shorthaired cats

Thousands of years ago, domestic cats spread from Egypt to varying environments. The early African wildcat type—lean, moderately sized, with a fine coat—was not naturally suited to all the new conditions.

In northern climates, survival of the fittest favored stocky individuals with dense, insulating undercoats of down hair to protect them from the cold. These cats also developed "cobby" bodies, a type later developed into the British shorthair and exported as the foundation stock for many of the world's cats, including the American shorthair. At the same time, the cat was also spreading east across Asia. In warm climates, natural selection favored sparser coats and a smaller body to increase the surface-area-to-weight ratio and help lose excess heat. These cats grew longer and leaner, and their smoother, thinner coats often

lacked any down hair. Such cats are called foreign or, if extremely slender, Oriental types.

Mutations in coat type always occurred, but they have died out without human intervention. Some shorthairs have wavy or curled "rex" coats, first bred in the Cornish rex. The extreme mutation of hairlessness is often a lethal trait that naturally disappears, but with selective breeding it has formed the basis of the sphynx's extraordinary appearance.

A new trend in breeding is that of creating a new look rather than refining what nature has already achieved. Many new breeds emulate wildcats. The Bengal was the first breed produced by mating the domestic cat with a wildcat. It has been followed by the chausie, crossed to the *Felis chaus*, or jungle cat.

**The silver spotted tabby** variety of British shorthair first appeared in the 1880s.

# Exotic shorthair

- Shorthaired Persian
- Lively and inquisitive
- Softly spoken

The exotic shorthair has the conformation, gentle personality, and soft, squeaky voice of a Persian *(see p.103)*, but it has a highly original coat: not quite short, but not semilong either. Outcrossing to produce the short coat has given the exotic a slightly livelier and more inquisitive disposition than its parent breed; it has not, however, eliminated the anatomical problems of the flat face inherited from the Persian.

**History** In the early 1960s, US breeders of the American shorthair *(see p.64)* attempted to introduce the Persian's coat texture into their breed. Instead, they produced cats with the shorthair's coat on the Persian's cobby, compact body. The exotic shorthair was recognized by the CFA in 1967.

### Key facts

**Place of origin**
United States

**Date of origin**
1960s

**Weight range**
7–14 lb (3–6.5 kg)

**Temperament** Gently inquisitive

**Breed colors**
All colors and patterns, including pointed, sepia, and mink

Legs are short, thick, and strong

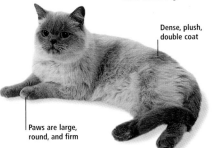

Dense, plush, double coat

Paws are large, round, and firm

### Physical characteristics

| | |
|---|---|
| Head | Round and massive, with full cheeks |
| Eyes | Large, round, and prominent |
| Ears | Small, with rounded tips, set wide and low |
| Body | Medium to large and cobby, carried low on legs |
| Coat | Dense, plush, standing out from body |
| Tail | Relatively short |

# British shorthair

- Easy-going temperament
- A natural hunter
- Unusual blood type

The impressively built British shorthair is self-possessed and undemanding. Numerous firm guard hairs give the coat a distinctively crisp feel, and the protective undercoat insulates on the frostiest of days. The British shorthair has a gentle disposition but, if prey appears, it is a successful hunter.
**History** British shorthairs were developed in the 1880s from British farm, street, and household cats. Although by the 1950s the breed had almost died out, it was revived by dedicated breeders. In the 1970s, the British shorthair arrived in the United States, where its calm, reserved manner immediately won it admirers. Unlike most shorthaired cats, 40 percent of all British shorthairs have Type B blood, a rare trait.

## Key facts

Place of origin
**Great Britain**

Date of origin
**1880s**

Weight range
**9–18 lb (4–8 kg)**

Temperament Genial and relaxed

Breed colors A wide variety of colors and color combinations is acceptable

Good width in shoulders

Short, strong legs

Broad nose

## Physical characteristics

| | |
|---|---|
| Head | **Round face with full cheeks** |
| Eyes | **Large, round, and copper or gold in most colors** |
| Ears | **Medium in size, with round tips** |
| Body | **Cobby and strong, carried low on legs; broad chest** |
| Coat | **Dense, with crisp feel** |
| Tail | **Short and thick, with blunt tip** |

# Manx

- Naturally tailless
- Careful breeding required
- Some have tails!

The lack of a tail is this breed's most obvious visible feature. Manx may be "rumpies" (with no tail), "stumpies" (with short tails), and "tailies" (with almost natural tails). The Manx gene carries potentially lethal consequences; rumpy-to-rumpy breedings, for example, can result in Manx syndrome, in which kittens either die at or soon after birth or they develop fatal problems by four months of age.

**History** The Manx originated on the Isle of Man in the Irish Sea before the 18th century. Taillessness occurs occasionally in feline populations as a spontaneous mutation, but it only survives in isolated groups, such as those on islands. The breed was recognized by the CFA in the 1920s.

## Key facts

**Place of origin**
**Isle of Man, UK**

**Date of origin**
**Pre-1700s**

**Weight range**
**8–12 lb (3.5–5.5 kg)**

**Temperament** Mellow and even-tempered

**Breed colors** A wide variety of colors and color combinations is acceptable

Ears are angled outward

Legs are relatively short and powerful

Hind legs are longer than forelegs

## Physical characteristics

| | |
|---|---|
| Head | Large and round, with medium-length nose |
| Eyes | Color in keeping with coat color |
| Ears | Fairly tall and high set, with rounded tips |
| Body | Solid and compact, with short back |
| Coat | Thick and double, with quality more important than pattern |
| Tail | No rise of bone or cartilage is discernible when stroked |

# American shorthair

- A powerful physique
- Calm and collected
- Adapted to its environment

This self-sufficient and no-nonsense cat is popular in North America but uncommon elsewhere. American shorthairs can be quite large, and the full-cheeked face and muscular, robust body exude strength. American shorthair breeders aim to produce kittens that have the best qualities of household cats.

**History** Domestic cats arrived in North America with the first settlers. They eventually developed thick coats to protect them from the cold and grew bigger than European cats to cope with their many natural predators. In the early 1900s, it was decided to preserve these cats' characteristics in a breed. The first litter, born in 1904, was from a mating of American and British shorthairs *(see p.62)*.

## Key facts

**Place of origin**
United States

**Date of origin**
Early 1900s

**Weight range**
8–15 lb (3.5–7 kg)

**Temperament**
Easy-going

**Breed colors** A wide variety of colors and color combinations is acceptable

Neck is medium-sized and muscular

Tail tapers to blunt end

Legs are heavily muscled

## Physical characteristics

| | |
|---|---|
| Head | Large, slightly longer than it is wide |
| Eyes | Large, rounded, and very slightly tilted |
| Ears | Medium-sized and well spaced, with rounded tips |
| Body | Solid, powerful, and muscular |
| Coat | Short, thick, and hard in texture |
| Tail | Medium length, thick at base |

# American wirehair

- ■ "Steel wool"-texture coat
- ■ Enjoys human contact
- ■ Developed in the 1960s

The most notable feature of this relaxed, friendly breed is its coat, which feels like steel wool. Every hair is thinner than usual and crimped, hooked, or bent, giving the appearance of wiring. The most prized coat is dense and coarse, but its appearance in kittenhood is no guarantee of its appearance at maturity. Curly whiskers are also highly valued. The wirehair is rarely destructive and enjoys being handled.

**History** The breed descends from a kitten born in 1966 in upstate New York. For a while its standard, apart from the coat, was the same as the shorthair's *(see opposite)*. The wirehair's own standard was written in 1967. This rare breed remains largely unrecognized outside of North America.

### Key facts

**Place of origin**
**United States**

**Date of origin**
**1966**

**Weight range**
**8–15 lb (3.5–7 kg)**

**Temperament** Relaxed, occasionally bossy

**Breed colors** A wide variety of colors and color combinations is acceptable

Eyes are large and round

Coat is dense and coarse

Legs are sturdy, with rounded paws

### Physical characteristics

| | |
|---|---|
| Head | Rounded, with high cheekbones |
| Eyes | Large and round, widely spaced, with a slight tilt |
| Ears | Medium-sized, with rounded tips |
| Body | Level back and rounded torso |
| Coat | Springy and tight, medium length |
| Tail | Tapers down to rounded—but not blunt—tip |

# Snowshoe

- Distinctive white paws
- Chatty and loving
- Growing in popularity

Named after its characteristic white paws, this breed combines the pointing of the Siamese with white spotting. Two patterns exist: the mitted, with limited white, and the bicolor, with more white on the face and body. Snowshoes are affectionate and, although they are talkative, they have soft voices.

**History** In the 1960s, a Philadelphia breeder began to cross her Siamese *(see p.96)* with American shorthairs *(see p.64)*. The resulting hybrid faced some opposition from Siamese breeders at first, partly due to fears that the spotting might find its way into Siamese bloodlines. Since being recognized by TICA in the 1980s, the snowshoe has gained wider popularity, but it remains a fairly rare breed.

Body has semi-foreign build

Ears continue lines of face

Medium-sized paws are oval and white

## Key facts

**Place of origin**
**United States**

**Date of origin**
**1960s**

**Weight range**
**6–12 lb (2.5–5.5 kg)**

**Temperament** Active and friendly

**Breed colors** Seal, chocolate, blue, and lilac in mitted and bicolors with white

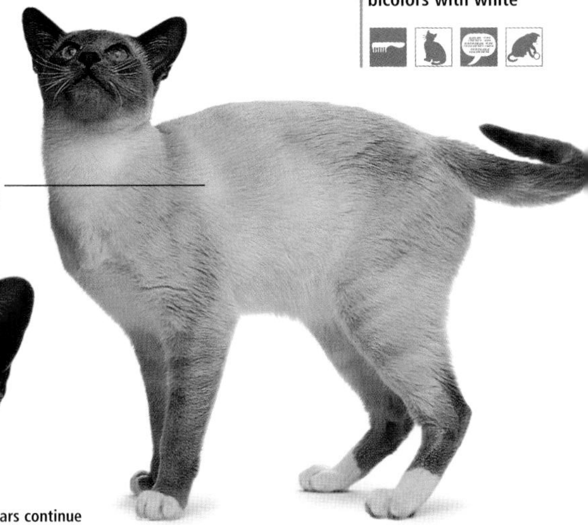

## Physical characteristics

| | |
|---|---|
| Head | **Broad modified wedge, with slight stop in profile** |
| Eyes | **Medium-sized, oval, and blue** |
| Ears | **Medium to medium-large** |
| Body | **Moderate size and musculature** |
| Coat | **Short, smooth, and close-lying, with no noticeable undercoat** |
| Tail | **Medium thickness, tapering slightly** |

# European shorthair

- The least-known shorthair
- Coat for all weathers
- "Ready-made" breed

The European shorthair is not as well known as its British or American counterparts. The breed is less cobby than the British type, with a slightly longer and less heavily jowled face. It has many of the same basic traits as the British cats, however, being a strong, hardy cat with an all-weather coat. Its personality tends to be calm and affectionate.

**History** Until 1982, European shorthairs were classified with British shorthairs *(see p.62).* FIFé then gave the breed its own category, and it began effectively as a "ready-made" breed. European shorthairs are selectively bred, with no British shorthair crosses permitted in the pedigree by most major breed registries.

## Key facts

**Place of origin**
**European mainland**

**Date of origin**
**1982**

**Weight range**
**8–15 lb (3.5–7 kg)**

**Temperament**
**Intelligent and reserved**

**Breed colors** A wide variety of colors and color combinations is acceptable

Medium-length tail

Dense,
all-weather coat

Muscular neck

Legs are
well muscled

## Physical characteristics

| | |
|---|---|
| Head | Triangular to rounded, well-defined muzzle |
| Eyes | Large, round, and well spaced, with colors to match coat |
| Ears | Medium-sized and upright, rounded tips |
| Body | Medium to large, well muscled, but not cobby |
| Coat | Short and dense, standing away from body |
| Tail | Thick at base, tapering to rounded tip |

# Chartreux

- Ancient French feline
- A hunter, not a fighter
- Late developer

A keen observer of life, the Chartreux is a tolerant breed, less talkative than most, with a high-pitched meow and a rarely used chirp. A big, late-maturing cat, the Chartreux is also a good hunter, if not a fighter: individuals tend to withdraw from conflict rather than display aggression.

**History** The Chartreux's ancestors arrived in France by ship, possibly from Syria. By the 1700s, it was known as the "cat of France." After World War II it became almost extinct and was reestablished by outcrossing survivors with blue Persians *(see p.103)* and blue British shorthairs (British blues; *see p.62*). The Chartreux reached North America in the 1970s.

## Key facts

**Place of origin**
**France**

**Date of origin**
**Pre-18th century**

**Weight range**
**7–17 lb (3–7.5 kg)**

**Temperament** Calmly
attentive

**Breed colors** Blue self

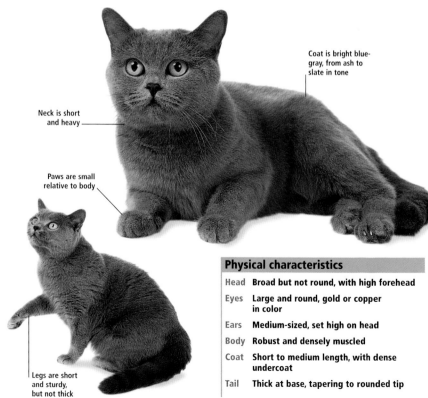

Coat is bright blue-gray, from ash to slate in tone

Neck is short and heavy

Paws are small relative to body

Legs are short and sturdy, but not thick

## Physical characteristics

| | |
|---|---|
| Head | Broad but not round, with high forehead |
| Eyes | Large and round, gold or copper in color |
| Ears | Medium-sized, set high on head |
| Body | Robust and densely muscled |
| Coat | Short to medium length, with dense undercoat |
| Tail | Thick at base, tapering to rounded tip |

# Russian shorthair

- Double-thick coat
- Elegant green eyes
- Allegedly non-destructive

The most vivid features of this slightly reserved cat are its thick, lustrous coat—described in the British breed standard as "the truest criterion of the Russian"—and its emerald-green eyes. This is a gentle breed, among the least destructive of all cats, and an ideal indoor companion.

**History** Legend has it that the Russian shorthair descends from ships' cats from the Russian port of Archangel in the 19th century. The modern Russian shorthair contains bloodlines from blue British shorthairs (British blues; *see p.62*), and even blue-pointed Siamese *(see p.96)*. White and black versions have also been developed; these are accepted in Britain, but not by FIFé or North American fancies.

## Key facts

**Place of origin**
**Possibly Russian port of Archangel**

**Date of origin**
**1800s**

**Weight range**
**7–12 lb (3–5.5 kg)**

**Temperament**
**Reserved and shy**

**Breed colors** **Black, blue, or white self**

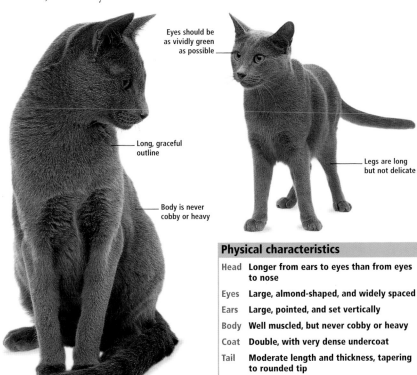

Eyes should be as vividly green as possible

Long, graceful outline

Body is never cobby or heavy

Legs are long but not delicate

## Physical characteristics

| | |
|---|---|
| Head | Longer from ears to eyes than from eyes to nose |
| Eyes | Large, almond-shaped, and widely spaced |
| Ears | Large, pointed, and set vertically |
| Body | Well muscled, but never cobby or heavy |
| Coat | Double, with very dense undercoat |
| Tail | Moderate length and thickness, tapering to rounded tip |

# Havana brown

- ■ Climbing cat
- ■ Outcrossing allowed
- ■ Confusing color history

This breed's origins are the same as for the Oriental shorthair *(see p.97)*, but it has come to resemble the Russian shorthair *(see p.69)*. Over the past decade, the breed has struggled to exist. To overcome this, in 1998 the CFA agreed to allow outcrossing again. As graceful as they look, Havana browns are very physical cats—they are, for example, great climbers.

**History** In the 1950s, British cat breeders developed a solid chocolate of Siamese type, which was registered as a chestnut-brown foreign in Britain and as Havana brown in North America. In 1973, after the CFA accepted the Oriental shorthair breed, Havana browns were registered as chestnut Oriental shorthairs. Confusingly, the chestnut color is now called Havana in Britain.

## Key facts

**Place of origin**
**Great Britain and United States**

**Date of origin**
**1950s**

**Weight range**
**6–10 lb (2.5–4.5 kg)**

**Temperament** Sweet and sociable

**Breed colors**
Chocolate self, *lilac*

Tail has _____
tapered tip

_____ Oval, compact
paws

Long head
narrows to
slim muzzle _____

## Physical characteristics

| | |
|---|---|
| Head | Long and slender, with narrow, almost squared muzzle and strong chin |
| Eyes | Oval in shape, green in color |
| Ears | Large and wide set, but upright |
| Body | Medium length, carried level |
| Coat | Not open nor extremely close-lying; short, smooth, and shiny |
| Tail | Medium length and thickness, tapering toward tip |

# Abyssinian

- North African origin
- Top-five breed in the US
- Attention-seeking athlete

This breed's "ticked" coat pattern is due to a gene that gives each hair several dark bands evenly spread on a lighter background. Although Abyssinians are often almost silent, their personalities are far from quiet: they are natural athletes, climbers, and investigators. Occasionally they can suffer inherited forms of retinal atrophy, a form of blindness.

**History** This breed's coat is a perfect camouflage in North Africa's sunburned habitat. The founding cats were brought to Britain from Abyssinia (now Ethiopia) in the late 1860s and accepted in 1882. The breed was almost extinct in Britain in the early 1900s, but by the 1930s it was established in the US. Today it is the fifth most popular breed in North America.

## Key facts

**Place of origin**
**Ethiopia (formerly Abyssinia)**

**Date of origin**
**1860s**

**Weight range**
**9–16 lb (4–7.5 kg)**

**Temperament**
**Attention-demanding**

**Breed colors** Ruddy, red (sorrel), blue, or fawn in ticked tabby (no other colors are officially accepted)

Only faint necklaces are acceptable

Ticking requires at least four bands of darker color

Almond-shaped eyes are green, hazel, or amber

## Physical characteristics

| | |
|---|---|
| Head | Wedge-shaped face |
| Eyes | Rounded, almond-shaped eyes; dark rims set in "spectacles" of lighter hair |
| Ears | Large and cupped, ideally with tufted tips |
| Body | Medium-sized and muscular |
| Coat | Close-lying, fine but not soft |
| Tail | Gently tapering; same length as body |

# Australian mist

- Loves being indoors
- Popular "down under"
- Sociable with humans

This rare breed has a playful and home-loving nature. Its appearance is moderate in all ways: medium in size, foreign in build but not extremely so, with a short, but not close-lying, coat. The delicate markings create a misty appearance (hence the name); the background ticking is essential to this effect.

**History** Dr. Truda Straede in New South Wales, Australia, started a program to produce an indoor-loving, people-oriented breed, mixing the build and companionability of the Burmese *(see pp.93 and 94)* and the ticking and lively disposition of the Abyssinian *(see p.71)*. Domestic tabbies gave the spots and offset the tendency toward early sexual maturity. The first half-Burmese, quarter-Aby, quarter-domestic tabby kittens were born in January 1980.

### Key facts

**Place of origin**
**Australia**

**Date of origin**
**1980**

**Weight range**
**8–13 lb (3.5–6 kg)**

**Temperament** Lively and harmonious

**Breed colors** Blue, brown, chocolate, gold, lilac, or peach in spotted-and-ticked tabby

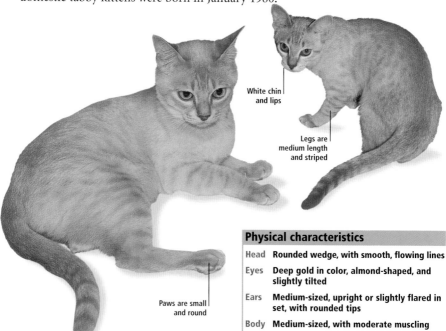

White chin and lips

Legs are medium length and striped

Paws are small and round

### Physical characteristics

| | |
|---|---|
| Head | Rounded wedge, with smooth, flowing lines |
| Eyes | Deep gold in color, almond-shaped, and slightly tilted |
| Ears | Medium-sized, upright or slightly flared in set, with rounded tips |
| Body | Medium-sized, with moderate muscling |
| Coat | Short, stands out softly from body |
| Tail | Medium length, tapering slightly to rounded tip |

# Korat

- Boss cat
- A rare Thai beauty
- Fine-coated

Similar to the Russian shorthair *(see p.69)* in size and color, the Korat has a single rather than double coat, and peridot-green rather than emerald-green eyes. Despite their innocent expression, Korats are strong-willed and thrive on having their own way. Very rarely, individuals carry neuromuscular disorders.

**History** The *Cat Book Poems* of the Ayutthaya Kingdom (1350–1767) describes the silver-blue Si-Sawat from Korat, a remote Thai plateau. Korats were introduced into the United States in 1959 and recognized there in 1965. The first pair was imported into Britain in 1972, and the breed was recognized in 1975. It remains rare everywhere.

## Key facts

**Place of origin**
Thailand

**Date of origin**
Pre-1700s

**Weight range**
6–10 lb (2.5–4.5 kg)

**Temperament**
Demanding and opinionated

**Breed colors** Blue self

Paws are oval and compact

Oversized eyes and heart-shaped face

## Physical characteristics

| | |
|---|---|
| Head | Large, flat forehead and firm, rounded muzzle |
| Eyes | Luminous, prominent, and rounded |
| Ears | Large, wide at base, with rounded tips |
| Body | Strong and semicobby build |
| Coat | Glossy, fine, and close-lying, with no undercoat |
| Tail | Heavy at base, tapering to rounded tip |

# Bombay

- Heat-seeking feline
- Low-maintenance coat
- Miniature black panther

This majestic breed thrives on human company and is a real heat-seeker. The Bombay's brilliant copper-colored eyes can fade or turn slightly green with age, while the jet-black coat is almost maintenance-free: a rubdown with a chamois, or even your hand, is all that is needed to keep its sheen. Although litters are large, the Bombay remains rare, especially outside North America.

**History** In the 1950s, a Kentucky breeder tried to create a "mini black panther" from black American shorthairs *(see p.64)* and sable Burmese *(see pp.93 and 94)*. By the 1960s, she had produced cats with black coats, muscular bodies, rounded heads, and copper eyes. The Bombay was recognized in 1976.

### Key facts

**Place of origin**
United States

**Date of origin**
1960s

**Weight range**
6–11 lb (2.5–5 kg)

**Temperament** Genial, relaxed, and gregarious

**Breed colors**
Black self,
*sable*

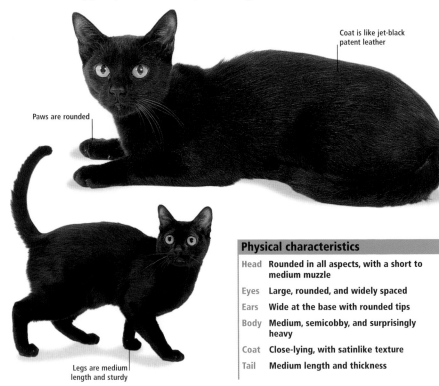

Coat is like jet-black patent leather

Paws are rounded

Legs are medium length and sturdy

### Physical characteristics

| | |
|---|---|
| Head | Rounded in all aspects, with a short to medium muzzle |
| Eyes | Large, rounded, and widely spaced |
| Ears | Wide at the base with rounded tips |
| Body | Medium, semicobby, and surprisingly heavy |
| Coat | Close-lying, with satinlike texture |
| Tail | Medium length and thickness |

# Cornish rex

■ Velvety coat
■ Long-legged acrobat
■ Originating in Cornwall, England

Extrovert and curvaceous, with washboard waves of hair, the Cornish rex has dramatic ears set high on a relatively small head and fine, lean legs. The coat lacks guard hairs and is gloriously soft to touch, much like cut velvet.
**History** In 1950, a farm cat from Cornwall, England, had a litter with one curly-haired male kitten, Kallibunker. Breeding Kallibunker back to his mother confirmed that the rex mutation was recessive. Descendants were crossed to British shorthairs *(see p.62)* and Burmese *(see pp. 93 and 94)*. In 1957, the Cornish rex arrived in the US, where Oriental shorthair *(see p.97)* and Siamese *(see p.96)* lines were introduced.

## Key facts

**Place of origin**
**Great Britain**

**Date of origin**
**1950s**

**Weight range**
**6–10 lb (2.5–4.5 kg)**

**Temperament**
**Enterprising acrobat**

**Breed colors** All colors and patterns, including pointed, sepia, and mink

Coat is short and velvety, with regular waves

Ears set high on head

Neck is slender and elegant

Paws are small and oval

## Physical characteristics

| | |
|---|---|
| Head | Medium length, with rounded muzzle and strong chin |
| Eyes | Medium-sized and oval |
| Ears | Large, wide at base, with rounded tips |
| Body | Medium-sized, hard, and muscular |
| Coat | Short, plushy, and silky |
| Tail | Long, fine, and tapering |

# Devon rex

- Elfin "extraterrestrial" looks
- Fun-loving personality
- Smaller than average

Startling eyes and oversized ears give the Devon rex the look of an elfin clown. The temperament follows suit: a Devon is seldom elegant and always finds life amusing. This, together with its coat, earned it the nickname "poodle cat." Its coat has also led to unsubstantiated claims of non-allergenic qualities.

**History** In 1960, a curly-coated cat in Devon, southwest England, and a local female produced a normal litter with one curly-coated kitten, named Kirlee. Kirlee's parents were almost certainly related, and inbreeding was needed to perpetuate the Devon rex. Unfortunately, early inbreeding brought to light a genetic spasticity syndrome, which is being studied as part of the Feline Genome Project.

## Key facts

**Place of origin**
**Great Britain**

**Date of origin**
**1960**

**Weight range**
**6–9 lb (2.5–4 kg)**

**Temperament**
Appealing clown

**Breed colors** All colors and patterns, including pointed

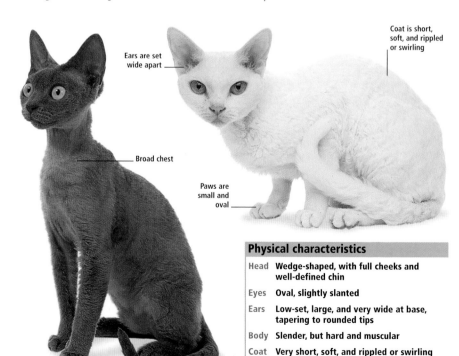

Ears are set wide apart

Broad chest

Paws are small and oval

Coat is short, soft, and rippled or swirling

## Physical characteristics

| | |
|---|---|
| Head | Wedge-shaped, with full cheeks and well-defined chin |
| Eyes | Oval, slightly slanted |
| Ears | Low-set, large, and very wide at base, tapering to rounded tips |
| Body | Slender, but hard and muscular |
| Coat | Very short, soft, and rippled or swirling |
| Tail | Long and tapering, well covered but not bushy |

# Selkirk rex

- On-and-off rexing
- Brushing straightens the hair
- Available in two coat lengths

Rexing is apparent in the soft coat of this breed immediately after birth, but it then disappears, only to reappear at eight to 10 months. While the coat needs routine grooming, excessive brushing straightens the hair. Selkirks come in two versions, the plush shorthair and the more dramatic longhair. In body shape, these cats resemble the British shorthair *(see p.62)*.

**History**  In 1987, in Montana, a female calico kitten was born, the only one in a litter of seven to have curly hair and whiskers. Miss DePesto, as she was called, was bred and three in her litter of six had curly coats, indicating that the rexed coat was genetically dominant. The breed, recognized by TICA, was named after the nearby Selkirk Mountains.

## Key facts

**Place of origin**
**United States**

**Date of origin**
**1987**

**Weight range**
**7–11 lb (3–5 kg)**

**Temperament**  Patiently tolerant

**Breed colors**  All colors and patterns, including pointed, sepia, and mink

Whiskers are curly

Legs are medium length and substantially boned

Curl on neck prominent

Curl on body is variable

## Physical characteristics

| | |
|---|---|
| Head | Rounded with distinct stop to nose, full-cheeked |
| Eyes | Round and widely spaced |
| Ears | Medium and pointed, set well apart |
| Body | Medium in build, cobby, with good musculature |
| Coat | Thick, medium length, in loose curls |
| Tail | Thick, tapering to rounded tip |

# LaPerm

- Quirkily named rexed breed
- Excellent hunter
- Loving and nosey

LaPerm cats are born with fur, but then, usually during infancy, they become completely bald. The new coat that grows after this is thick, silky, and curly. There are both longhaired and shorthaired versions: shorthairs may have wavy, rather than curly, hair. LaPerms are excellent hunters.

**History** In 1982, a farm cat in Oregon produced a litter that included a bald kitten. At the age of eight weeks, the kitten finally grew a coat that, unlike that of her littermates, was curly and soft. The gene is dominant, so wide outcrossing to increase the gene pool can be done while still producing reasonable numbers of rexed kittens.

Neck is long and carried vertically

Paws are medium-sized and round

Legs are medium length and well muscled

### Key facts

**Place of origin**
United States

**Date of origin**
1982

**Weight range**
8–12 lb (3.5–5.5 kg)

**Temperament**
Affectionate and inquisitive

**Breed colors** All colors and patterns, including sepia, pointed, and mink

## Physical characteristics

| | |
|---|---|
| Head | Broad, modified wedge, with prominent muzzle |
| Eyes | Large, almond-shaped, and slightly slanted |
| Ears | Medium-sized, with wide base and rounded tip |
| Body | Medium-boned, muscular, and heavy for size |
| Coat | Short, thick, and silky, with moderate undercoat |
| Tail | Long and tapering, with wavy hair |

# California spangled

- Miniature wildcat looks
- A sociable Californian
- Not widely recognized

The active California spangled (a term meaning spotted) has a lean body but is surprisingly heavy for its size. Its dense double coat has spotting over the back and sides, and striping between the ears and down the neck to the shoulders. Its round head is reminiscent of many small wildcats.

**History** Californian Paul Casey set out to create a wild-looking spotted cat without wildcat bloodlines. Using non-pedigreed cats from Asia and Cairo and a range of pedigreed breeds, he produced the desired cat in 1971. Rosetted and ringed coats mimic those of the ocelot, margay, and jaguar.
The breed has not as yet gained wide recognition.

## Key facts

**Place of origin**
**United States**

**Date of origin**
**1971**

**Weight range**
**9–18 lb (4–8 kg)**

**Temperament** Gently sociable

**Breed colors** Black, charcoal, brown, bronze, red, blue, gold, or silver in spotted tabby and snow leopard

Coat is spotted over the back and sides

Legs are medium length and muscular, with tabby bars

Dark rims to eyes

Spots can be round, oval, or triangular

## Physical characteristics

| | |
|---|---|
| Head | Wild in appearance, with broad, high cheeks and full whisker pads |
| Eyes | Oval and slightly slanted |
| Ears | Upright, with rounded tips, set far back on head |
| Body | Long and muscular |
| Coat | Short and sleek, but not close-lying |
| Tail | Tapering from heavy base |

# Egyptian mau

- Fastest domestic cat?
- Natural worried look
- Originally from Cairo

The mau resembles the cats featured on ancient wall paintings in Egypt. Its body and face are both moderate in form, and the coat has a spotted pattern in shades of the original brown color. However, while early portraits show wild-looking eyes, maus have wide, round eyes with a worried look. This is perhaps the fastest breed of domestic cat, able to run at speeds of almost 30 mph (50 km/h).

**History** Exiled Russian Nathalie Troubetskoy was taken with the spotted markings of street cats in Cairo, so she imported a female to Italy to mate with a local tom. In 1956, she went to the United States, where the kittens were registered. Recognized by the CFA in 1977, the breed remains almost unknown in Europe.

## Key facts

**Place of origin**
**Egypt and Italy**

**Date of origin**
**1950s**

**Weight range**
**5–11 lb (2.25–5 kg)**

**Temperament** Friendly and intelligent

**Breed colors** Black smoke, bronze spotted tabby, silver spotted tabby (no other colors are officially accepted)

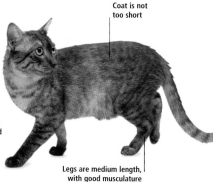

Coat is not too short

Legs are medium length, with good musculature

Nose curves smoothly from tip to forehead

Paws are small, with long toes

## Physical characteristics

| | |
|---|---|
| Head | Medium, rounded wedge without flat planes |
| Eyes | Large, rounded, and gooseberry-green in color |
| Ears | Medium to large, upright or slightly flared in set |
| Body | Well muscled, neither cobby nor foreign |
| Coat | Fine and silky, close-lying |
| Tail | Medium length, tapering from base to tip |

# Ocicat

- Siamese–Abyssinian hybrid
- Trainable feline
- Mini ocelot looks

A successful blend of Siamese and Abyssinian blood, the ocicat is playful and curious, and a real lap cat. It also responds well to early training. The breed's most distinctive feature is its spotting: the distribution should follow the classic tabby pattern, swirling around the center of the flank.

**History** Virginia Daly of Michigan crossed a Siamese *(see p.96)* with an Abyssinian *(see p.71)*, aiming to develop an Aby-pointed Siamese. In 1964, when one of the kittens was bred to a Siamese, the litter included not only Aby-pointed Siamese, but also a spotted kitten. Daly's daughter, noting its resemblance to the ocelot, called the kitten an "ocicat." In 1986 this still-uncommon breed was recognized by TICA.

## Key facts

**Place of origin**
**United States**

**Date of origin**
**1964**

**Weight range**
**6–14 lb (2.5–6.5 kg)**

**Temperament** Social and responsive

**Breed colors** A variety of spotted and silver spotted tabby colors is acceptable (no other colors are officially accepted)

Neck is
graceful
and arching

Tail has
dark tip

Graceful,
athletic build

Legs are
medium
length and
well muscled

## Physical characteristics

| | |
|---|---|
| Head | Modified wedge with broad muzzle, strong chin, and firm jaw |
| Eyes | Large, almond-shaped, and slightly tilted upward |
| Ears | Moderately large and set out at an angle |
| Body | Large, solid, and powerful, but graceful |
| Coat | Short, fine, and sleek, close-lying |
| Tail | Fairly long and slender |

# Bengal

- Wildcat origins
- Bred for dependable disposition
- Well muscled and large

The rare Bengal has a distinctively thick coat. Because of its wildcat origins, a dependable temperament is another vital feature. Early breeding introduced some undesirable genes for dilution—long hair and spotting—but also the Siamese coat pattern, which resulted in the extraordinary "snow" shades. Initially this was a nervous feline family, but continued development has led to a more outgoing breed. **History** The first mating of the Asian leopard cat with a domestic cat was accidental and took place in California in 1963. Ten years later, the University of California continued this hybridization to examine the Asian leopard cat's resistance to feline leukemia virus (FeLV). Out of these beginnings, in 1983, appeared the Bengal.

## Key facts

**Place of origin**
United States

**Date of origin**
1983

**Weight range**
12–22 lb (5.5–10 kg)

**Temperament**
Elegantly conservative

**Breed colors**
Brown or snow spotted or marbled tabby, *black self*

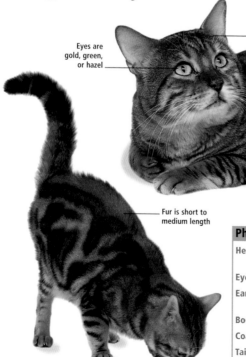

Eyes are gold, green, or hazel

Head is slightly longer than it is wide

Fur is short to medium length

## Physical characteristics

| | |
|---|---|
| Head | Relatively small, rounded wedge with broad muzzle and strong, round chin |
| Eyes | Large and oval, with slightly slanted set |
| Ears | Short, with wide base and rounded tips, no tufts |
| Body | Large, very muscular, and sleek |
| Coat | Dense, thick, and soft to touch |
| Tail | Thick and even, with rounded tip |

# Chausie

- Domestic–wildcat hybrid
- Temperament still developing
- Not yet recognized

The chausie (pronounced "chow-sea") is a hybrid cross between a domestic female and a male jungle cat (*Felis chaus*). Breeders claim that chausies make loyal pets if they are properly socialized from birth. The cat has a large, athletic body, long legs, and a ticked shorthaired coat.

**History** Since the 1960s, cat breeders have accidentally and intentionally crossed domestic cats with closely related wildcats, producing fertile hybrids. Within the cat-breeding world there is still intense debate over the ethics of creating domestic–wildcat hybrids. However, in 1995 the US-bred chausie was officially registered with TICA, and it is likely to eventually reach championship status.

## Key facts

**Place of origin**
**United States**

**Date of origin**
**Late 1960s**

**Weight range**
**10–22 lb (4.5–10 kg)**

**Temperament** Lively and devoted

**Breed colors** Brown ticked tabby, solid black, silver tip

Tufted ears are wide at base

Dense, shorthaired coat

Large, athletic body

## Physical characteristics

| | |
|---|---|
| Head | **Modified wedge, with high cheekbones and a strong chin** |
| Eyes | **Large and walnut-shaped** |
| Ears | **Wide at the base, large, and tufted** |
| Body | **Large, rectangular body, with full chest** |
| Coat | **Dense and shorthaired** |
| Tail | **Three-quarter length, extending just below the hock** |

# American bobtail

- Origins unknown
- Short-tailed show cat
- Remains quite rare

The background of the American bobtail is uncertain: bobcat parentage is unconfirmed, but both Manx *(see p.63)* and Japanese bobtail *(see p.98)* genes may be present, since tailless rumpies and cats with kinked tails appear. Show cats should have a short tail that stops just above the level of the hock. **History** This breed can be traced back to a random-bred, bobtailed, tabby kitten from Arizona. Early breeding aimed to produce bobtailed cats with a pattern similar to that of the snowshoe *(see p.66)*, but the cats became inbred and unhealthy. In the 1960s more colors and patterns were introduced, and the health of the breed improved. Both CFA and TICA have granted American bobtails "new breed" status.

### Key facts

**Place of origin**
United States

**Date of origin**
1960s

**Weight range**
7–15 lb (3–7 kg)

**Temperament** Friendly and inquisitive

**Breed colors** All colors and patterns, including sepia, pointed, and mink

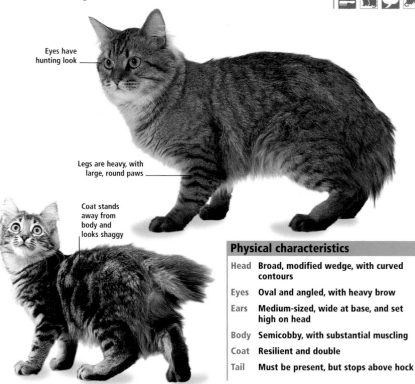

Eyes have hunting look

Legs are heavy, with large, round paws

Coat stands away from body and looks shaggy

### Physical characteristics

| | |
|---|---|
| Head | Broad, modified wedge, with curved contours |
| Eyes | Oval and angled, with heavy brow |
| Ears | Medium-sized, wide at base, and set high on head |
| Body | Semicobby, with substantial muscling |
| Coat | Resilient and double |
| Tail | Must be present, but stops above hock |

# Pixiebob

- Bred to look like a bobcat
- Doglike temperament
- Rules the roost

Developed to resemble the bobcat's wild appearance, pixiebobs are claimed to have the temperament of faithful dogs; they do not readily change homes, and are often happiest as a single-cat "ruler of the roost."

**History** Pixie, the founding cat of the pixiebob, was the result of breeding two "legend cats"—said to be the result of wild bobcats matings with domestic barn cats—in Washington State. In truth, legend cats simply had bobcat good looks. Recognized by TICA in 1995, the breed is not known outside North America. Legend cats are still found in rural areas, and may be refined to produce pixiebobs; no other pedigreed breeds or wildcats can be used in this process.

## Key facts

**Place of origin**
**North America**

**Date of origin**
**1990s**

**Weight range**
**9–18 lb (4–8 kg)**

**Temperament** Quiet but affectionate

**Breed colors** Brown spotted or rosette tabby

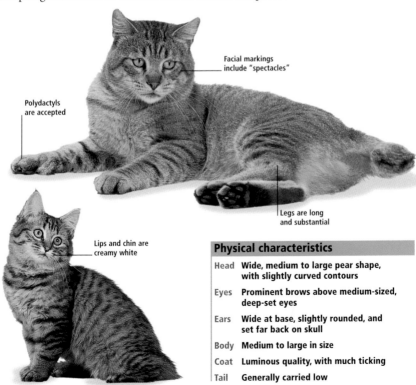

Facial markings include "spectacles"

Polydactyls are accepted

Legs are long and substantial

Lips and chin are creamy white

## Physical characteristics

| | |
|---|---|
| Head | Wide, medium to large pear shape, with slightly curved contours |
| Eyes | Prominent brows above medium-sized, deep-set eyes |
| Ears | Wide at base, slightly rounded, and set far back on skull |
| Body | Medium to large in size |
| Coat | Luminous quality, with much ticking |
| Tail | Generally carried low |

# Scottish fold

- Distinctive flat ears
- Reserved and placid
- Not recognized in its homeland

Folded ears, a short neck, and a round head ensure this breed's distinctive look. While the first Scottish fold had a "single" fold (ears bent forward), today's show cats have tight "triple" folds. Straight-eared cats are still essential for breeding healthy folds. The breed has a placid personality. **History** Susie, the fold's founding mother, was a Scottish farm cat. In the 1960s, a local shepherd was given one of her kittens and bred it to a British shorthair *(see p.62)*. In 1971, the shepherd's wife sent some folds to a geneticist in the US, and development continued with British and American shorthairs *(see p.64)*. Folds were recognized by 1994. In Britain, genetic problems associated with the breed prevent its recognition.

## Key facts

**Place of origin**
**Scotland**

**Date of origin**
**1961**

**Weight range**
**6–13 lb (2.5–6 kg)**

**Temperament** Quietly confident

**Breed colors** All colors and patterns, including pointed, sepia, and mink

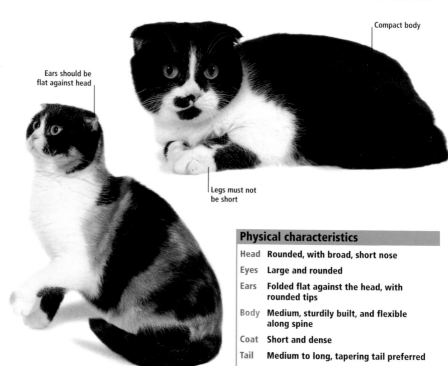

Compact body

Ears should be flat against head

Legs must not be short

## Physical characteristics

| | |
|---|---|
| Head | Rounded, with broad, short nose |
| Eyes | Large and rounded |
| Ears | Folded flat against the head, with rounded tips |
| Body | Medium, sturdily built, and flexible along spine |
| Coat | Short and dense |
| Tail | Medium to long, tapering tail preferred |

# American curl

- Handle curl with care
- Quiet and friendly
- Available in two coat lengths

This elegant and sweet-tempered breed comes in two coats, short and long. The extent of curl to the ears is graded in three stages: cats with ears just turned back (first degree) become pets, those with more curl (second degree) are used for breeding, and those with full crescents (third degree) are shown. The curled ears should be handled with care: uncurling them may damage the cartilage.

**History** American curls are the result of a genetic mutation that occurred in the US in the early 1980s in a black, longhaired, stray kitten named Shulamith. Half of her kittens also showed curled ears, a genetically dominant characteristic, and were distributed to form a breeding program.

Coat has minimal undercoat

Ears curl permanently at about four months

Body is moderately muscled

Tail tapers to tip

## Key facts

**Place of origin**
**United States**

**Date of origin**
**1981**

**Weight range**
**7–11 lb (3–5 kg)**

**Temperament** Quietly affable

**Breed colors** A wide variety of colors and color combinations is acceptable

## Physical characteristics

| | |
|---|---|
| Head | Modified wedge with gentle curves |
| Eyes | Upper rim oval, lower rim rounded |
| Ears | Curving at least 90° in smooth arc |
| Body | Semiforeign shape, moderately muscled |
| Coat | Soft and close-lying, with minimal undercoat |
| Tail | Equal to length of body, wide at base, tapering to tip |

# Munchkin

- Short "dwarfed" legs
- Accepted after health checks
- Playful personality

The short-legged munchkin has stirred up unprecedented controversy. While its playful personality is unmistakably feline, the breed's dwarfism represents a radical departure from normal feline anatomy. The breed has had to undergo rigorous health investigations before gaining acceptance.
**History** The munchkin has been bred since the 1980s in North America. After health investigations, TICA granted it "new breed" status in 1995. Some breeders are working with pedigreed breeds, producing rexed and curled-ear munchkins. A short-legged, curly coated type, called a Skookum, was produced by crossing a LaPerm (*see p.78*) with a munchkin in 1996.

## Key facts

**Place of origin**
**United States**

**Date of origin**
**1980s**

**Weight range**
**5–9 lb (2.25–4 kg)**

**Temperament**
Appealing and inquisitive

**Breed colors** All colors and patterns, including pointed, sepia, and mink

Legs are short but not misshapen

Round paws point outward

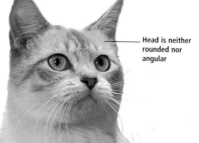

Head is neither rounded nor angular

## Physical characteristics

| | |
|---|---|
| Head | Almost triangular, with nose of medium length |
| Eyes | Walnut-shaped, large, and slightly tilted |
| Ears | Moderately large, wide at base, and upright |
| Body | Medium-sized, substantially muscled, neither svelte nor cobby |
| Coat | Moderately dense, with medium undercoat |
| Tail | Set high, medium-thick, tapering to rounded tip |

# Burmilla (Asian shaded)

- Burmese–chinchilla Persian hybrid
- Quiet attention-seeker
- Backcrossing permitted

These striking cats' type is inherited from their Burmese *(see p.94)* parentage, and the coat comes from their chinchilla Persian *(see p.103)* side. Less boisterous than the Burmese but more sociable than Persians, burmillas are attention-seekers. Despite this, they are moderate in their vocal demands and remarkably even-tempered.

**History** In 1981, in London, a mating between a Burmese and a chinchilla Persian resulted in shaded silver kittens. A breeding program began. The original litter was of Burmese type, and initial policy was to breed back to Burmese every other generation. Backcrossing still helps to enlarge the genetic base. The burmilla was recognized by the GCCF in 1989.

### Key facts

**Place of origin**
**Great Britain**

**Date of origin**
**1981**

**Weight range**
**9–15 lb (4–7 kg)**

**Temperament** Relaxed and engaging

**Breed colors** A wide variety of colors in sepia and solid shaded and silver shaded is acceptable

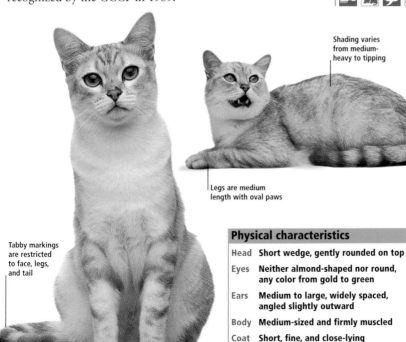

Shading varies from medium-heavy to tipping

Legs are medium length with oval paws

Tabby markings are restricted to face, legs, and tail

### Physical characteristics

| | |
|---|---|
| Head | Short wedge, gently rounded on top |
| Eyes | Neither almond-shaped nor round, any color from gold to green |
| Ears | Medium to large, widely spaced, angled slightly outward |
| Body | Medium-sized and firmly muscled |
| Coat | Short, fine, and close-lying |
| Tail | Medium to long, tapering to rounded tip |

# Asian self

■ Considered distinct from Asian shaded
■ Previously named Bombay
■ Many colors available

Breeders tend to see Asian selfs as distinct from their shaded counterparts *(see p.89)*, and some do not use cats from chinchilla Persian lines in their breeding programs.
**History** Black Burmese-type cats, called Bombays (not to be confused with America's Bombay breed), were being bred as early as the 1980s. Although the Bombay program had used nonpedigreed cats, it was then integrated into the continuing development of the Asian group as a whole. Other self colors were also developed, and there is now a wide range of colors.

## Key facts

**Place of origin**
**Great Britain**

**Date of origin**
**1981**

**Weight range**
**9–15 lb (4–7 kg)**

**Temperament** Relaxed and engaging

**Breed colors** A wide variety of colors is acceptable

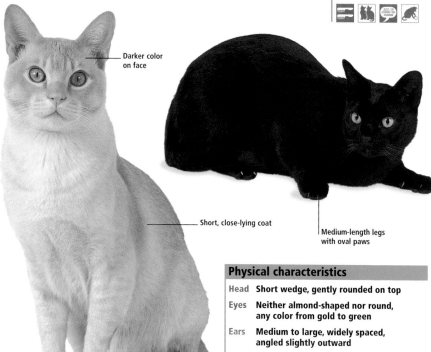

Darker color on face

Short, close-lying coat

Medium-length legs with oval paws

## Physical characteristics

| | |
|---|---|
| Head | Short wedge, gently rounded on top |
| Eyes | Neither almond-shaped nor round, any color from gold to green |
| Ears | Medium to large, widely spaced, angled slightly outward |
| Body | Medium-sized and firmly muscled |
| Coat | Short, fine, and close-lying |
| Tail | Medium to long, tapering to rounded tip |

# Asian smoke

- Halfway between shaded and self
- Shimmering undercoat
- Easy-going disposition

The Asian smoke combines the white undercoat of the burmilla (or Asian shaded, *see p.89*), with the solid coat of the Asian self *(see opposite)*. Smokes come in all the colors of the selfs, and Burmese color restriction is also permitted. With a coat slightly longer than that of the Burmese *(see p.94)*, the smoke's undercoat shows in a faint gleam over curves when the cat is still, and as a gentle shimmer when it moves. This coat type appeared in the second generation of crosses from burmillas.

**History** Asian smokes originated in the early 1980s from a British breeding program developed after the accidental creation of the burmilla.

**Key facts**

Place of origin
**Great Britain**

Date of origin
**1981**

Weight range
**9–15 lb (4–7 kg)**

Temperament  Relaxed and engaging

Breed colors  A wide variety of colors in sepia and solid smoke is acceptable

Ghost tabby marks give look of watered silk on coat

Eyes can be any color from gold to green

Up to half of hair length is white

## Physical characteristics

| | |
|---|---|
| Head | Short wedge, gently rounded on top |
| Eyes | Neither almond-shaped nor round, any color from gold to green |
| Ears | Medium to large, widely spaced, angled slightly outward |
| Body | Medium-sized and firmly muscled |
| Coat | Short, fine, and close-lying |
| Tail | Medium to long, tapering to rounded tip |

# Asian tabby

- Available in four patterns
- Ticking introduced from Abyssinians
- Enjoys companionship

The Asian tabby is one of the few cats recognized in Britain in which all four tabby patterns are bred; the ticked pattern is the most popular of them. The slightly disparate origins of these various coat patterns were a factor in the unusual decision to grant the Asians status as a group, rather than as a breed.

**History**  In Britain in the early 1980s, tabbies began to appear in the second generation of Asian crosses. The chinchilla Persian *(see p.103)*, one of the group's founding cats, has an agouti coat, although its tabby markings are rendered invisible by the inhibitor gene. It was then found that some breeders had also been bringing Abyssinians *(see p.71)* into their programs to introduce the ticked gene, and this work was then incorporated into the Asian breed.

## Key facts

**Place of origin**
**Great Britain**

**Date of origin**
**1981**

**Weight range**
**9–15 lb (4–7 kg)**

**Temperament**  Relaxed and engaging

**Breed colors**  A wide variety of colors in solid, sepia, silver, and ticked tabby is acceptable

Strong tabby markings on head

Necklace must be broken

Dark tip on tail

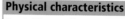

## Physical characteristics

| | |
|---|---|
| Head | Short wedge, gently rounded on top |
| Eyes | Neither almond-shaped nor round, any color from gold to green |
| Ears | Medium to large, widely spaced, angled slightly outward |
| Body | Medium-sized and firmly muscled |
| Coat | Short, fine, and close-lying |
| Tail | Medium to long, tapering to rounded tip |

# American Burmese

- Enjoys human company
- Round head favored by breeders
- Originated in Rangoon, Burma

The American Burmese is fond of human company but is less vocal or demonstrative than other Oriental breeds. This breed has a rounder head than its European counterparts. The extremely round, "contemporary" look was developed in the 1970s; unfortunately, so was the Burmese head fault, an inherited skull deformity that is often lethal.

**History** The Burmese begins with Wong Mau, a Burmese–Siamese hybrid from Myanmar (formerly Burma), brought to the US in 1930. A natural Tonkinese *(see p.95)*, Wong Mau was bred to a Siamese *(see p.96)*, and the kittens bred back to Wong Mau. Three types emerged: Siamese-pointed; dark brown with minimal pointing (the first true Burmese); and a dark body with darker points, like Wong Mau.

## Key facts

**Place of origin**
**Myanmar (formerly Burma)**

**Date of origin**
**1930s**

**Weight range**
**8–14 lb (3.5–6.5 kg)**

**Temperament** Friendly and relaxed

**Breed colors** Sable, champagne, blue, or platinum in sepia

Muzzle is short and broad, with rounded chin

Close-lying coat

Well-developed neck

## Physical characteristics

| | |
|---|---|
| Head | Pleasingly rounded, with full cheeks |
| Eyes | Rounded in shape and golden in color |
| Ears | Medium-sized, widely spaced, and tilting forwards |
| Body | Medium-sized, muscular, and compact |
| Coat | Short and fine, with satinlike texture and glossy shine |
| Tail | Medium length |

# European Burmese

- Easy-going and relaxed
- Closer to "original" Burmese looks
- Gregarious and friendly

While the American side of the Burmese family has developed into a rounded cat, European breeders opted for a well-muscled but more angular shape and a more Oriental look. Regardless of type, the Burmese is ideally suited to living in active households.

**History** The Burmese breed started with Wong Mau, a cat brought from Myanmar (formerly Burma) to the US in the 1930s. European Burmese descend from American Burmese cats *(see p.93)* imported into Europe after World War II. The wide range of colors was developed by the introduction of the red gene. In the 1970s this range was broadened to create tortie versions of all the recognized colors.

## Key facts

**Place of origin**
**Myanmar (formerly Burma)**

**Date of origin**
**1930s**

**Weight range**
**8–14 lb (3.5–6.5 kg)**

**Temperament** Friendly and relaxed

**Breed colors** A variety of self and tortie colors is acceptable

Muzzle is blunt, with deep chin

Oval paws

Underparts may be slightly lighter than rest of coat

Hind legs longer than forelegs

## Physical characteristics

| | |
|---|---|
| Head | Short, blunt wedge |
| Eyes | Large, widely spaced, and slightly slanted |
| Ears | Medium-sized, rounded at tip |
| Body | Strong and muscular; also surprisingly heavy |
| Coat | Short and fine, lying close to body |
| Tail | Has a rounded tip |

# Tonkinese

- Burmese–Siamese hybrid
- Curious and affectionate
- First recognized in Canada

A hybrid of the Burmese *(see p.93 and opposite)* and the Siamese *(see p.96)*, Tonkinese produce variants in the pointing patterns of their parent breeds. Their type is a successful blend of their parent breeds, and their temperament has the lively affection of an Oriental breed, without the more vociferous traits. Tonkinese have a distinctive eye color known as "aqua."

**History** The first documented Tonkinese was Wong Mau, the mother of the Burmese breed. Her natural hybrid features were bred out of her offspring, however, and not until the 1950s did controlled breeding programs begin. Early work was carried out in Canada, where the breed was first recognized in the 1960s.

## Key facts

**Place of origin**
United States and Canada

**Date of origin**
1960s

**Weight range**
6–12 lb (2.5–5.5 kg)

**Temperament** Sociable and intelligent

**Breed colors** A wide variety of self and tortie-mink colors and tabby patterns is acceptable

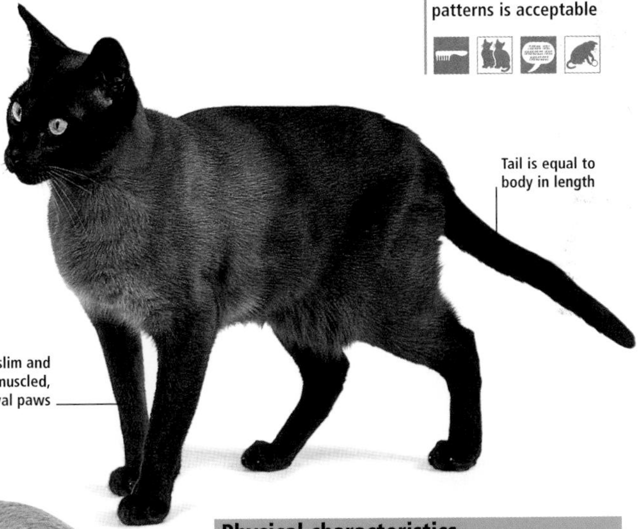

Tail is equal to body in length

Ears are slightly taller than wide

Legs are slim and well muscled, with oval paws

## Physical characteristics

| | |
|---|---|
| Head | Moderate wedge with slight nose break and whisker pinch |
| Eyes | Upper edge oval, lower edge rounded |
| Ears | Slightly taller than wide, with broad base and oval tips |
| Body | Medium to long, muscular, and surprisingly heavy |
| Coat | Short, silky, and close-lying |
| Tail | Neither heavy nor thin |

# Siamese

- The chatty cat
- Early sexual maturity
- Elegant beauty

In recent decades, selective breeding has altered Siamese cats considerably. Indeed, some requirements of the early standards (such as crossed eyes) are now regarded as faults. Siamese have a svelte body, long, slim legs, and a long head. They also have a gregarious, chatty nature: this is the most vocal breed, even strident in its talking. It is also one of the most sexually precocious, often mating by five months of age.
**History** Siamese originated in a mutation in Asia more than 500 years ago. Revered by Buddhist monks and royalty in Siam (now Thailand), they made their way to the West in the late 19th century. The breed remains the most popular CFA shorthair. New colors and tabby stripes have augmented the original four Siamese colors since the 1960s.

## Key facts

**Place of origin**
**Thailand (formerly Siam)**

**Date of origin**
**Pre-1700s**

**Weight range**
**6–12 lb (2.5–5.5 kg)**

**Temperament**
**Energetically enterprising**

**Breed colors** Seal, chocolate, blue, or lilac in Siamese point. Some colorpoint shorthair point colors are also acceptable.

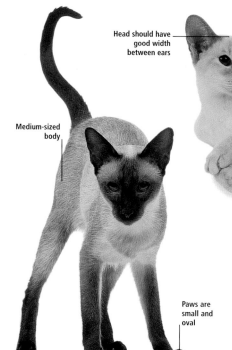

Head should have good width between ears

Slanting eyes

Medium-sized body

Paws are small and oval

## Physical characteristics

| | |
|---|---|
| Head | Long, narrowing to muzzle in straight lines, with long, straight nose |
| Eyes | Oriental in shape, slanted in set |
| Ears | Strikingly large, following lines of face outward |
| Body | Medium-sized, long, and svelte |
| Coat | Very short and fine, with no undercoat |
| Tail | Long, tapering, and free of kinks |

# Oriental shorthair

- Naturally athletic
- Highly sociable
- Attention-seeking

These athletic cats are outrageously gregarious. In physique and temperament, the Oriental is a Siamese, but in solid coat colors. Orientals may suffer from inherited heart problems, but their long lives belie their reputation as a delicate breed.
**History** The historical *Cat Book Poems* shows Siamese cats in varied colors. Indeed, there were self cats among the first Siamese brought to the West, but in the 1920s the Siamese Club of Britain vetoed "any but blue-eyed Siamese" and numbers declined. Work on a solid chocolate in Britain in the 1950s led to the chestnut brown foreign, recognized in 1957, and the origin of the Havana brown.

## Key facts

**Place of origin**
**Great Britain**

**Date of origin**
**1950s**

**Weight range**
**9–14 lb (4–6.5 kg)**

**Temperament** Devoted and demanding

**Breed colors** A wide variety of colors and color combinations is acceptable

Coat is short and glossy

Legs are long and slim, but muscular

Slanted, widely set eyes

Triangular face

## Physical characteristics

| | |
|---|---|
| Head | Long, triangular wedge, described by straight lines |
| Eyes | Slanted and widely set; always green |
| Ears | Large, wide at base, pricked, continuing lines of head |
| Body | Medium-sized, long, and svelte |
| Coat | Very short, fine, and glossy |
| Tail | Long, tapering to point |

# Japanese bobtail

- ■ Not the devil in disguise
- ■ A symbol of good fortune
- ■ Well-established in North America

Superstition may have helped to perpetuate this affectionate breed's most notable feature, its short 3–4 in (8–10 cm) tail. In Japan, a cat with a bifurcated tail—one with two tips—was considered a demon in disguise. Cats with normal tails may have been persecuted, but those with short tails left alone. The bobtail is immortalized in Japan as the famous *Maneki-neko*, or beckoning cat, popular as a good-luck symbol.

**History** Among the first feline immigrants from mainland Asia to Japan were cats with stumpy or bobbed tails. Favored by Japan's restricted gene pool, these individuals flourished, giving rise to this breed sometime before the 19th century. The first breeding program outside Japan was established in the United States in 1968.

## Key facts

**Place of origin**
**Japan**

**Date of origin**
**Pre-19th century**

**Weight range**
**6–9 lb (2.5–4 kg)**

**Temperament** Playful and vibrantly alert

**Breed colors** A variety of colors and color combinations is acceptable

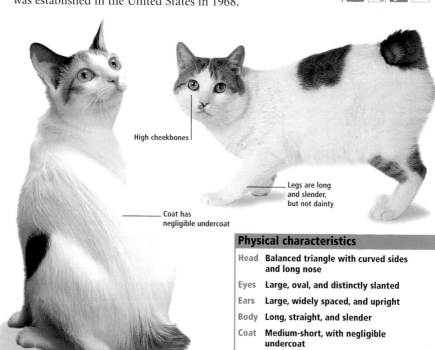

High cheekbones

Legs are long and slender, but not dainty

Coat has negligible undercoat

## Physical characteristics

| | |
|---|---|
| Head | Balanced triangle with curved sides and long nose |
| Eyes | Large, oval, and distinctly slanted |
| Ears | Large, widely spaced, and upright |
| Body | Long, straight, and slender |
| Coat | Medium-short, with negligible undercoat |
| Tail | Short, with fanned hair resembling pompom |

# Singapura

- Quiet and refined
- Adapted through pressure
- Comparatively rare

The Singapura's temperament and build may be the result of selective pressures. In Singapore, most cats are feral and those attracting least attention are more likely to breed successfully, leading to small size, a quiet voice, and a retiring disposition.

**History** This breed's name is Malaysian for Singapore, from where Hal and Tommy Meadows brought cats to the US in 1975; all registered Singapuras originate from their breeding program. Because Tommy Meadows also bred Burmese and Abyssinians, there are claims that these were used to create the Singapura. Whether this is true or not, some believe that the closed register could work to the detriment of Singapuras, of which there are still fewer than 2,000. The breed was recognized in 1982.

## Key facts

**Place of origin**
**Singapore and United States**

**Date of origin**
**1975**

**Weight range**
**4–9 lb (2–4 kg)**

**Temperament** Retiring and affectionately introspective

**Breed colors** Sepia agouti in ticked tabby

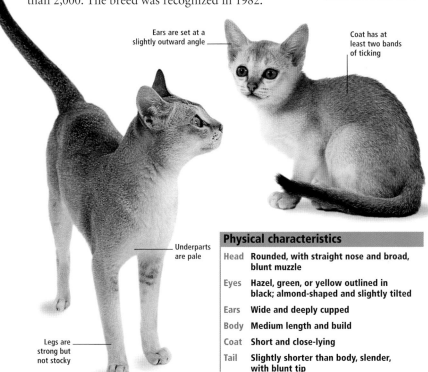

Ears are set at a slightly outward angle

Coat has at least two bands of ticking

Underparts are pale

Legs are strong but not stocky

## Physical characteristics

| | |
|---|---|
| Head | Rounded, with straight nose and broad, blunt muzzle |
| Eyes | Hazel, green, or yellow outlined in black; almond-shaped and slightly tilted |
| Ears | Wide and deeply cupped |
| Body | Medium length and build |
| Coat | Short and close-lying |
| Tail | Slightly shorter than body, slender, with blunt tip |

# Sphynx

- Regular grooming required
- Sensitive to climate extremes
- Indoor cat

The most successful hairless cat is the sphynx, which is covered in short, silky, "peach-fuzz" down. Each empty hair follicle has an oil-producing gland. With no hair to absorb the oil, sphynx cats need daily rubbing down with a chamois. Lacking the insulating protection of a coat, these cats are vulnerable to both heat and cold and must be kept indoors.

**History** The first sphynx was born in 1966, but his line died out. In 1978, a longhaired cat in Toronto had several litters with one or more hairless kittens. One of them was exported to Europe and bred to a Devon rex *(see p.76)*. Hairless offspring resulted, implying that this recessive gene may have some dominance over the Devon gene.

### Key facts

**Place of origin**
**North America and Europe**

**Date of origin**
**1966**

**Weight range**
**8–15 lb (3.5–7 kg)**

**Temperament**
Mischievous and playful

**Breed colors** All colors and patterns, including pointed, sepia, and mink

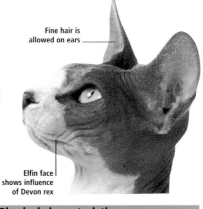

Fine hair is allowed on ears

Elfin face shows influence of Devon rex

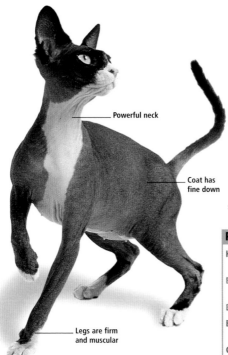

Powerful neck

Coat has fine down

Legs are firm and muscular

### Physical characteristics

| | |
|---|---|
| Head | **Slightly longer than it is wide, with high cheekbones and strong chin** |
| Eyes | **Large, slightly slanted, and set wide apart** |
| Ears | **Very large, wide at base, and open** |
| Body | **Rounded, hard, and muscular, with broad chest** |
| Coat | **Apparently hairless, but has fine down** |
| Tail | **Tapering and whiplike** |

# Random breeds

- Anything goes
- Most popular cats in the world
- Environmentally adaptive

The random-bred cat has no clubs to promote it and no romantic history or royal connections to beguile the public, yet the "household pet" is still the most popular and widely owned cat worldwide. Types vary from place to place, with stocky, sturdy cats found in cold countries and lighter, more slender cats in evidence in warmer climates. Typically Oriental colors and pointed patterns remain rare in Western nonpedigreed cats, although these genes have occasionally filtered from pedigreed breeds into the general population through the determined ingenuity of all felines in matters of mating.

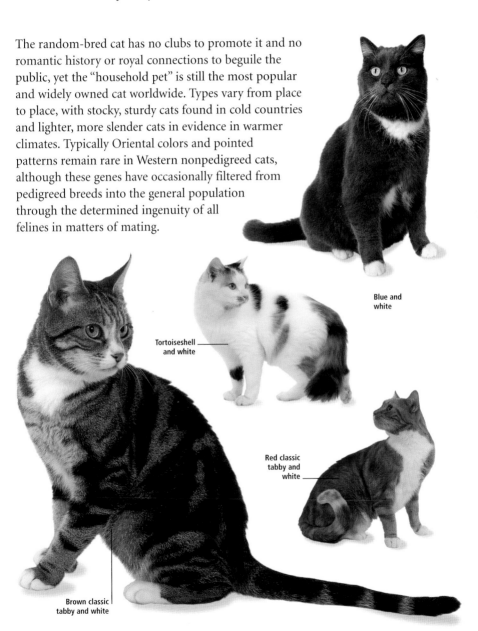

Blue and white

Tortoiseshell and white

Red classic tabby and white

Brown classic tabby and white

# Longhaired cats

Genetically, all longhaired cats share the recessive gene that causes their coats to grow longer than those of their wildcat ancestors. The difference between full-coated longhairs and silky semilonghairs is one of polygenetic factors. Some sources still state that the gene for long hair was introduced into these domestic cats from the wild Pallas' cat of Tibet, but there is no evidence that this is so: a simple genetic mutation is almost certainly the cause.

Although their exact origins are unknown, longhairs occurred naturally centuries ago in Central Asia. Some of these cats reached Europe: the French authority Dr. Fernand Mery reported that specimens were brought to Italy around 1550 and to France soon after. After the Crystal Palace Cat Show—the first formal cat show—held in London in 1871, standards were published for both Persians and Angoras.

The most popular longhair in early American shows was the Maine coon. This breed's coat may have come from Central Asia via Britain, but some early settlers' cats may have carried the longhair gene from another mutation. What is certain is that New England's harsh climate favored the survival of big cats with long, insulating coats.

Other longhaired breeds are the results of introducing the longhair gene into shorthaired breeds. New breeds, such as the tiffanie and the nebelung, have been developed on both sides of the Atlantic. Perhaps the most extraordinary and striking of all longhaired breeds are the rexed longhairs, with a curl or ripple to the coat, such as the LaPerm and the Selkirk rex.

**Longhaired breeds** come in almost as many shapes and sizes as their shorthaired cousins.

# Persian

- Quiet, inactive breed
- Requires daily grooming
- Former status symbol

In surveys of vets, the Persian is cited as the quietest and least active cat breed, and the one most likely to accept other cats into its home. However, the Persian will guard its territory and catch prey with surprising ease, given its shortened face. The coat needs daily care—vets are often called on to clip matted coats—and breed problems include kidney disease and retained testicles.

**History** The Persian's first documented ancestors were imported from Persia (now Iran) into Italy in 1620 and from Turkey into France at about the same time. For the next 200 years their descendants were status-symbol pets. In Britain, in the late 1800s, the Persian was developed within the guidelines of Harrison Weir's first written breed standards, and by the early 1900s it was recognized by all registries.

## Key facts

**Place of origin**
**Great Britain**

**Date of origin**
**1800s**

**Weight range**
**8–15 lb (3.5–7 kg)**

**Temperament**
Interested observer

**Breed colors** A wide variety of colors and color combinations is acceptable

Short, broad nose with definite stop

Short, thick, and sturdy neck

Large, round paws, preferably tufted

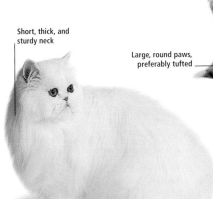

Short, thick legs

## Physical characteristics

| | |
|---|---|
| Head | Round, massive, and broad |
| Eyes | Large, round, and widely spaced |
| Ears | Small, round-tipped, and set low on the head |
| Body | Large and cobby, with good muscling |
| Coat | Long and thick, but not woolly |
| Tail | Full and short, but not disproportionate to body |

# Himalayan Persian

■ The original "designer cat"
■ Twenty years in the making
■ Outgoing but relaxed

Possibly the first deliberate hybridization of two breeds, the Himalayan Persian (known as colorpoint longhair in Britain) features the first recognized "export" of the Siamese *(see p.96)* pointed pattern. Eye color is less intense than in the Siamese, and the pointing is softer in the longer coat. Himalayan Persians are outgoing but relaxed. The sexual precociousness of the Siamese can also manifest itself in these cats.

**History** In the 1930s in the US, a black Persian was bred with a Siamese. The first generation consisted entirely of longhaired, black cats, but a pointed longhaired cat—the Himalayan— was produced when back-crossed. British efforts at creating a pointed Pesian progressed through the 1930s and 1940s. The colorpoint Persian was accepted in 1955, and recognition of the Himalayan Persian was universal by 1961.

## Key facts

**Place of origin**
**Great Britain and United States**

**Date of origin**
**1950s**

**Weight range**
**8–15 lb (3.5–7 kg)**

**Temperament** Calm and friendly

**Breed colors** A wide variety of self, tortie, and tabby points is acceptable

Frill on shoulders and chest

Body is set low on legs

Short, thick, strong legs

Large, round, tufted paws

## Physical characteristics

| | |
|---|---|
| Head | Round and massive, with full cheeks |
| Eyes | Large, full, round, and brilliant blue |
| Ears | Small and round-tipped, not unduly open at base |
| Body | Large to medium-sized, cobby, set low on legs |
| Coat | Long, thick, and silky, with no woolliness |
| Tail | Short, but in proportion to body, and bushy |

# Birman

- Striking beauty
- Daily grooming required
- Heritage unknown

The Birman is a strikingly marked breed whose silky hair requires daily grooming. Neutered males demand attention, while neutered females can be bossy. At the end of World War II, the last two remaining Birmans in France were outcrossed to perpetuate the breed. As with all breeds with a small genetic base, inbreeding can increase hereditary problems, but only rare skin and nerve disorders are hereditary in this breed.

**History** According to tradition, the Birman descends from the temple cats of Burma, specifically from Sita, a pregnant female brought to France in 1919. A less romantic notion exists that Birmans were created in France at the same time as the Himalayan Persian *(see opposite)* was developed.

### Key facts

**Place of origin**
**Myanmar (formerly Burma) or France**

**Date of origin**
**Unknown**

**Weight range**
**10–18 lb (4.5–8 kg)**

**Temperament**
Friendly and reserved

**Breed colors** A wide variety of self, tortie points, and tabby points is acceptable

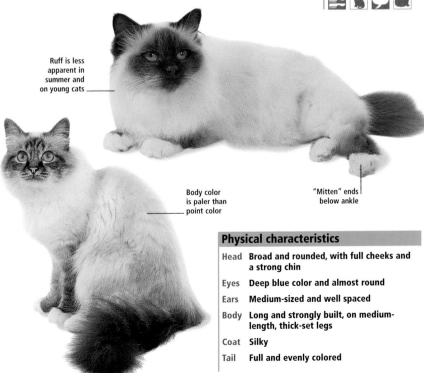

Ruff is less apparent in summer and on young cats

Body color is paler than point color

"Mitten" ends below ankle

### Physical characteristics

| | |
|---|---|
| Head | Broad and rounded, with full cheeks and a strong chin |
| Eyes | Deep blue color and almost round |
| Ears | Medium-sized and well spaced |
| Body | Long and strongly built, on medium-length, thick-set legs |
| Coat | Silky |
| Tail | Full and evenly colored |

# Ragdoll

- Gentle giant
- Unenthusiastic hunter
- CFA newcomer

Best known for its placid disposition, the ragdoll is a big, heavy cat whose coat does not mat as readily as that of the Persian *(see p.103)*. Ragdolls are born white and slowly develop color and pattern over two years, becoming pointed cats. The breed shows little enthusiasm for hunting, making it popular in Australia, where cats have threatened indigenous wildlife. Tales of a high pain threshold have been disproved.
**History** In the 1960s, Californian breeder Ann Baker bred the first ragdolls from a white, probably nonpedigreed, Persian and a Birman-type tom. Baker formed a ragdoll breed association but its cats were not accepted by other registries. Some individuals later bred her ragdolls to produce the breed accepted by major registries today. The ragdoll won full CFA acceptance in 2000.

## Key facts

**Place of origin**
**United States**

**Date of origin**
**1960s**

**Weight range**
**10–20 lb (4.5–9 kg)**

**Temperament**
Genial and relaxed

**Breed colors** Seal, chocolate, blue, or lilac, in pointed, mitted, or bicolor patterns

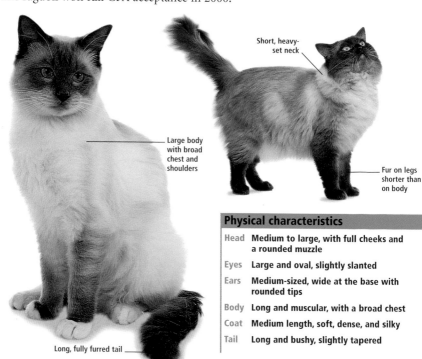

Short, heavy-set neck

Large body with broad chest and shoulders

Fur on legs shorter than on body

Long, fully furred tail

## Physical characteristics

| | |
|---|---|
| Head | Medium to large, with full cheeks and a rounded muzzle |
| Eyes | Large and oval, slightly slanted |
| Ears | Medium-sized, wide at the base with rounded tips |
| Body | Long and muscular, with a broad chest |
| Coat | Medium length, soft, dense, and silky |
| Tail | Long and bushy, slightly tapered |

# Maine coon

- Welcoming cat
- Highly sociable
- Heavy coat

Strong and tranquil, the Maine coon looks its best in winter, when its heavy coat is at its most luxurious. A quirk that sets this breed apart is the frequent happy chirping trill it uses to greet its human or feline family. The Maine enjoys the company of people but is not a dependent or lap cat.

**History** Probable ancestors include British cats that came with early settlers and longhaired Russian or Scandinavian cats on ships in Maine's ports. The black-and-white Captain Jenks of the Horse Marines was the "first" Maine, noted at shows in 1861. Despite losing favor to the Persian *(see p.103)* in the early 1900s, the Maine coon survived as a breed because farmers recognized its excellent hunting ability. Interest was rekindled in the 1950s, and by 2000 it had become the CFA's second most popular longhaired breed.

## Key facts

**Place of origin**
United States

**Date of origin**
1860s

**Weight range**
9–22 lb (4–10 kg)

**Temperament**
Gentle giant

**Breed colors** A wide variety of colors and color combinations is acceptable

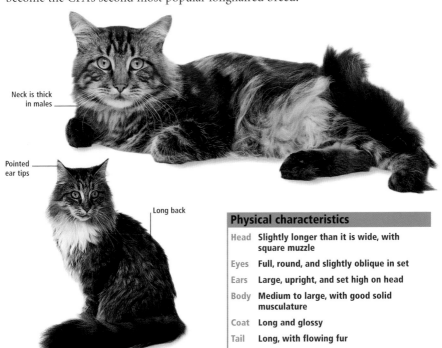

Neck is thick in males

Pointed ear tips

Long back

## Physical characteristics

| | |
|---|---|
| Head | Slightly longer than it is wide, with square muzzle |
| Eyes | Full, round, and slightly oblique in set |
| Ears | Large, upright, and set high on head |
| Body | Medium to large, with good solid musculature |
| Coat | Long and glossy |
| Tail | Long, with flowing fur |

# Norwegian forest cat

- Confident companion
- Great hunter
- Feline fisherman

Reserved with strangers but confident with people it knows, the Norwegian forest cat shares attributes with the Maine coon *(see p.107)* and the Siberian *(see opposite)*. A commanding physical presence, this gentle cat can defend its territory vigorously. It is a superb climber and hunter, and owners living near streams say their "Wegies" like to fish. **History** By AD 1000, Vikings had established trade routes with the Byzantine East. Proof that cats were traded from Byzantium (now Istanbul) to Norway comes from Norwegian cats with colors common in Turkey but rare across Europe. The Wegie was not regarded as a breed until the 1930s, and planned breeding began in the 1970s. The first Wegies arrived in America in 1979 and in Britain in the 1980s.

## Key facts

**Place of origin**
Norway

**Date of origin**
1930s

**Weight range**
7–20 lb (3–9 kg)

**Temperament**
Reserved and contained

**Breed colors** A wide variety of colors and color combinations is acceptable

Full ruff is desirable

Angular, alert-looking face

Legs are long but not delicate

Large, round paws with tufts between toes

## Physical characteristics

| | |
|---|---|
| Head | Triangular, with a long, straight profile and strong chin |
| Eyes | Large and open, but not round, and slightly oblique in set |
| Ears | Open, wide at base, and set high on head |
| Body | Large, with good bone and muscle structure |
| Coat | Smooth, glossy, water-repellent topcoat and woolly undercoat |
| Tail | Long and bushy, same length as body |

# Siberian

- Winter warrior
- Active and agile
- Resourceful Russian

Every aspect of this cat is honed for survival in the harsh Siberian winter: its topcoat is strong, plentiful, and oily; its undercoat dense enough to keep out the fiercest winds; and its build large. Siberians are active, highly agile cats that, while sociable, are disinclined to play the passive lap cat. **History** Longhaired cats are found across the northern wastes of Russia. Like many natural breeds, the Siberian was regarded as noteworthy only recently. Serious breeding began in the 1980s, and the breed is recognized by a wide range of registries in its homeland. Siberians were imported into the United States in 1990. Among major registries, FIFé and TICA accept the Siberian.

## Key facts

**Place of origin**
**Eastern Russia**

**Date of origin**
**1980s**

**Weight range**
**10–20 lb (4.5–9 kg)**

**Temperament** Sensible and resourceful

**Breed colors** A wide variety of colors and color combinations is acceptable

Broad chest

Paws are large, round, and tufted

Short, sturdy neck

## Physical characteristics

| | |
|---|---|
| Head | Broad, and flat between ears |
| Eyes | Large, oval, and slightly slanted in set |
| Ears | Medium in size, with rounded tips, and angled out |
| Body | Long, well muscled, and powerful |
| Coat | Long, with a slightly oily topcoat |
| Tail | Medium length and thick, with a rounded tip |

# Exotic longhair

- Identical in looks to the Persian
- Playful and sociable
- Longhaired version of the shorthaired version of the Persian!

Although there are genetic differences between the exotic longhair and the Persian *(see p.103)*, it is impossible to tell them apart by appearance. According to breeders, however, the exotic longhair is more outgoing and adventurous than the Persian. This is a playful, inquisitive breed, and most individuals get along well with other cats and dogs.

**History** After recognizing the exotic shorthair *(see p.61)* in 1967, the CFA's breeding policy allowed for them—as it still does—to be bred periodically to Persians in order to retain the Persian's body and head type. However, the longhaired offspring of this union could not be registered, neither as Persians nor as exotics. To overcome this dilemma, US cat breeders created this new breed.

## Key facts

**Place of origin**
United States

**Date of origin**
1960s

**Weight range**
7–14 lb (3–6.5 kg)

**Temperament**
Gently inquisitive

**Breed colors**
All Persian and exotic shorthair colors and patterns

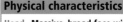
Short tail

Large, round paws

## Physical characteristics

| | |
|---|---|
| Head | Massive, broad face with full cheeks |
| Eyes | Large, round, and widely spaced |
| Ears | Small, tilted forward, rounded at tips; set low on the head |
| Body | Large and cobby, with good strong musculature |
| Coat | Long and glossy |
| Tail | Short; must not be carried high |

# Munchkin

- Short of stature
- Available in three sizes
- Limited recognition

The munchkin is defined by a single factor: the long bones in its legs are simply not long. The flexible feline spine may save the breed from the back and hip problems of dwarfed dog breeds but, in all other species, dwarfs are prone to arthritis. There are three munchkin sizes: standard; "super-short," or "rug-hugger," which has very short legs; and a controversial, exceptionally small type called the "mini," provisionally recognized by the United Feline Organization under the name Mei Toi.

**History** The munchkin originated in Louisiana in 1983 in a mutation that breeders outcrossed to nonpedigreed cats. TICA recognized the munchkin in 1995, but so far it is the only major registry to have done so.

## Key facts

**Place of origin**
**United States**

**Date of origin**
**1983**

**Weight range**
**5–9 lb (2.25–4 kg)**

**Temperament**
Appealing and inquisitive

**Breed colors** All colors and patterns, including pointed, mink, and sepia

Eye color is unrelated to coat color

Paws turned slightly outward

Short but straight legs

## Physical characteristics

| | |
|---|---|
| Head | Medium-sized, neither round nor wedge-shaped |
| Eyes | Large and walnut-shaped, with open expression |
| Ears | Triangular, moderately large in size |
| Body | Medium-sized, with level spine or slight rise from shoulder to rump |
| Coat | Lustrous, medium length |
| Tail | Medium thickness, tapering to rounded tip |

# American curl

- Ear mutation is dominant
- Pixielike features
- Selectively bred in California

This quiet, gentle breed is simply the household cat of the United States with a single, striking mutation: its ears curl back toward the back and center of the head. This feature gives the curl a pixielike face, full of astonishment. The trait is dominant, so a curl bred to any cat should give at least 50 percent curls.

**History** In 1981, a stray kitten with a long, silky coat and unusual ears appeared at the California home of Grace and Joe Ruga, who named her Shulamith; all curls trace their origins to this cat. Shulamith had four kittens, including two with curly ears. Fully recognized in North America, the curl is the first breed ever to win CFA acceptance in two coat lengths. The first curls to reach Europe arrived in Britain in 1995.

## Key facts

**Place of origin**
**United States**

**Date of origin**
**1981**

**Weight range**
**7–11 lb (3–5 kg)**

**Temperament** Quietly affable

**Breed colors** A wide variety of colors and color combinations is acceptable

Curled-back ears

Sweet, surprised-looking face

Semiforeign build

Long, fluffy tail

## Physical characteristics

| | |
|---|---|
| Head | Rounded, modified wedge |
| Eyes | Walnut-shaped and slightly tilted |
| Ears | Point back toward the center and back of the head |
| Body | Moderately muscled and semiforeign in build |
| Coat | Silky and flowing, with minimal undercoat |
| Tail | Full plume equal to length of body |

# Scottish fold

- Luxurious winter coat
- Prone to problematic joints
- Longhaired rarity

The longhaired Scottish fold is best seen in winter, when it sports an imposing ruff, elegant breeches, and a huge fluffy tail. Kittens are born with straight ears, which begin to fold at about three weeks of age. The joint problems that result from breeding fold-to-fold appear at four to six months: a short, thickened tail is a sign that might be missed in a longhaired kitten, so tails should be checked carefully—and always gently. **History** All Scottish folds can be traced back to Susie, a white farm cat born in 1961 in Scotland. Two geneticists found that Susie carried the longhair gene, which could be carried in shorthaired offspring and appear in later generations. The fold is still rare: the absence of any longhaired outcross breed makes the longhaired version even rarer.

## Key facts

**Place of origin**
**Scotland**

**Date of origin**
**1961**

**Weight range**
**6–13 lb (2.4–6 kg)**

**Temperament** Quietly confident

**Breed colors** All colors and patterns, including pointed, sepia, and mink

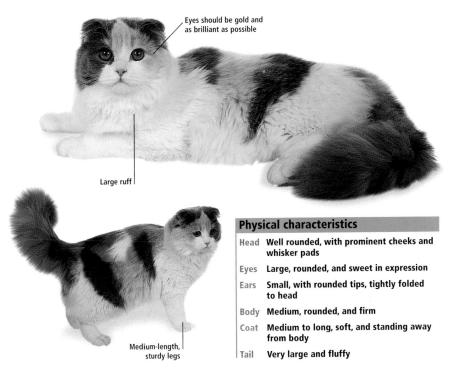

Eyes should be gold and as brilliant as possible

Large ruff

Medium-length, sturdy legs

## Physical characteristics

| | |
|---|---|
| Head | Well rounded, with prominent cheeks and whisker pads |
| Eyes | Large, rounded, and sweet in expression |
| Ears | Small, with rounded tips, tightly folded to head |
| Body | Medium, rounded, and firm |
| Coat | Medium to long, soft, and standing away from body |
| Tail | Very large and fluffy |

# Selkirk rex

- One of only two rexed longhaired breeds
- Thick, ringleted coat
- Loving and tolerant

The longhaired Selkirk rex looks quite unique and is possibly the most striking of all of the rexed breeds. The long, thick coat is at its best in heterozygous cats, with one rexing and one straight-haired gene: this combination gives a loose, ringleted effect. All three hair types are present in the coat.

**History** The very first Selkirk rex was a shorthaired kitten from Montana. Born in 1987, she came into the household of Jeri Newman, who mated her to a black Persian *(see p.103)*. The resulting litter included longhaired and shorthaired kittens, with a mixture of straight and curly coats. The Selkirk rex's longhaired and shorthaired classes are not formally separated, and the allowed outcrosses for the breed include the Persian.

## Key facts

**Place of origin**
**United States**

**Date of origin**
**1987**

**Weight range**
**7–11 lb (3–5 kg)**

**Temperament** Patiently tolerant

**Breed colors** All colors and patterns, including pointed, sepia, and mink

Coat is soft and curly

Curly whiskers

Untidy-looking coat is typical of young Selkirk cats

## Physical characteristics

| | |
|---|---|
| Head | Rounded, with short, squared-off muzzle |
| Eyes | Round and widely spaced |
| Ears | Medium, pointed, and set well apart |
| Body | Muscular and rectangular, with slight rise to hindquarters |
| Coat | Soft, falling in loose, individual curls |
| Tail | Thick, tapering slightly to rounded tip |

# LaPerm

- Born in the US from farm cats
- Dominant curly coat gene
- Excellent hunter

Along with the Selkirk, the LaPerm is the only longhaired rexed cat accepted by major registries. Although they descend from random-bred American stock, they have a foreign appearance with a wedge-shaped head and lean build. They are very active, inquisitive cats and excellent hunters.

**History**  In 1982, a farm cat in Oregon produced a litter of kittens that included a single bald kitten that eventually grew a curly, soft coat. The owner and founder of the breed named this kitten Curly, and over the next five years she bred a number of curly coated kittens, the basis of the breed. The gene is dominant, so outcrossing to increase the gene pool can be done while still producing rexed kittens.

## Key facts

**Place of origin**
United States

**Date of origin**
1982

**Weight range**
8–12 lb (3.5–5.5 kg)

**Temperament**
Affectionate and inquisitive

**Breed colors**  All colors and patterns, including sepia, pointed, and mink

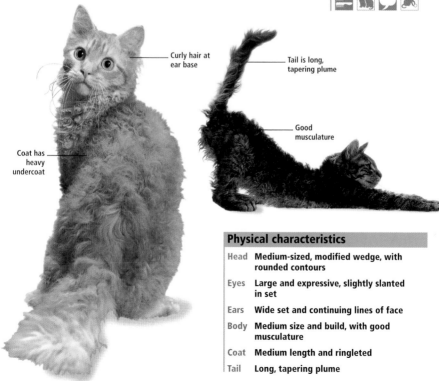

Curly hair at ear base

Tail is long, tapering plume

Good musculature

Coat has heavy undercoat

## Physical characteristics

| | |
|---|---|
| Head | Medium-sized, modified wedge, with rounded contours |
| Eyes | Large and expressive, slightly slanted in set |
| Ears | Wide set and continuing lines of face |
| Body | Medium size and build, with good musculature |
| Coat | Medium length and ringleted |
| Tail | Long, tapering plume |

# Turkish Van

- Swimming cat
- Distinctive coat pattern
- Independent personality

Although they might appear to be ideal lap cats, Turkish Vans descend from rural cats in an area where life was far from easy, and they retain minds and spirits of their own. The breed is distinguished for two reasons: the distinctive pattern of its coat, called Van even in other breeds, and its reputation for enjoying a dip in hot summer weather.

**History** This breed originated in the Lake Van region before the 18th century. After two Vans were brought to Britain in 1955, the breed spread across Europe, but registry acceptance was slow. In the 1970s, the first Van kittens reached the US, where the breed is now accepted by the CFA and TICA. In the GCCF, only the original red and the more recently accepted cream are allowed.

## Key facts

**Place of origin**
**Lake Van region of Turkey**

**Date of origin**
**Pre-18th century**

**Weight range**
**7–19 lb (3–8.5 kg)**

**Temperament**
**Self-possessed**

**Breed colors** White with auburn or cream (no other colors are officially accepted)

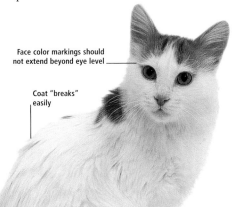

Face color markings should not extend beyond eye level

Coat "breaks" easily

White blaze divides color on forehead into two separate areas

## Physical characteristics

| | |
|---|---|
| Head | Short wedge with long, straight profile |
| Eyes | Large and oval |
| Ears | Large and set high on head, fairly close together |
| Body | Long and sturdy, with males particularly muscular |
| Coat | Long and silky, with no undercoat |
| Tail | Full brush as long as body |

# Cymric

- Longhaired Manx
- Welsh only by name
- Friendly and relaxed

This breed matches the shorthaired Manx *(see p.63)* in all but coat, which is semilong and double. The Cymric produces variant "stumpies" and "longies," both with some degree of tail, as well as the showable tailless "rumpies."

**History** Although Cymric is the Welsh word for "Welsh," this is an exclusively North American breed. Manx cats have always produced the occasional longhaired kitten and, in the 1960s, breeders worked to gain recognition for these variants. By the 1980s, the CFA and TICA both recognized the Cymric breed, but the CFA has now reclassified it as longhaired Manx. Cymrics are not recognized in Britain.

## Key facts

**Place of origin**
**North America**

**Date of origin**
**1960s**

**Weight range**
**8–12 lb (3.5–5.5 kg)**

**Temperament** Friendly and even-tempered

**Breed colors** A wide variety of colors and color combinations is acceptable

Neck is short and thick

Hind legs are much longer than forelegs

Sturdy legs

No hint of tail

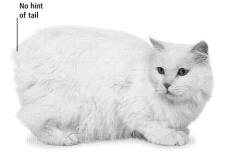

## Physical characteristics

| | |
|---|---|
| Head | Rounded, with gentle dip from forehead to nose |
| Eyes | Large, round, and set at slight angle |
| Ears | Medium-sized, wide at base, rounded tips |
| Body | Medium-sized, sturdy, and well muscled |
| Coat | Thick and plush, shorter on face and lower legs |
| Tail | Should feel completely rounded, with no hint of tail |

# Nebelung

- German "mist-creature"
- Longhaired version of blue Russian shorthair
- Shy, quiet personality

Its silver-tipped blue hair gives the Nebelung a luminous elegance. Light reflects off its guard hairs, creating a misty incandescence; there is a solid-blue ground color beneath. This rare breed, whose name is German for "mist-creature," is based upon a longhaired strain of the Russian blue *(see p.69)*.

**History** Blue shorthairs and longhairs from Russia were exhibited more than 100 years ago. Shorthairs became known as Russian blues, but the longhairs lost their identity. In 1986 in the US, Siegfried, the founding father of this revived breed, was mated to his longhaired sister, producing longhaired blue kittens. The Nebelung was recognized by TICA in 1987 and by the TCA in 1993.

## Key facts

**Place of origin**
**United States**

**Date of origin**
**1980s**

**Weight range**
**6–11 lb (2.5–5 kg)**

**Temperament** Retiring

**Breed colors** Blue self

Coat has silver-tipped guard hairs

Neck is long and slender under ruff

Small, round paws

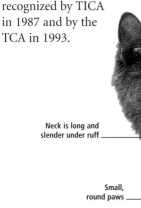

Eyes are yellow in younger cats

## Physical characteristics

| | |
|---|---|
| Head | Modified wedge, with flat forehead and straight profile |
| Eyes | Very slightly oval, green, and widely spaced |
| Ears | Wide at base, with slightly rounded tips |
| Body | Lithe and slender, but not tubular |
| Coat | Fine, double, and medium length |
| Tail | Long and fluffy, tapering from thick base to fine tip |

# Turkish Angora

- Protected breed in its homeland
- Vivacious and athletic
- Not recognized in Britain

With fine bones and a silky coat, the Turkish Angora is a vivacious, quick-witted, and quick-moving cat. Its medium-long coat is probably the result of a mutation that occurred centuries ago in an isolated population of domestic cats in central Asia. As with other breeds, white blue-eyed cats may be partially or totally deaf. This is due to a color gene defect.

**History** Originating in the 1400s, Turkish Angoras reached France and Britain in the 17th century. However, by the early 1900s, cross-breeding with other longhaired cats had led to the virtual extinction of the breed outside Turkey. The breed is said to have been saved through a program at Ankara Zoo. Although this may be a rather romanticized tale, the breed is now protected in Turkey. Turkish Angoras are not recognized in Britain.

## Key facts

**Place of origin**
Turkey

**Date of origin**
1400s

**Weight range**
6–11 lb (2.5–5 kg)

**Temperament**
Energetic exhibitionist

**Breed colors** A wide variety of colors and color combinations is acceptable

Slim, graceful neck

Hind legs are longer than forelegs

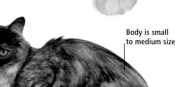

Body is small to medium size

Tail is full plume of hair

## Physical characteristics

| | |
|---|---|
| Head | Modified wedge of small to medium size, with a narrow muzzle |
| Eyes | Large and oval, slightly slanted |
| Ears | Large and high set, slightly pointed |
| Body | Long and slender, but muscular |
| Coat | Fine and silky, with negligible undercoat |
| Tail | Very fluffy, tapering from wide base to fine tip |

# Chantilly/Tiffany

- Extremely rare breed
- Coos like a pigeon
- Angora beginnings

This rare breed has a moderate disposition, neither as quiet as a Persian *(see p.103)* nor as active as Oriental-type longhairs. The Chantilly will communicate happiness with an endearing chirp that sounds like a pigeon cooing.

**History** In 1967, a Florida breeder bought a pair of gold-eyed, longhaired cats of unknown background, although the chocolate coat implied a Burmese *(see p.93)* parentage. She also coined the name Tiffany. In the 1980s, confusion led to the breed almost vanishing. The breed was reestablished in 1988 in Canada and traced to the breeding program that created the Angora *(see p.124)*. Because the name Tiffanie was now being used by British breeders for the longhaired Burmilla, Canadian breeders altered the name to Chantilly/Tiffany.

**Key facts**

Place of origin
**Canada and United States**

Date of origin
**1970s**

Weight range
**6–12 lb (2.5–5.5 kg)**

Temperament **Gentle and conservative**

Breed colors
**Chocolate, cinnamon, blue, lilac, or fawn in self, mackerel, spotted, or ticked tabby**

Coat matures at two to three years of age

Legs are medium length, well muscled, but not stocky

Eye color in kittens is less intense

**Physical characteristics**

| | |
|---|---|
| Head | Triangular, with gently curved profile, slightly indented at eye level |
| Eyes | Golden or copper, oval, and slightly slanted |
| Ears | Medium-sized, wide at base, with rounded tips |
| Body | Medium length, slender, and elegant |
| Coat | Medium length, single |
| Tail | Plumed, equal in length to body |

# Tiffanie

- Longhair–Burmese hybrid
- Accidental origins
- Easy-going feline

Essentially longhaired Asians, Tiffanies take their coat from chinchilla Persians *(see p.103)* and their build from Burmese cats *(see p.94)*. In temperament, they combine the traits of their parent breeds to great advantage, with more liveliness than the Persian and more restraint than the Burmese. A relaxed, easy-to-care-for longhair, the Tiffanie deserves wider popularity.

**History** The Tiffanie is the only longhaired member of the Asian group. Its origins can be traced back to an accidental mating, in London in 1981, of a chinchilla Persian and a Burmese. The first-generation offspring were shorthaired, shaded Burmillas *(see p.89),* but subsequent breedings brought the recessive longhair and sepia-pointing genes back to the surface.

## Key facts

**Place of origin**
**Great Britain**

**Date of origin**
**1980s**

**Weight range**
**8–14 lb (3.5–6.5 kg)**

**Temperament** Lively and affectionate

**Breed colors** A wide variety of colors in solid and sepia self, shaded, and tabby colors

Good musculature on body

Round paws

Fine, silky coat

Medium to long tail is elegantly plumed

## Physical characteristics

| | |
|---|---|
| Head | Short wedge, with distinct nose-break in profile |
| Eyes | Neither almond-shaped nor round, slightly oblique in set |
| Ears | Medium to large, continuing lines of face |
| Body | Medium build, with straight back and good musculature |
| Coat | Semilong, fine and silky |
| Tail | Medium to long, elegantly plumed |

# Somali

- Longhaired Abyssinian
- Loves the outdoors
- Excellent hunter

Like its Abyssinian forebear *(see p.71)*, the Somali has a ticked coat: each hair on its body has three to 12 bands of color that produce a vibrant shimmer when the cat is in full coat. The striking facial markings resemble eyeliner. The Somali is a natural hunter that thrives on outdoor activities and will only accept confinement if introduced to it at an early age.

**History** In 1963, a Canadian breeder entered one of her longhaired Abyssinian cats in a local show. The judge, Ken McGill, asked her for one to breed from, and the first official Somali was McGill's May-Ling Tutsuta. Evelyn Mague, a US Aby breeder, was also developing longhairs, which she named Somalis. By the late 1970s the breed was fully accepted in North America. Somalis appeared in Europe in the 1980s.

## Key facts

**Place of origin** Canada and United States

**Date of origin** 1963

**Weight range** 8–12 lb (3.5–5.5 kg)

**Temperament** Quiet but extrovert

**Breed colors** A wide variety of ticked tabby and ticked silver tabby colors is acceptable

Full ruff preferred
Ticking requires at least three dark bands on each hair

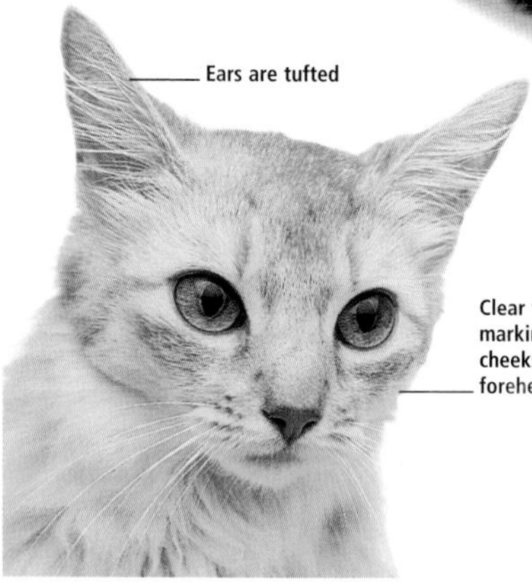

Ears are tufted
Clear tabby markings on cheeks and forehead

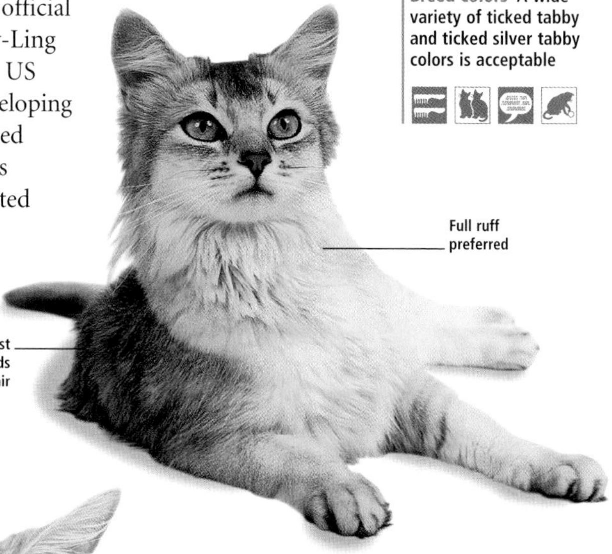

## Physical characteristics

| | |
|---|---|
| Head | Moderate wedge, with smooth lines and slight nose-break in profile |
| Eyes | Large and almond-shaped; amber, hazel, or green in color |
| Ears | Wide-set, large, cupped, and tufted |
| Body | Medium-sized, lithe, and muscular |
| Coat | Soft and fine, medium length |
| Tail | Long, with full brush of hair |

# Balinese

- Remarkable escape artist
- Longhaired Siamese
- Delicate as a dancer

Happiest at the center of activity or investigating cupboards and shopping bags, the Balinese is also a superb escape artist. A talkative cat, it sometimes appears, like its cousin the Siamese *(see p.96)*, to talk to itself. The Balinese does not have very long hair, and from a distance some might be mistaken for a Siamese, were it not for the graceful plume of a tail. **History** A longhaired Siamese was registered with the CFA in Britain in 1928, but it was only in the 1950s that a program began in the US to breed them. Longhaired Siamese were recognized in 1961 and named Balinese by a breeder who thought the cats reminded her of Balinese temple dancers. The breed arrived in Europe in the mid-1970s.

## Key facts

**Place of origin**
**United States**

**Date of origin**
**1950s**

**Weight range**
**6–11 lb (2.5–5 kg)**

**Temperament**
**Energetic and exhibitionist**

**Breed colors** A wide variety of point colors is acceptable

No woolly undercoat

Eyes are widely spaced

Points clearly contrast with pale body

Straight nose

Strong chin

## Physical characteristics

| | |
|---|---|
| Head | Long and wedge-shaped, with elegant lines |
| Eyes | Widely spaced, and Oriental in shape and set |
| Ears | Large, wide at base, and pricked |
| Body | Medium-sized, lithe and graceful |
| Coat | Medium-long, fine and silky, lying flat |
| Tail | Long and plumed |

# Angora (British)

- ■ Different names for different places
- ■ Oriental temperament
- ■ Developed in Britain

This breed is similar in temperament and type to the Oriental breeds—lively and inquisitive, with long and lean limbs. In mainland Europe it is called Javanese to avoid confusion with the Turkish Angora *(see p.119)*, but some North American associations use Javanese for certain colors of Balinese *(see p.123)*. In North America, it has been called Oriental longhair, with the misleading implication that it is descended from the Oriental shorthair *(see p.97)*. It is hoped that Angoras can simply remain Angoras from now on.

**History**  The Angora was developed in Britain in the 1970s, following the mid-1960s mating of a sorrel Abyssinian *(see p.71)* to a seal-point Siamese *(see p.96)* in an attempt to produce a Siamese with ticked points. The descendants inherited both the cinnamon trait and the gene for long hair, which eventually led to the Angora.

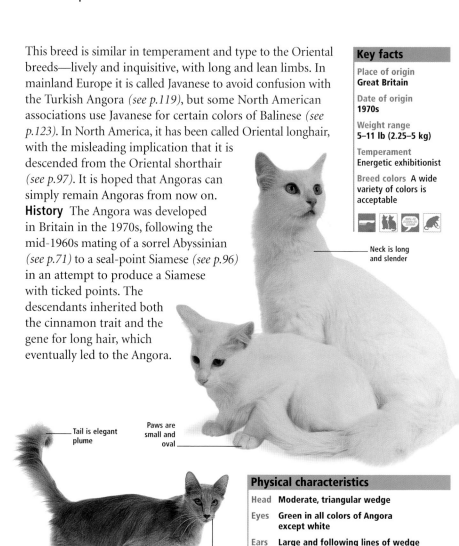

Neck is long and slender

Tail is elegant plume

Paws are small and oval

Fine muzzle

## Key facts

Place of origin
**Great Britain**

Date of origin
**1970s**

Weight range
**5–11 lb (2.25–5 kg)**

Temperament
**Energetic exhibitionist**

Breed colors  **A wide variety of colors is acceptable**

## Physical characteristics

| | |
|---|---|
| Head | **Moderate, triangular wedge** |
| Eyes | **Green in all colors of Angora except white** |
| Ears | **Large and following lines of wedge** |
| Body | **Medium-sized, svelte, and muscular** |
| Coat | **Medium length, fine and silky, with no woolly undercoat** |
| Tail | **Long, tapering to fine end** |

# Oriental longhair

- Not really longhaired
- Oriental shorthair–Balinese hybrid
- Confusion abounds

This beautiful, fully colored, semilonghaired version of the Oriental shorthair *(see p.97)* reflects its family in all respects: it bears the colors of the Oriental, and the soft coat and plumed tail of the Balinese *(see p.123)*. In summer, but for the plumed tail, it may look similar to shorthairs. **History** In 1985 in the US, an Oriental shorthair and a Balinese mated to produce a litter of silky, semilonghaired Orientals. The breed was then developed, and it is now recognized by TICA and FIFé. There may be some confusion in name between this cat and the British Angora *(opposite)*, which has been called an Oriental longhair in North America, but visually and historically the two are distinct.

## Key facts

**Place of origin**
**North America**

**Date of origin**
**1985**

**Weight range**
**10–13 lb (4.5–6 kg)**

**Temperament** Friendly and inquisitive

**Breed colors** All colors and patterns, except pointed, sepia, and mink

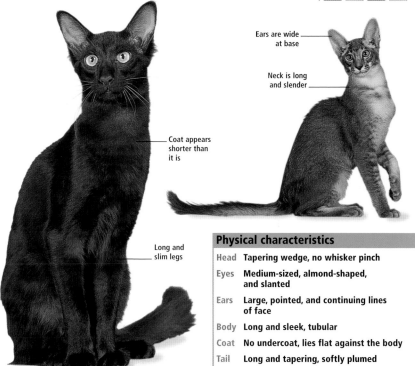

Ears are wide at base

Neck is long and slender

Coat appears shorter than it is

Long and slim legs

## Physical characteristics

| | |
|---|---|
| Head | Tapering wedge, no whisker pinch |
| Eyes | Medium-sized, almond-shaped, and slanted |
| Ears | Large, pointed, and continuing lines of face |
| Body | Long and sleek, tubular |
| Coat | No undercoat, lies flat against the body |
| Tail | Long and tapering, softly plumed |

# Kurile Island bobtail

- Russian or Japanese?
- Friendly, independent temperament
- Short-tailed feline

The Kurile Island bobtail is quite different from the Japanese bobtail *(see opposite)*, although it has the same short tail. Its coat, conditioned by harsh winters, is longer and thicker than that of its more southerly relation, and its build sturdier. A friendly breed, it nonetheless retains its independence.

**History** With the advent of a more open attitude in the countries of the former Soviet Union, new breeds are emerging. The Kurile Island bobtail represents the same mutation as the Japanese bobtail, and has probably been present on the Kurile Islands for centuries. While this genetic similarity causes no problems to the Russian bodies that register the Kurile, the shared mutation that causes its bobtail might be a barrier to the breed's acceptance in Europe.

## Key facts

Place of origin
**Kurile Islands**

Date of origin
**Pre-18th century**

Weight range
**7–10 lb (3–4.5 kg)**

Temperament Busy
and friendly

Breed colors A wide
variety of colors and
color combinations is
acceptable

Coat is
semilong

Round
paws

Legs are
sturdy, but
not heavy
for build

## Physical characteristics

| | |
|---|---|
| Head | Broad, with gentle nose-break at eye level, and slight whisker pinch |
| Eyes | Oval, slightly tilted, wide range of colors |
| Ears | Medium-sized and upright in set |
| Body | Medium-sized, strong, and muscular |
| Coat | Semilong, with discernable undercoat |
| Tail | Short, curled, and carried high |

# Japanese bobtail

- Still rare outside Japan
- Pompomlike tail
- "Entertain me or else!"

This sociable and inquisitive breed exists throughout Japan. The short tail, which makes a full, fluffy pompom, does not carry spinal or bone deformities with it. Highly gregarious, the Japanese bobtail is easily bored and, when bored, can be mischievously destructive.

**History** Examples of both short- and longhaired bobtails can be found in Japanese art going back over the last three centuries. A natural variant of the shorthaired Japanese bobtail (*see p.98*), these longhaired cats would have had an advantage in the cold climate of Japan's northernmost areas. Shorthaired bobtails were brought to the United States in 1968, carrying with them the longhair gene, which was noticed in the early 1970s. It has yet to gain recognition in Britain.

## Key facts

**Place of origin**
Japan

**Date of origin**
1700s

**Weight range**
6–9 lb (2.5–4 kg)

**Temperament** Vibrantly alert

**Breed colors** A wide variety of colors and color combinations is acceptable

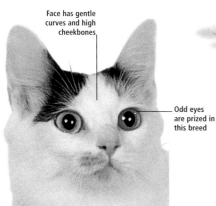

Tail can be straight or curled

Legs are long and slender but not dainty

Face has gentle curves and high cheekbones

Odd eyes are prized in this breed

## Physical characteristics

| | |
|---|---|
| Head | Broad, with noticeable whisker-break and gentle dip at eye level in profile |
| Eyes | Large and oval, with definite slant when viewed in profile |
| Ears | Large, set wide apart and upright |
| Body | Long, straight, and slender, but well muscled |
| Coat | Semilong, soft and silky |
| Tail | Short pompom, either straight or curled |

# Random breeds

- Most popular longhair
- May not be particularly longhaired
- Anything goes

By far the most commonly owned domestic cat is the humble, random-bred household pet. Even in countries with high populations of pedigreed cats, these self-selected pets outnumber them four to one. While some people are set on the looks and personality traits of a certain breed, random-bred cats usually satisfy those of us with less-definite needs.

A cat's personality depends on its early experiences, so a random-bred cat is as friendly as one makes it, although it may not achieve the chattiness of Oriental breeds or the extreme placidity of some longhaired breeds. Only a few of these naturally developed felines have long hair, because it is a recessive trait, but cats in the style of the Angora or the Maine Coon do turn up: after all, these breeds sprang from such non-pedigreed cats.

Shaded silver

**The color,** "eyeliner," and outlined nose of the silver shaded Persian all appear in random-breds, and many household pets have coats that would not have disgraced early Persians.

**The majority** of tortie-and-white cats are female, and no two cats have the same markings.

Tortie-and-white

Cream-and-white

**Bicolored cats** are quite common, and cream-and-whites and black-and-whites are among the most popular.

Black-and-white

**Tabby random-breds** have been around for centuries. Their markings, though, may be slightly obscured in a longhaired cat.

Brown tabby

# CHAPTER THREE

# Behavior

Cats that are well socialized to humans before seven
weeks of age develop a warm, often physical
relationship with people. They are vocal, demanding,
and responsive. Selective breeding has perpetuated the
"kitten" in cats. The cat's inherited behavior potential
is set in its genes. The way it thinks, eats, hunts, marks
territory, grooms itself, mates, gives birth, and cares
for its young is immutable. Through contact with us
very early in life, the cat comes to look upon us as
lifelong providers. Ultimately the cat is a taker, taking
food, contact comfort, and security from us in a
relationship not unlike the one it had with its mother.

# Natural selection

- Interference from humans has had little effect
- Domestic cats inherit wildcat potential
- Color and personality are possibly linked

Unlike most other domesticated animals, the cats of today look and behave much as they did before they evolved from the wild. However, there is one vital difference: given the right early social experience, domestic cats are at ease around other species, especially humans.

### Breeding for temperament

Domestic cats are more manageable, docile, and fertile than their wild cousins. They are easier to handle and have a reduced fight-or-flight response. Due to their tamability, we create playful, sociable adult cats by perpetuating into adulthood attractive juvenile behavior

**The cat is probably** "more natural" in terms of the way it looks and behaves than any other domesticated species.

characteristics. This is virtually impossible with wildcats, but, through careful breeding of wildcat to domestic cat, tamability can be selected.

### Sex differences in behavior

Male cats roam over larger territories, urine-mark more, and fight more than females. They are more active and more destructive. Neutering has no effect on excitability or destructiveness but reduces their general activity level. Neutered males demand more attention, tolerate handling better, are more affectionate and hygienic, and are likely to be friendly to other cats.

Females are generally more playful and affectionate than males. Neutering has little effect on the personality, although neutered females demand more attention and are less active, more tolerant of other cats, and more playful with us.

### Color differences in behavior

In foxes there is a link between color and the function of hormones associated with the fight-or-flight response. In Russian foxes, three mutant colors— non-agouti, blue, and chocolate—are related to reduced fear and aggression.

These colors exist in cats, too, and, together with blotched tabby and sex-linked orange (tortoiseshell, calico, and marmalade), may be associated with altered hormone activity and the effect of reducing fear-related behavior.

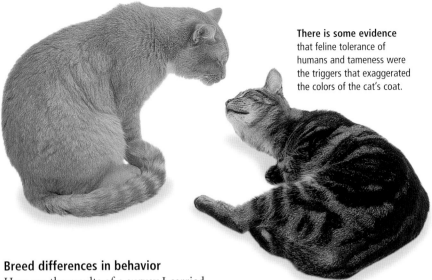

**There is some evidence** that feline tolerance of humans and tameness were the triggers that exaggerated the colors of the cat's coat.

## Breed differences in behavior

Here are the results of a survey I carried out, asking 100 practicing vets about breed differences in behavior.

• **Attention demanding:** Siamese, Burmese, Abyssinians, foreigns, and Orientals demand the most attention.

• **Activite:** The above breeds demand the most activity, and Persians demand the least.

• **Tolerant of handling:** Domestic shorthairs are best.

• **Affectionate:** All cats give affection but Persians give the least.

• **Destructive:** Persians are least destructive, and Orientals and Siamese are the most destructive.

• **Friendly to other cats:** Domestic shorthairs are most friendly; Siamese and Burmese are the least friendly.

• **Vocal:** The Siamese is the most vocal, the Persian the least.

## It's all in the genes

Zürich University ethologist Dennis Turner asked cat-research personnel to rank their cats' friendliness to people. He found no relationship to sex or color, but a strong relationship to who their fathers were.

### The dominant tabby

For whatever reason, attractiveness or tamability, the blotched tabby color increases along the old trade routes out of northern Africa and reaches its highest level in British cats. In turn, these cats accompanied traders, soldiers, and settlers from Great Britain throughout the world. This color is so successful that in time it may engulf all available feral-cat populations.

# Feline social behavior

- Feline social behavior is adaptable
- Blood ties do matter
- Cohabiting can work with encouragement

The cat's potential social behavior is enormously varied, from fiercely independent to gregariously sociable with other cats. Some experts feel the cat's social personality is "in transition" from independent to interdependent. In truth, its personality and consequent social interactions with other cats depend upon its early learning, the population density of local cats, and how much food is available locally.

## Population density varies

The domestic cat is a lone hunter. If foraging for itself, it needs a large enough territory to supply sufficient prey, and it will defend that territory against other cats.

In farming regions of North America, Europe, and Australasia, an area of ⅖ sq mile (1 sq km) will support up to five cats. In suburban regions, where there is both prey and garbage for food, the same area will support up to 50 cats.

## Food influences behavior

Social interactions increase when food is plentiful because there is less reason to fight. Thinly scattered hunting cats restrict their social gestures to defensive postures, while well-fed cats in colonies are sometimes surprisingly gregarious in their social interactions.

Since food is plentiful in our homes, this is where cats are most sociable, even sleeping in contact with each other.

**Where there is unlimited food,** such as around harbors or where cat lovers feed feral cats, an area of ⅖ sq mile (1 sq km) can support 2,000 cats.

## Family is important

Just because its stomach is full and life is easy for your resident housecat, do not expect it to appreciate the arrival of a new cat. Far from it.

The greatest predictor for cats getting along is blood relationship. The other great predictor is early neutering. While feral toms make far fewer social contacts than unneutered females, neutered toms make as many contacts with other cats as neutered females. Neutering greatly enhances male feline sociability.

## The matriarchy

Cat sociability is strongly matriarchal. Feral colonies usually consist of three or more generations of blood-related females. Licking is the most common social interaction between females, more than twice as common as rubbing.

As male kittens mature, and as their play behavior between four and six months becomes rougher, they are driven out of the colony by their mother, her sisters, and their mother and grandmother. These males join other, older, ejected males, forming a loose brotherhood of cats who, if food is plentiful, generally do not fight with each other but hang out around the colony and attack any unrelated adult male that comes near.

## Group dynamics

The social dynamics of a group of cats responds to changing conditions such as absences, new cats, or new people.

In a typical group of domestic cats living with humans, social contacts are made by females and kittens, seldom by unneutered adult males.

Once there is stability within a housed group, disputes are settled by eye contact or by an occasional swipe of a paw. A ranking hierarchy develops but this is more fluid than the type of ranking that develops among dogs.

## Social hierarchy

Rank is not static. When two cats meet unexpectedly, the cat on the higher ground is usually the social superior on that occasion. The same might not be true on the next meeting. Rank is also affected by health and odor. It is not uncommon for a cat to return home after being treated or hospitalized for a medical condition only to be attacked by a healthy resident cat. In a multicat household, however, once rank is established, disputes are rare.

## Feline faceoffs

When cats have a demarcation dispute, they are likely to try body language to settle their problems before turning to force. Rituals used include arching their backs, baring their teeth, bristling their fur, hissing, and spitting. Anyone confronted by this display knows how impressive a little cat can be. Cats stare at each other until one breaks eye contact and turns its head. That is the signal it is about to withdraw. If it moves too quickly it risks being physically attacked by the victor. Vanquished cats get bitten on their bottoms. Those that stand their ground get bitten on the head and neck.

Hissing indicates anger at other cat's presence

Making itself look small, this cat shows its submission

# The lone hunter

- Cats are selective about their prey
- Dawn and dusk are favored hunting times
- Hunting can be prevented

All cats hunt. There is a tendency among urban and "new-breed" cat owners to deny the cat its origins as the world's most efficiently packaged, small, land-based predator, but cats need to hunt, and this has little to do with hunger.

Even the most perfectly bred, expensive, well-fed, lovable house cat will be a hobby hunter, impelled by its basic need to stalk, leap or pounce.

## Cats cannot help it

Hunting is a "hard-wired," natural activity, at the very core of feline behavior. While rural feral cats refine their hunting techniques according to the available prey, urban feral cats scavenge more than hunt, eating the leftovers thrown away by us.

### Should cats hunt?

When cats are introduced into an isolated ecological environment, the effects on wildlife can be devastating. The debate over whether cats should be allowed to follow their hunting instincts has been most passionate in Australia, a continent with few natural land-based predators. In 1989, a small suburb of Melbourne passed a local law compelling cat owners to have their cats in their homes from just before sunset to just after sunrise. By 2002, whole states had passed cat-control laws.

Pet cats hunt for the thrill of the stalk and pounce, rather than out of hunger.

Most cats are attracted to land-based mammals, but some become bird specialists. This can have a huge effect on the population of land-based birds, especially in regions where, historically, there have been no land-based predators.

**When stalking prey,** cats crouch low. As they approach their prey, they raise and "spring-load" their hindquarters to facilitate a pounce.

## How cats hunt

While their senses suggest they should hunt at dawn, dusk, and under a full moon, cats will hunt throughout hot summer nights or at noon in winter. These altered activities may be related to the changing activities of prey.

A cat is attracted to a location by scent, such as mouse urine. Its strategy is to wait beside a small mammal's semipermanent pathway. Cats with full stomachs are more patient than hungry cats, feral cats are better hunters than pet cats, but nursing mothers are best.

When a cat pounces it may throw itself on its side and rake its prey with its hind claws while pinning it down with its forepaws. If it is hungry, it kills its prey with a bite to the neck. A cat's canine teeth slip perfectly between the neck vertebrae of a small rodent, killing it instantly. Whether the prey is eaten immediately, or even killed, depends on the cat and the context of the hunt.

Tormenting, batting, and throwing the prey may serve some function, but equally it may be a form of torture.

After the hunt, many pet cats literally dance with delight, taking high, curving, pantomime leaps. This activity is rarely seen in feral cats.

## Hunting birds

A different strategy is needed when hunting birds. A cat uses long grass as cover when it stalks prey. Keeping close to the ground, it slinks forward, "freezing" if it thinks it is detected.

With its head stretched fully forward and its ears positioned to catch the slightest sound, the cat leaps on its prey.

On well-mown lawns or smooth floors, cats employ the same low, slow slink in approaching prey,

**Playing with prey** before the kill is normal feline behavior. Notice how this kitten's ears are pointed forward in the classic pounce pose.

but hunting birds on manicured lawns is seldom productive.

Bird kills seem high because hunting is carried out in daylight in the garden and few birds are consumed. The remains are left in a visible "pantry," a virtual cemetery of avian corpses.

A backyard is a great place for cats to successfully hunt birds seeking worms and insects. You can reduce the number of birds killed by cats each year simply by putting a bell on your cat's collar.

# Feline genetics

- Inheritance is controlled by genes
- Genes influence physical and mental traits
- Random mistakes happen

A gene stores information in four proteins, which are called A, T, C, and G. Together, these proteins make up deoxyribonucleic acid, or DNA.

The combination of four states is phenomenally greater than the two states of a computer microchip, and that colossal storage space is available in almost every cell of your cat's body.

Let's put that in context. I could store all the information from 100 books like this one in the genetic code of just one feline cell. And I could accurately reproduce all the information in those 100 books each time that cell divides and copies.

## Why cats are not clones

But if copying is so accurate, then all cats should be clones, perfect copies of their ancestors. This would be true but for eggs and sperm. A string of genes is called a chromosome, and cats have 19 pairs of chromosomes—38 in total—in each cell. All cells have 38 chromosomes, except eggs and sperm, which have 19, each one half of a pair.

When cats mate, the combination of the egg and sperm's 19 chromosomes into a new set of 38 chromosomes creates new sets of alleles *(see below)* at each site on each chromosome.

**Every living cell** contains a nucleus, in which 19 pairs of chromosomes are stored. All chromosomes are X-shaped, except the male gender chromosome, which is Y-shaped. Each chromosome, when unfurled, is a complex helix of four proteins. This helix is called DNA.

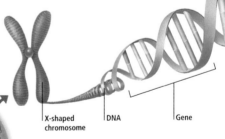

X-shaped chromosome | DNA | Gene

Chromosome

Nucleus

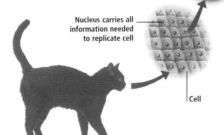

Nucleus carries all information needed to replicate cell

Cell

## Alleles

Specific information about a trait, like eye color, is always carried at the same site on each chromosome: in a pair of chromosomes, the pair of sites is called an allele. If the data is the same at both sites, the instructions are homozygous; if not, they are heterozygous.

Allele of two genes

## Dominant and recessive traits

Characteristics such as coat length are called dominant if only one half of an allele is needed to show its effect, and recessive if both parts of an allele are needed. In general, ancient wildcat traits tend to be dominant, while newer mutations are recessive.

## Genetics in isolated populations

In a large population, genetic mutations usually vanish in a short time, but in small, isolated populations they are far more influential on the new population. This is why tailless cats were perpetuated primarily on what were previously cat-free islands, such as the Isle of Man, Japan, or the Kuriles off northeast Asia.

**Polydactyl (many-toed) cats** were among the first cats to arrive in America, which is why they are still more common along the East Coast, from Halifax to Boston, than elsewhere in the world.

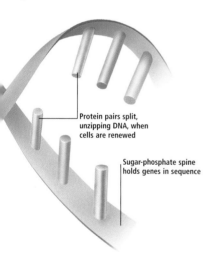

Protein pairs split, unzipping DNA, when cells are renewed

Sugar-phosphate spine holds genes in sequence

## A breed is an isolated population

In selecting for a color, body type, or even personality, we unwittingly create isolated populations that may harbor dangerous genes. This is how genetic disease gains a foothold within a pure-bred line. Advances in feline gene-mapping and genetic fingerprinting will eventually reduce disease risks.

### How dominant traits work

As an example, let's say a cat has an allele where both genes are for short hair, and let's call that SS (capital letters mean dominant traits). It mates with a cat that has an allele where both genes are for long hair—let's call that *ll* (lower-case means recessive traits). Because short hair is dominant, crossing them produces four shorthaired kittens, each with S*l* alleles.

$$SS + ll$$

| S*l* | S*l* | S*l* | S*l* |

Now let's cross two of these descendants. We end up with three shorthaired cats and one longhaired because this is what happens:

$$Sl + Sl$$

| SS | S*l* | S*l* | *ll* |

Looking at the three shorthaired descendants gives no clues as to which have the potential, through appropriate breeding, to produce longhaired kittens. Unfortunately, genetics is not usually that simple. Most physical and behavioral characteristics are polygenetic, controlled by an as-yet-unknown combination of genes.

# Courtship and mating

- Mating is a dramatic spectacle
- The female is in control of the proceedings
- Eggs are precious

Because so many pet cats are neutered early in life, few urban cat owners other than breeders have the opportunity to observe sexual behavior in males and females. Cats are noisy, promiscuous, and enthusiastic about sex. The female controls the timing of mating activity, only permitting the male to mate when she is emotionally and biologically ready. Repeat matings occur throughout the day, a repetition that is necessary to induce eggs to be released from the female's ovaries. Without frequent matings, eggs are not released, but another heat period follows within a few weeks.

**The female** often shows she is receptive after the male grooms behind her ears. She will stretch out and allow the male to sniff her, drawing scent into his vomeronasal organ.

## The onset of heat

The female's first signs of impending heat are increased restlessness and a heightened desire to rub her body sensuously against objects or even other animals. She urinates more frequently and is likely to use her urine as a scent marker to indicate her impending condition to territorial toms.

Soon after, she begins to make her plaintive and distinctive sexual call to toms, signaling that she is receptive. Inexperienced people can mistake her calling and dragging herself around for pain. If you now touch the base of her tail, she crouches with her hindquarters

**As the male mounts,** he grasps the female's neck skin in his jaws, which helps to subdue her. Mating is over within seconds but the male maintains his grasp to prevent her from turning on him.

raised and her tail turned to the side, ready for mating. Often she purrs, kneads with her front paws, and stretches her body.

## Ever-ready males

The male cat is a sexual opportunist. If unneutered, he patrols his territory, spraying urine and responding to the scent posts and calls that tell him a female is receptive. Often, however, he is not the only male who has been alerted by the female's activities.

Dominant males use intimidation or brute strength for the right to mate. Feline courtship itself is perfunctory.

## Sensible behavior

Compared to other mammals, the cat appears overwhelmingly promiscuous, but there is sound biological logic in its behavior. The female cat is an induced ovulator: she does not release eggs from her ovaries until she has been mated.

More sociable species—such as humans, dogs, or any domesticated livestock—have no need for the female to save eggs because males are always available. Cats, however, evolved as lone hunters. When a female comes into season it is possible that no males are in the vicinity. Saving eggs until mating is a sound solution to naturally independent behavior. So is the female's plaintive

### Who is the father?

Females do not release eggs until there have been repeated matings, which stimulate a cascade of hormones. The hormones induce egg release, and fertilization occurs 24 hours later. This rewards either the male who physically subdued other males, the low-ranking male who gains the female's attention through intelligent courtship, or the persevering male who takes over after the dominant male is exhausted. In each of these instances, the female is selecting for excellent qualities for her young.

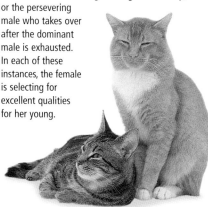

call, which carries over a greater distance than scent, indicating her impending receptivity.

Releasing eggs after a single mating rewards the opportunist male, but this is not necessarily the best father.

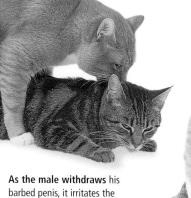

**As the male withdraws** his barbed penis, it irritates the lining of the vagina and stimulates egg release. The female cries out, hisses, spits, and attempts to bite him.

# Expecting kittens

- Early on, there are few outward signs of pregnancy
- The cat may adopt a more serene disposition
- Sensible nesting activity begins

Pregnancy in cats lasts about nine weeks, but during the first half of that time a typical expectant cat gives few clues that she is pregnant. She hunts, rests, and generally behaves normally.

Under the influence of progesterone, the hormone of pregnancy, and with an ever-increasing weight in her abdomen, she soon moderates her behavior, gradually reducing her activity level and resting more.

### Is my cat pregnant?
If you think your cat might be pregnant, first check her nipples. These become more prominent and pinker by three weeks of gestation. By four to five weeks after conception, your vet will be able to feel golf-ball-sized swellings in her abdomen. At this time the developing fetuses are usually quite easy to count. Shortly afterward, her belly becomes visibly enlarged.

### Multiple fathers
Unplanned breeding of pedigree females by both pedigree and non-pedigree males, producing litters of both purebred and crossbred kittens, confirmed what breeders had long expected: a litter may be sired by several males. This could have a survival potential for the offspring.

In large cats, such as the lion, when a new male takes over a pride, it is not

**Cats do not become** visibly pregnant until after about five weeks. Shortly before this time, your vet will be able to tell you how large the litter will be.

uncommon for him to kill all cubs sired by the previous dominant male.

The frequency of infanticide in domestic cats is unknown, but at least one highly respected world authority, zoologist David MacDonald of Oxford University, England, has observed a strange male cat enter a communal nest among bales of hay and kill six kittens belonging to three mothers before the cries of the survivors brought the mothers running back.

## Risks during pregnancy

The greatest risk to unborn kittens occurs during the first three weeks of development in the womb. Both drugs and infections might seriously impair healthy development. If, for example, the mother is exposed to feline infectious enteritis (FIE, or panleukopenia) at this time, the surviving kittens will be born with severe brain damage. Even exposure to live panleukopenia vaccine is dangerous. Cats should be vaccinated before they are pregnant, to increase the amount of passive protection they pass in the first milk to their kittens.

Never vaccinate pregnant cats to increase the level of inherited protection. Never vaccinate other cats in the household of a pregnant cat. Live vaccine virus can be shed by vaccinated cats and affect the pregnant cat's fetuses.

## Pregnancy and hormones

During pregnancy, the production of progesterone rapidly increases, peaking at around the 35th day after conception. This induces the more serene disposition of pregnancy. At the same time, the belly starts becoming visibly more rotund.

### Pregnancy checklist

1. Do not even think of breeding from your cat unless you know you can find homes for the resulting litter.

2. Do not breed from your cat until she is emotionally as well as physically mature.

3. Ensure that your cat is well nourished during pregnancy and especially after, during her period of milk production.

4. Test your cat and the proposed father to ensure they are not carriers of viral diseases such as FIV or FeLV.

5. Do not let your cat "follow nature's course" and breed with a feral tom. Feral toms are excellent breeders. The are also the most likely source of life-threatening infections such as FIV, FeLV, and feline infectious peritonitis (FIP).

Pregnancy can be as short as 57 days or as long as 70 days, but a few days before birth the female becomes restless and searches out her chosen shelter.

She rearranges her bedding material and spends increasing amounts of time in her chosen nest. This impregnates the region with her own scent, something that will eventually help her kittens orient themselves toward home.

As birth approaches, the mother loses her appetite and restlessly paces in the nest until contractions begin.

**A few days before the birth,** a pregnant cat will begin looking for a good nest, which she will scent-mark. This will help her newborns recognize home.

# Giving birth

- Problems are rare
- Do not fuss with your cat when she's giving birth
- Monitor her activities during the birth

Feline birth is usually uncomplicated. In her chosen, secluded, warm den the mother-to-be digs at the surface, often purring rhythmically. Soon her breathing quickens and contractions begin. Once contractions occur every 30 seconds, delivery is imminent. About 70 percent of kittens are born in a diving, head-and-front-feet-first position.

## Cleaning up

A good mother licks away the membranes and stimulates each kitten to take its first breath. If she fails to do this, you must intervene.

Further contractions expel the placenta, which is eaten after the cat chews through the umbilical cord. A mother consumes all birth wastes to prevent predators from knowing there is a litter of helpless kittens.

## The mothering instinct

Good mothering is based on genetics, emotional maturity, and the experience the cat had with its own mother.

There is no more fearsome form of aggression than that of a mother cat defending her litter. She will not bluff but will defend her kittens ferociously.

Shortly after birth, her first instinct is to keep her litter together and remove it from danger. The family will probably move again about four days later.

**The mother lifts her leg** out of the way. The kitten emerges from the birth canal in a lubricated amniotic sac, which the mother instinctively licks away.

## The scruff response

To move her kittens, the mother carries them, one at a time, by the scruff.

When scruffed, a kitten instinctively stops wriggling and draws its limbs close to its body to prevent injury in transport. The scruff response remains intact throughout a cat's life.

## Feeding

A kitten uses heat receptors in its nose to find a teat and then returns to the same teat throughout its suckling period. It stimulates milk release by kneading on its mother's breast with its forepaws, a behavior that some cats continue to perform on soft textures, such as woolen garments, into adulthood.

Mother's milk is highly concentrated in both fat and protein, which help kittens grow rapidly. Kittens that initially latch on to the most productive teats grow fastest, unless they are displaced by more dominant littermates. Suckling for nourishment lasts for five to six weeks, but it continues for emotional benefits for an equal length of time.

In Italy, Dr. Eugenia Natoli has observed how other females within a cat community may act as midwives, vigorously licking the newborn and even chewing through their umbilical cords.

**Ask the vet**

**Q:** How soon after giving birth will my cat's next heat follow?

**A:** At birth the mother produces more of the hormone prolactin, which stimulates both milk production and milk release. The suckling of her kittens stimulates the continued release of prolactin, which suppresses other hormone activity. When her kittens stop suckling, the mother's prolactin level drops again. She can be calling again within seven days.

### After birth

During the first few weeks, a kitten depends on its mother to stimulate all of its body functions. Her licking prompts each kitten to release its bladder and bowels. She also continues to consume her kittens' waste products, to hide their presence from predators.

### Absent fathers

Mating is the only time that most cats come in close contact with others.

After mating, the male leaves and rarely has any role in the upbringing of his young.

**After cleaning up** the area around the newborn kitten, the mother eats the amniotic sac. She licks the kitten dry to prevent it from getting cold.

**The mother licks** the kitten's face to clear the mouth and nostrils of mucus. She is vigorous and rough, making the kitten gasp for its first breath.

# Dependent on mother

- Kittens learn by observation
- They have a natural curiosity
- Independence comes early

At birth a kitten is totally helpless—it cannot even regulate its own body temperature—but within four days it can find its mother and crawl to her from over 20 in (0.5 m) away. In another 10 days its brain is sufficiently developed for it to coordinate its front legs. At three weeks old, it is tentatively standing, scenting, hearing, seeing, and responding. By seven weeks, it seems to have developed near-perfect balance.

## Shared responsibility

Within a feline community with other unneutered females, a kitten may be suckled by its own mother or by half-sisters or aunts.

Early actions are guided by instinct, but learning begins early. Even a two-day-old kitten knows which teat is most productive.

By a week of age it knows the smell of its own nest and, if separated, returns to it. At just 18 days old a kitten can use a litter box (see pp.172–5).

## Mother provides food

For the first few weeks the mother had to induce her kittens to suckle, but now they pester her for a meal. At three weeks a kitten starts to eat solid food. By five weeks it has a full set of pin-sharp baby teeth. Feral mothers bring back prey and cut it up for their young. As they grow older they will do more of the cutting up for themselves. Soon she will bring back live prey—an exciting learning experience for young kittens.

### Learning to walk

Kittens can crawl from birth, and at two weeks they start to develop fluid movement. By seven weeks they move like an adult cat, and by ten weeks they can walk along narrow ledges and have perfect balance.

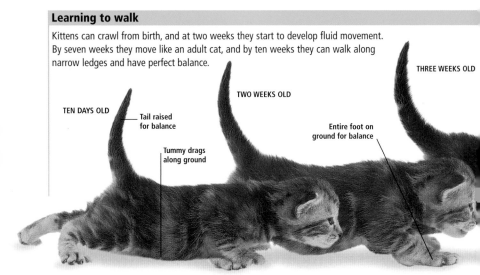

THREE WEEKS OLD

TWO WEEKS OLD

TEN DAYS OLD

Tail raised for balance

Entire foot on ground for balance

Tummy drags along ground

**For the first three weeks** the kittens' only food source is their mother's milk, which has almost twice the nutritional value of either cow's or goat's milk.

## The breakup of the family

As the mother's milk and prolactin levels diminish, so does her need to mother. Those pin-sharp baby teeth play a role, too: they begin to hurt her when the kittens suckle. Single kittens are allowed to suckle for longer. Within six months, large litters split up; smaller ones stay together longer.

## Starting to learn

While a kitten still depends on its mother for most of its grooming, at five weeks it is capable of fully grooming itself: even at this young age, the seeds of separation are being sown.

Mothers educate their young. They teach them how to use cat-flaps and even which human sex to prefer. Without a demonstration kittens either cannot perform a task or do so only by chance.

### Playing rough

At about six months, play between the littermates becomes increasingly rough—between males and females, even vicious. A mother and her daughters become seemingly so exasperated with the males' rough play that they are expelled from the nest.

The remaining females form the nucleus of the blood-related colony of females that is the basic feline social group.

Males join the brotherhood of toms, each with its own territory but all willing to spend time together, awaiting a chance to father another generation.

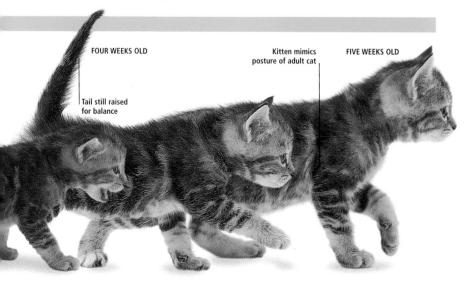

FOUR WEEKS OLD

Kitten mimics posture of adult cat

FIVE WEEKS OLD

Tail still raised for balance

# Early socialization

- Cats' brains mature quickly
- Frequent handling is essential
- Personality develops rapidly

The cat's brain is already well developed at birth and continues to develop at an astonishing rate for the next three months.

When it enters this world, a kitten is only 3 percent of its adult weight, yet its brain is already 20 percent of adult weight. Even so, the size and weight of the adult brain are one-third smaller than those of the African wildcat.

One of the reasons for this shrinkage in brain is that the cat's life is, compared to the wildcat's, easy. Early sensory stimulation results in greater brain power, more control over emotions, and ease with living with people.

## Frequent handling

At Temple University in Philadelphia in the early 1980s, Dr. Eileen Karsh showed that early and routine handling, from three to seven weeks of age, produced adult cats that head- and flank-rubbed, chirped, and purred when humans approached.

Routine handling also helps kittens grow faster and possibly bigger. If social contact with people does not begin until after seven weeks, kittens develop into more withdrawn adults.

Dr. Karsh also showed that calm mothers, at ease with people, teach their kittens to be equally at ease in the presence of such potentially intimidating predators as we are.

## How kittens learn

German ethologist Paul Leyhausen has described how a mother cat talks to her kittens in different ways. One sound means "I'm bringing a mouse back," and the kittens become excited. Another sound means "I'm bringing a rat back," and the kittens become more agitated or even hide.

Through trial and error the kitten learns about the natural world, what tastes good, what bites back, what is dangerous, and what is fun. Its natural inquisitiveness is profound early in life. Young cats are also open-minded about training (see pp.184–9).

**Regular handling** of kittens will ensure they grow into socially adept adults.

## Sensitive periods in development

Kittens develop their social manners at between three and seven weeks of age. If during this time a kitten frequently meets a member of another species—a dog, rat, horse, or human, for example—it will develop a social rapport with that species and not look upon it as predator or prey. That is at the very heart of a contented relationship with cats. If a cat does not learn how to live in harmony with us or with other animals at this early stage in life, natural fears are likely to develop.

John Bradshaw at Southampton University in England has shown that, if the conditions are right, some cats over seven weeks old can still be conditioned to live harmoniously and fearlessly with us. Although it can be difficult, some older cats retain the ability to learn new social lessons.

**Regular contact between** very young cats and other animals will reduce the chance that they will look on other species as prey or predator.

### Giving kittens a head start

① Ensure that potential mothers are emotionally competent to raise their kittens. Never breed from young females who have not yet reached emotional maturity.

② Offer balanced nourishment to the mother while she is pregnant and during her period of milk production. Good nourishment is necessary for proper development.

③ For proper social development, allow kittens to continue to suckle up to 10–12 weeks.

④ Handle kittens frequently, especially from birth to seven weeks, and expose them to mild sensory stimulations.

⑤ Think of how the kitten will live as an adult, and introduce it to other species early in life.

### You are mother

If, through early learning, your kitten comes to depend upon you for food, security, and warmth, it will probably, for the duration of its lifetime, think of you as its mother. That is the essence of the social relationship that we humans have with cats.

More independent cats will have a more restricted relationship with you. You are simply a useful resource. But kittens who learn early in life that you are Mom will continue to enjoy contact with you—stroking and petting—just as they enjoyed the comfort of grooming by their natural mother.

# How cats communicate

- Voice is varied
- Body language is explicit
- Why and how cats purr remains a mystery

Cats communicate successfully with other cats but less well with us. Social relationships are of little importance to cats, so the nuances of facial expression and "distance-reducing" body language are not highly defined. Our smile or the dog's wagging tail do not have overt equivalents in cat communication. Methods by which cats exchange information include the voice, touch, scent, and visual displays, or markers.

## Understanding cats

It is easy to misunderstand exactly what a cat is attempting to say or do, but with experience we learn to understand what they want. We are not nearly as good at understanding what a cat is communicating when it scratches the couch or leaves its feces unburied in the neighbor's yard. Cat sounds can be divided into three categories.

- **Murmurs:** These include purring and the happy, soft-sounding "chirp" used for greetings. The chirp is classified with the purr because it does not involve vowel sounds. It sounds like a "brrrp" or "brrrm" and is uniquely used in pleasurable circumstances. Some breeds chirp more than others.

- **Vowel sounds:** The classic "meow" varies according to context. Cats talk with meows. Requests, commands, demands, complaints, and bewilderment are all easy to understand. The Siamese and its close relatives have notoriously loud meows.

- **High-intensity sounds:** Usually reserved for other cats, some high-intensity sounds are familiar to owners and vets. Changing the shape of the open mouth creates different sounds—a grumbling, irritated growl, a threatening snarl or hiss, a defensive spit. Shrieks of fear or pain are produced in the same way, as is the high-pitched mating wail of females.

**You can almost hear** the demanding meow being issued by this kitten simply by observing the shape of its mouth!

## Where does the purr come from?

The source of the purr remains a mystery. The oldest theory is that the sound comes from two folds of membrane in the windpipe behind the voice box. These "false vocal cords" vibrate, producing the purr. It is certainly possible to stop the purr by applying gentle pressure just below the voice box.

Anatomists say it is not possible for these folds to vibrate, and suggest that turbulence in the vena cava, the main vein carrying blood to the heart, creates vibrations that are transferred up the windpipe.

Another explanation is that cats can control voluntary skeletal muscle fibers in the soft palate to make it flutter. Whatever its source, the purr is not simply a sign of contentment. Stressed or traumatized cats also purr, a phenomenon familiar to vets who treat cats after traffic accidents.

## Vibrant body language

Body language remains the favored, logical method for cats to communicate with other cats or people. The whole body can be used to send signals and also to indicate complete relaxation.

For all forms of visible communication the ears and tail are the cat's most expressive parts.

## Go away!

Feline body language is most refined in sending "go away" signals: aggressive and defensive displays are simple to understand.

An offensive display involves direct eye contact, often with constricted pupils, and a posture permitting instant attack. The head and whiskers lean forward, and the ears are held up and out so that the opponent sees the back of them.

Apprehension is communicated by crouching, the most common position for a cat that feels unsure of itself.

If a cat feels threatened, it shows its willingness to defend itself by rolling over and assuming a defensive position that reveals its claws and teeth. Hair may stand on end all over the body. Nervous cats may avert their eyes and yawn.

**Increased apprehension** in a cat leads it to adopt a lower crouch and dilated pupils. Eventually, the ears are laid back against the head.

# Marking territory

- Cats like to leave visible signposts
- Odor is memorable
- Touch is subtle

Cats leave visual markers on their territory to communicate either their presence or ownership of the domain.

While scratching keeps the claws sharp and efficient, it is also a technique used by a cat to leave a visible sign of its presence. This is why house cats prefer to scratch something highly visible, like the arm of a couch, and why scratching posts should be left in the middle of a room, not tucked away in a corner.

### Powerful scent markers

Feces is used by a dominant cat to visibly mark the extent of its jurisdiction. This is why some cats leave their feces unburied in neighbors' yards but not in their own. The cat feels that its territory extends beyond its own yard, and its feces is a visible sign of this.

Each time a cat empties its bowels, it squeezes a watery soup of chemicals out of its adjacent anal sacs. French researchers have identified at least 12 different chemicals in this discharge, which suggests it can transmit a lot of information. So does cat urine, which is either deposited normally as body waste or sprayed against upright objects and used as a scent marker.

Both males and females are capable of scent-marking and may continue to do so even after neutering. Male urine has a sour, pungent odor, potent enough even to our relatively insensitive noses to tell us that a male has claimed a territory.

**Scent-marking** allows a cat to clearly define the boundaries of its territory. Those boundaries may bear no relation to its owner's property boundaries!

## More subtle communication

Scent from the sweat glands on the paws also leaves an aromatic trail, defining where a cat has visited.

Further glands on the chin, around the lips, and at the base of the ears all produce substances that cats use as scent markers. Scent-marking is also used by many cats as part of their greeting ritual when their human family returns home.

## Touch is meaningful

While a cat communicates by leaving scent markers on objects or even on people, its ability to communicate its needs or demands, using touch, is also quite exquisite. Many cat owners are familiar with the feather-light touch of their cat's paw on the face early in

**Cats gently touch** nose to nose not only to scent each other, but also to make physical contact.

the morning—a gentle reminder of a new day and impending mealtime.

Those foolish enough to disregard the gentle stroke know that it will soon become a more urgent tap. If this is disregarded, some cats quite literally turn the tap into a punch, all the time sitting there, inscrutable and overtly innocent, but knowing exactly how to communicate a demand.

And while feral cats abhor physical contact with people, cats that have been raised from kittenhood in the presence of humans derive a lifelong satisfaction in seeking physical comfort from people.

**Cats can often be seen** rubbing their heads against objects. They do this in order to leave a scent marker that is sniffed when the cat returns.

## Touching taboos

The comfort of stroking is similar to that of being licked by its mother. Physical contact demonstrates safety and security.

Taboos remain, though. The abdomen is the most poorly defended part of the body, and touching it often provokes a genuine or mock aggressive response.

Excess stroking may also provoke aggression, because stroking remains a learned rather than natural behavior. The cat instinctively reacts to excess stroking with a bite, then apologizes, returns, and asks for more maternal care.

# The importance of play

- Social order is enhanced through play
- Play teaches hunting skills
- Gender has an impact on play

Feral kittens go through a play period, then mature into the serious business of independently capturing prey. Selective breeding and altered early experiences have allowed the cat's natural inclination toward play to blossom; well-socialized cats maintain a lifelong interest in play.

## Kitten play

Kittens start to play at about three weeks of age. Play begins with flamboyant, seemingly aggressive rushes at each other. By four weeks kittens wrestle, grasp with the forepaws, and kick with the hind legs. By five weeks the pounce is perfected, and by six weeks kittens are chasing each other with great dexterity.

Kittens play with other cats and with things. Social play with littermates and mother teaches social graces. It can be so rough that some owners are concerned about the severity of their activity. Playing with objects exercises what will become a cat's hunting skills.

## Playing with other cats

Social play between kittens involves sparring, hugging, licking, or simply lying belly up waiting for something to happen. During play, kittens learn how to inhibit their biting and how to play with sheathed claws. If the kitten claws or bites a littermate too severely and hurts it, the hurt kitten bites back or squeals in pain and stops playing. Soon kittens learn what is permissible.

Play with other kittens, or cats, increases when the mother becomes less tolerant and reduces her time with the litter. She swats and growls at her kittens if they annoy her. Other adult cats rarely show this anger when kittens play with them.

At about 14 weeks of age, social play enters a natural decline. Play between female kittens continues a little longer, but females become less tolerant of males. By 18 weeks, play between males and females occurs at 10 percent of its previous level, while play between males drops to 5 percent of its highest level. Social relationships naturally disintegrate, a necessary stage for the smooth dispersal of the litter.

**A litter of kittens** will play with each other for hours, inquisitively pawing at each other's extremities. This play will later turn rough or even vicious.

## Playing with things

Some of the maneuvers used in social play, such as leaps and pounces, are also used in object play. Other actions are used uniquely with objects, like pats, bats, pokes, scoops, and tosses. Kittens also grasp, mouth, and chew objects.

All of these activities would seem to be geared toward teaching a kitten to hunt, but repeated experiments show that neither the quantity nor the quality of object play is related to hunting proficiency later in life.

## Playful activity declines

Although both sociable and object play naturally decline, they do not disappear completely. A cat of almost any age can be enticed to play. Kittens that continue to live together into adulthood continue social play. This could be a natural way that cats in social groups bond with each other, or the perpetuation of juvenile characteristics into adulthood.

In the absence of other cats, cats treat us as cat substitutes. Many carry out their playful leaps and pounces on us.

### Perpetuating play

The natural decline in playful activity can be avoided by neutering your cat before it reaches sexual maturity. Under these circumstances, the neutered male's play activity is very similar to the neutered female's play activity. These individuals are likely to continue playing with each other well into adulthood with the same intensity and frequency of two adult female siblings.

# Grooming

- A necessary daily ritual
- Mutual grooming is social
- Lack of grooming is medically important

Grooming is an instinctive, or "hard-wired," behavior. A cat typically spends 8–15 percent of its waking hours cleaning itself. It doesn't need to watch its mother to learn how to groom. By six weeks of age kittens groom themselves as proficiently as adult cats and follow a set ritual.

Grooming begins with the head, proceeds along the back and sides, and ends at the base of the tail. Thorough bathing extends over the anogenital region, across the belly, down the legs, and between the toes of the feet.

Grooming significantly reduces numbers of skin parasites.

### Messy faces

Catching, killing, and eating small mammals is a messy business. More than 40 percent of grooming time is spent cleansing the cat's messiest parts—the head, forepaws, and neck.

The head and neck cannot be licked directly, so washing is a two-step process. A paw is licked, then wiped over the head,

licked again, and wiped over the head again. Cats are ambidextrous, using both forepaws equally well to wash both sides of the face and neck.

Grooming appears to be controlled by a biological clock. A certain amount of grooming is necessary each day. When cats are unable to groom for three days, they spend the first 12 hours afterward catching up on missed grooming.

**A cat's grooming ritual**
invariably begins with its head. This instinctive behavior is important to the cat; if your cat stops grooming, something is wrong.

## The problem with long hair

The cat's tongue is superb for removing dead hair from its coat. However, long hair sticks to the barbs on the tongue and is swallowed, forming a ball of hair in the stomach. Cats usually regurgitate these hairballs, but they can enter the intestines, needing laxatives to expel them. Longhaired cats need our help. Use a wide-toothed comb and a bristle brush at least twice weekly to remove dead hair and prevent mats from forming *(see p.197)*.

## Ask the vet

**Q:** Why doesn't my cat groom itself?
**A:** If a cat stops grooming itself, that is a powerful sign that something is wrong. Your cat may have a significant medical problem, so **contact your vet.**
 Cats certainly groom excessively because of skin wounds, infections, or parasites, but they also groom in excess when anxious. This is a displacement behavior, similar to our twisting our hair or pulling our earlobes when we are anxious or tense.

## Grooming controls overheating

Cats evolved in a hot climate, where regulating body temperature can be a matter of life and death. When properly maintained, there is an insulating layer of air captured in the coat, which protects the cat from overheating. On really hot days, the evaporating saliva left from licking has an even greater cooling effect on the body.

## Group grooming

Mother is responsible for all of a kitten's grooming needs for the first weeks of life and, occasionally, this can evolve into mutual grooming.

 This behavior occurs almost entirely between related females living in a matriarchal colony— a mother and her descendants or her sister's descendants.

 Unrelated cats that grow up from kittenhood in the same household, or that have socially bonded with each other, may also groom each other into adult life.

 Sometimes a new young household cat latches on to an older cat as a mother figure and allows it to groom it. In that sense, cats permit us to groom them or to stroke them because we are, in essence, mother substitutes. Under these circumstances, some cats will even groom humans.

**Mutual grooming** in adult cats is most common between blood-related females, but it may occur between any two cats with a strong social bond.

### Cats grooming people

Some cats try to lick and groom their owners with a perverse intensity. The cat licks and licks, favoring specific parts of the body. This is not simple grooming but a comforting behavior.

 These cats usually were taken from their mothers before 12 weeks of age, when comfort suckling ends. In these circumstances, a cat kneads with its paws on its owner (to stimulate milk release), then licks if it is allowed.

# Snoozing the years away

- Cats are living longer
- Sleep is blissful and necessary
- Do cats have extrasensory abilities?

In the wild, a cat's life expectancy depends upon finding food and avoiding injury, illness, or predators. In our homes there are fewer threats, so cats are naturally living very long lives, over twice as long as cats in the wild.

## A biological clock

Aging is controlled by a biological clock located in the part of the brain called the hypothalamus. As aging progresses, the chemical factory in the brain produces less of a neuroendocrine chemical called dopamine. If dopamine production is maintained, a cat probably lives longer. Some breeds, like the Siamese, have aging clocks set to last longer than others.

## Aging changes

Studies into the behavior changes of aging in cats found that by the age of 16, about 20 percent passed urine or feces outside as well as inside the litter box for no medical or acquired behavioral reason. Twenty-five percent slept more in the day but less at night, when they were more demanding of their owners. Over 60 percent were more irritable with their family, hissing or spitting with little or no provocation. Over 70 percent of 16-year-olds became disoriented, forgetting how to use the cat-flap, getting stuck in corners, or simply staring into space. Seemingly pointless, plaintive meowing also increased.

## Delaying aging changes

You can actively delay aging changes by doing the following:
- Feed smaller meals more frequently. Include high levels of antioxidants.
- Provide a litter box on each floor for easy access.
- Watch your cat's weight. Keep it trim.

**We do not know why** adult cats sleep for so many hours of the day, but in kittens, it is only during sleep that growth hormone is released.

- Provide warmth and comfort for sleeping and resting.
- Change your cat's diet according to its medical needs.
- Offer mental stimulation with toys and activities.
- Gently groom as often as possible. It helps circulation.

## Aging and illness are different

Over time, brain cells die and are not replaced. Bones get brittle, muscles receive less nourishment and shrink, and the elasticity of tissue diminishes. The senses become less acute. The lungs and intestines do not function as well as they once did. The kidneys allow nutrients to be lost from the system. These are all aging changes, not illness.

However, never assume that changes in an elderly cat's behavior are simply the result of growing older. Any change may be significant. Elderly cats benefit from annual or semiannual medical examinations.

## Sleep

The cat's natural need to be active when humans want to sleep and to sleep when humans are at their most active

### Psychic cats

It is often said that cats possess "psychic" qualities. Some of these attributes are vestiges of the mystique that has always enveloped cats. There is, however, scientific confirmation of their ability to find their way home or to foresee earthquakes.

Random tests have shown that unusual behavior increases in cats before certain earthquakes. Other studies suggest that older cats in particular have a homing ability when less than 8 miles (12 km) from home. These activities are thought to be related to the cat's awareness of electromagnetic fields. Indeed, when magnets are attached to cats' collars, their homing ability is disrupted.

is annoying but difficult to change. Cats sleep an average of 16 hours each day. Why they sleep so much is not yet understood, although in kittens, growth hormone is released only during sleep. Sleep is certainly necessary for a cat to maintain healthy body functions, and cat dreams may enable the cat to reorganize and reclassify information.

Cats have biological body rhythms. The most common is a 24-hour one (circadian rhythm), which dictates when a cat is most active—dawn and dusk— and when it is at its sleepiest—around noon and in the middle of the night.

# Do cats love us?

- The cat marches to its own drum
- People are good for cats
- Cats are good for people

Like all other species, including us, the cat instinctively strives to survive and leave descendants. However, unlike people, the cat does so in a uniquely independent manner.

Although through selective breeding and early learning we are countering its independent nature, the cat remains supremely detached and perfectly capable of taking care of itself. The cat behaves as if it were number one because in its mind, it really is.

## We are good for cats

Humans are good for cats in obvious physical ways. We provide them with safe and secure territories and with a constant supply of tasty food. We ensure good health, both through preventive inoculation and parasite control and through sometimes extraordinarily sophisticated medical treatments. We also provide emotional support; a leg to rub against, someone to snuggle up to, a hand to tickle a chin. But are cats good for us? And do they love us?

## Cats are good for us

In the early 1970s, it was observed that when cat owners stroked their cats their blood pressure dropped.

In the early 1980s, Dr. Erika Friedmann at New York's Brooklyn College found that cat owners are more likely to survive one year after a major heart attack than people without pets.

In the early 1990s, a study at Monash University in Australia revealed that cat owners are less at risk of heart disease than non–pet owners.

The health rewards of living with a cat seem straightforward, but on closer examination the relationship is more intriguing than it seems.

## Cats "care" for us

It would seem that we humans are our cats' caregivers. We nurture them and we mother them.

**Early socialization** encourages kittens to consider humans as members of their own family—and sometimes even as mother substitutes.

**Is a cat rubbing** its head against its owner's leg displaying real affection? Or is it subtly manipulating its human into doing what it wants to do?

But, in a subtle way, cats are caregivers too, offering us unexpected physiological and emotional rewards. American cultural anthropologist Constance Perin was the first to hypothesize about why our blood pressure drops when we stroke our cats. She theorized that the physiological rewards we get from stroking a cat evolved from the rewards we got from the reassuring physical contact with our mothers when we were infants. Stroking a pet cat stimulates the same chemical pathways in our bodies as were activated when, as infants, we were in physical contact with our mothers. In a physiological sense, perhaps even in a deeply submerged psychological way, our cats "parent" us; they, too, are caregivers.

## Cats think in a unique way

It is difficult to think like another animal, especially if that animal is emotionally quite different from us. The gregariously sociable dog is easier to understand. We make excellent dog substitutes because we share many similar needs, such as physical contact or a social hierarchy.

Cats think differently. If, however, a cat learns early in life to look upon humans as members of its extended family, that cat grows to think of people not only as nonthreatening but also as potential mother substitutes. This is the objective of most cat owners I know. They want their cats to be members of the family, there to cuddle and play with.

## Cat love

Pet cats may appear to be dependent but, examined more closely, their behavior often involves subtle dominance. Most cat owners I know are perfectly sensible people, yet they are slaves to their cat's whims. People are browbeaten into submission because it is mealtime or playtime. And most accede to these feline demands. Ever adaptable, the cat has found in us a soft touch, and rich pickings for a modified and highly successful lifestyle. In that sense, cats don't just love us, they adore us.

# CHAPTER FOUR

# Living with your cat

In your relationship with your cat, remember that the two of you are simply sharing a home. Know what equipment you need, whether your cat can go safely outdoors, what toys you will provide, what you will feed, and, very important, the essentials of basic cat training. Remember, you are living with a self-centered feline. It has a cat's brain and a cat's physical needs. Do not have unwarranted expectations. Do not expect it to respond like a sensible human adult or a pliable dog. If your cat is behaving like a cat—for example, climbing up curtains—this is not the cat's problem. It is up to you to train your cat and adapt to its needs.

# Choosing your cat

- Do not be impulsive
- Ensure there is adequate space
- Choose for tomorrow, not just today

Cats may be self-sufficient but that does not mean they do not need us. All cats need exercise and activity as well as mental stimulation. Because so many cats live their entire lives indoors, you are responsible for both your cat's physical health and its emotional well-being.

### Cats cost money

Do some planning. It is not difficult to project the costs of keeping a cat. Food and cat equipment are constants. So are preventive healthcare—yearly visits to the vet, parasite prevention—and boarding when you are on vacation.

For medical emergencies, consider pet health insurance. Alternatively, check out the monthly cost of a policy, then set up a bank account and deposit a similar amount into it each month. Whatever you do, be prepared for 15 or more years of cat expenses.

### Cats can cause problems

Allergy is an increasing problem. Think carefully before getting a cat—it is heartbreaking to get one and then have to part with it because someone in the family is allergic to it.

Cats can also carry a variety of parasites and germs that are dangerous if you have a compromised immune system—for example, if you are on chemotherapy or are HIV-positive.

Finally, cats can scratch and bite.

### Cats need space

On its own, no outdoor cat would choose a territory as small as a typical house. Under the right circumstances, however, with food, comfort, and security, most cats are content to live in our small spaces.

**Two or more cats** might keep each other company. However, make sure you can provide them with plenty of space.

Make sure your cat has as much space as possible. This might include creativity on your part to ensure safe exposure to the outside world.

**Looking for a longhair?**
Longhaired cats require more attention than shorthairs, since they need to be brushed regularly.

### The best sex for you
When choosing a cat, work with your natural preferences, but remember: there are pros and cons to both sexes. Neutering almost always eliminates sexual drawbacks without inhibiting the attractions of that sex.

### Young or older cat?
Kitten or adult: this is always a tough call. The advantage of a kitten is obvious. It is putty in your hands, ready to be molded to you and your family's lifestyle. Your cat will have fewer behavior problems if you acquire it when it is about ten weeks old and raise it in your own unique environment.

Adult cats bring their own advantages. Costs of purchase and neutering have been met. Virtually all adult cats, given the need or chance, are emotionally capable of building a powerful new bond with you.

### Purebred or random-bred?
The advantage of a purebred cat is knowing the coat-type, looks, size, and temperament it will have. The downside is that, when breeding for certain characteristics, we have unwittingly bred for higher risk of medical conditions *(see box, right)*. These risks vary from breed to breed.

Random-bred cats benefit from hybrid vigor, the enhancement of good health that comes from mixing stock from different genetic backgrounds.

### Longhair or shorthair?
Coat length is a personal preference. If you are attracted to longhairs, be aware that daily grooming is usually necessary.

| Some breed-associated medical issues ||
|---|---|
| **BREED** | **MEDICAL PROBLEM** |
| Abyssinian | Patellar luxation (slipping kneecaps) |
| American shorthair | Cardiomyopathy (heart disease) |
| Birman | Cataracts |
| Burmese | Hyperesthesia syndrome (rolling-skin disease) |
| Devon rex | Spasticity |
| Himalayan | Asthma |
| Maine coon | Hip dysplasia |
| Manx | Spina bifida (back vertebrae condition) |
| Oriental | Amyloidosis (a metabolic disease) |
| Persian | Polycystic kidney disease |
| Scottish fold | Osteodystrophy (joint thickening) |
| Siamese | Psychogenic alopecia (excessive self-grooming) |
| Somali | Gingivitis (gum inflammation) |
| Sphynx | Sun and cold sensitivity |

## Where to find the cat of your life

Cats are intentionally bred as a hobby by some and as a way to make money by others. What you are looking for is not just a breeder but a reliable breeder. As a general rule, if a breeder has only one breed, cat hair on the furniture and happy cats with their own beds throughout the house, you are in the home of a true addict, someone who will want to investigate you as much as you will want to investigate him or her.

Although some breeders sell kittens through pet shops, it is extremely rare for reliable breeders to do so. Some pet shops are okay. Most are not. Some are hotbeds of infection. Get pet supplies, not kittens, from a pet shop.

### Newspaper ads

Be very careful with the "cats for sale" sections of the classifieds in your paper. Most of those advertised are "surplus" cats in need of caring homes, but in many instances their medical history—for example, exposure to serious viral infections—is unknown. With careful selection, however, it is possible to get a great cat through an ad.

### Neighbors and vets

An unexpected litter born to a neighbor's cat is one of the most common sources of kittens. Sensible neighbors are an excellent source of kittens, but ensure they have had the litter examined and treated for internal parasites, such as roundworms, and external parasites, such as ear mites. Conscientious neighbors will ensure that the mother's appropriate inoculations are up to date.

Veterinary clinic notice boards are also an excellent source for both kittens and adult cats. Almost invariably the staff know these cats or the parents.

---

### Questions to ask a breeder

If you are planning to get a cat from a breeder, ask these questions.

➊ May I see its mother? (You should always be able to.)

➋ May I see its father? (Dad is likely to be there too, but as an unneutered and probably smelly male, he may live in a separate building.)

➌ Where do the kittens live? (Kittens raised indoors in a home, constantly touched and exposed to normal household activity, make better kittens than those raised in a kennel.)

➍ Have they been seen by a vet? (Good breeders usually have parents examined before mating, and kittens examined and vaccinated before they are sold.)

➎ When will they be ready? (Under eight weeks is too soon. Over 12 weeks is late. Eight to 11 weeks is usually just about right.)

**Try your local animal shelter** when looking for a cat or kitten. These shelters usually have no shortage of loving animals looking for a new home

## Cat shelters

Thousands of wonderful cats are always in need of loving homes. Rescue centers almost invariably neuter any cats not previously neutered. The supply of older cats is often greater than the supply of younger ones. While the possibility of a behavior problem is greater in older cats, and a behavior problem may have been the cause of its original abandonment, healthy recycled felines usually make great, rewarding companions.

## Assessing a cat's temperament

The more aware you are of potential problems, the better position you are in to know whether a cat has the temperament you are looking for in a feline companion.

Look for these characteristics:
• Sociability with people;
• Sociability with other cats;
• Sociability with dogs;
• Alertness, activity, and curiosity;
• Even-temperedness and equability.

### Questions to ask the animal shelter

If you are planning to rescue a cat, ask these questions.

1 Was it lost or handed in?

2 If surrendered, why was it handed in? (Many cats are discarded because they have behavior problems—for example, poor litter-box manners—that are not apparent until you live with the cat.)

3 Has the animal shelter done any behavior testing? (Progressive shelters analyze behavior such as sociability with other cats and with dogs and give reports to potential adopters.)

4 Can you help with any future problems? (The best animal shelters give continuing advice on behavior problems.)

Establish how easy it will be to share your home with the cat by observing it in the presence of adults, children, strangers, other cats, dogs, and loud noises, as well as when it is in the kitty carrier, in moving vehicles, or home alone. The more unfazed the cat is in each of these circumstances, the quicker it will adapt to its new environment.

# Cat-proofing your home

- Be prepared for the arrival
- Select practical cat accessories
- Ensure your cat's safety

Ensure your home is safe before you bring home your new pet. Visit the safety section of the home-improvement store—products that protect babies protect cats too. For accessories, choose items designed according to your cat's needs as well as to your fashion sense and your wallet.

## Safety first

Most cats are fearlessly curious. Make sure security is in place to prevent falls from windows. Remove poisonous houseplants and avoid seasonal ones, such as poinsettia and mistletoe, that are toxic if chewed *(see p.233)*.

Beware of the household chemical products you use. Some of these, such as carpet cleaner and bug-control products *(see p.233)*, may be toxic and can be absorbed through a cat's paws when walked in.

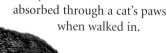

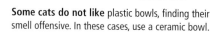

**Some cats do not like** plastic bowls, finding their smell offensive. In these cases, use a ceramic bowl.

### A little shopping list

Before bringing your cat home, there are other products you may consider purchasing.

- Alcohol-free spray to deter your cat from chewing furniture or fabrics;
- Sticky adhesive strips to arrange around plants to deter digging;
- Plexiglass shield to prevent your cat from jumping on the stove burners;
- Electric-outlet plugs to protect from electric shock;
- Simple locks for cabinets to prevent access to what is inside.

Keep cords from curtains and blinds, and electric cords, out of reach. Cats have a nasty habit of eating thread, rubber bands, and the elastic string that holds chicken together. Make sure none of these items is accessible to your cat.

## Food and water bowls

Choose sturdy, wide, not-too-deep bowls, ones that a cat can eat or drink from without its whiskers touching the sides. Wash the bowls daily.

Use a separate can opener for your cat's canned food and wash it routinely. Cover any partly used can of food with a plastic lid and store it in the refrigerator for a maximum of two days.

## Collars

Your cat should wear a soft collar and identification tag. A cat might scratch its neck a lot when it first wears a collar, but it will quickly get used to

**If you are planning** to let your cat wander outdoors, get it used to wearing a collar with an engraved identification tag.

it, usually within days. Do not tighten it too much. You should be able to slip two fingers under it.

If your cat goes outdoors, make sure the collar has an elastic section or a snap quick-release for safety.

## Feline ID

The most visible ID is an engraved name tag, but the most reliable method is the microchip—an electronic transponder the size of a grain of rice that is injected just under the skin in the neck. The transponder emits a signal that is read as a number when a reader is run over it.

If your cat goes outdoors, in many localities it must wear its color-coded rabies-inoculation tag to show that its rabies shots are up to date.

## Beds and bedding

Bedding should be hygienic, washable, protective, and comfortable.

Put comfortable bedding in the cat's carrier. If it feels secure in its own bed, it is less fearful when taken to the vet or the kennel. In cold climates, beds that can be suspended from radiators are feline favorites. Cats are sun worshippers—make sure you place the bed in a position your cat appreciates.

**Cats sleep for up to** 18 hours a day, so make sure bedding is comfortable, protective, and warm.

# The first 24 hours

- Start as you plan to continue
- Avoid excitement—create routines
- Expect problems to develop

A cat needs time to explore its new home. It should do so quietly, without fuss, so keep your family under control. Tell the children not to scream or jump around the kitten and that no yanking, tugging, or pulling is allowed. When it arrives home, restrict the kitten to one or two rooms. After it is settled in, knows where to hide and where its litter tray is, gradually let it inspect its new territory.

## Meeting your other cat

The first introduction of a resident cat to a new kitten should take place after the kitten has fallen into a deep sleep. Let the resident investigate and sniff the newcomer.

Do not interfere unless either one looks unhappy. Do not let your kitten get too excited. Older cats do not like exuberant kitten behavior, which may provoke a hiss or a bite. If you think your cat might attack the newcomer, ensure they are kept separate in your absence.

## Meeting your resident dog

Most cat–dog introductions go well. The cat hisses and the dog understands. If you have a terrier, sighthound, or any other dog full of bravado (or more than one dog), ensure that it is not tempted to chase your cat. If there is any sign of chasing, do not leave the cat and dog together without supervision.

**It is in the natural** order of life that cats rule. Most dogs (although not all) understand this.

**By offering an agreeable sleeping space** to your cat, you should be able to discourage it from attempting to share—or, more likely, claim—your bed.

## Who sleeps where?

This is your choice, but remember: early learning is powerful. Let your cat sleep in your bedroom now and it is likely it will aim to be under the covers with you within a week. This is fine if you and your partner do not mind becoming a feline threesome, but if there are any objections, prepare a comfortable bed for your cat elsewhere and shut the door to your bedroom to prevent nocturnal or dawn visits.

If your new cat is a yowler, especially if it has Siamese ancestry, invest in earplugs. It may be worthwhile taking a box of chocolates to your neighbors, too, if you have thin walls and a vocal pest. Vocal demands usually stop within a maximum of three weeks if there is no response from you.

### A name is important

Cats respond best to short, snappy names. One- or two-syllable names like Floss, Lick, Ditsy, or Thug are good. Names that do not sound like other words you regularly use are also recommended.

## Do not create problems

Put a kitten on your bed and it thinks it belongs to it. Give it some food while you are eating and it will expect it again. Be firm with yourself. Do not create problems for the future by thinking you can get away with something just once. Cats are smarter than you think.

### House rules

Create house rules for your whole family to follow. Keep them posted in the kitchen. For example:

1 Ditsy is the primary responsibility of… (specify which family member).

2 Ditsy will be restricted to… (specify area).

3 Ditsy will sleep in… (specify area).

4 Do not give Ditsy treats without Ditsy first meowing or coming to her name.

5 Always use Ditsy's name first when you want her attention.

6 Consider Ditsy when making your plans or arrangements.

7 Windows and exterior doors to the house are to be kept closed.

# The litter box

- Cats need little training
- Provide for your cat's expectations
- Try to supply one litter box for each cat

The cat is naturally clean. From about three weeks of age, and with its mother's guidance, a kitten intuitively chooses an elimination site with a "diggable" surface, and returns to this site each time it needs to empty its bladder or bowels.

By the time you acquire your cat it will need little training to use a litter box. What is important to a cat is the feel of the litter underfoot, the odor, and the location of the litter box. As always there are exceptions to the rule. Unneutered toms intentionally use their urine and unburied feces as territory markers.

### The cat's litter preference

In North Africa, where the domestic cat evolved, earth and sand were excellent for burying waste. They still are,

especially earth that we have already broken up to make digging easier. That's why cats enjoy burying their droppings in fresh flower beds.

The feel underfoot is especially important to cats and, generally speaking, the finer the feel, the more attractive the substance. Sand appeals to most cats, which is why children's outdoor sandboxes are likely to be contaminated by cats.

The amount of actual digging a cat does varies with each individual. While some are content to give their litter a cursory paw before and after eliminating, others carry out complex engineering works, creating excavations beforehand, and sculpting pyramids afterward.

**From a very young age,** cats are taught by their mother how to empty their bladder and bowels and how to cover it up afterward.

## Ask the vet

**Q:** What should I do if my cat refuses to use the litter box?

**A:** After eliminating possible medical causes, such as a painful case of cystitis *(see pp.174–5)*, try restricting your cat to an enclosure containing only its bedding and a clean litter box. When left with no other alternative, your cat will usually use the available litter box within 24 hours.

## Our litter preference

While each cat has its own personal litter preference, we also have preferences in what we want from them. Fortunately our requirements mostly coincide with theirs. Both of us want absorbable substances that control odor. However, what smells good to you does not necessarily smell good to your cat.

Commercial cat litter is a relatively recent product. Clay litters ground to a finer degree "clump" when wet, which allows for easy removal. Clumping litter tends to stick to long hair and get tracked out of the litter box.

The choice of which type of litter material is yours. Whatever your choice, remember that early learning is potent. What a kitten becomes used to is what it will likely prefer as an adult.

## Litter etiquette

Kittens are inquisitive and likely to taste any new type of cat litter. Some vets feel that kittens are more likely to taste clumping litters than other varieties. Supervise your kitten when introducing it to any form of litter until it understands what the litter is for. Remember, too, that an odor you find pleasant might be deeply offensive to your cat.

When possible, set up two litter boxes with different forms of litter, both of which are acceptable to you.

Your cat will use the one it prefers. Place the litter box in a secluded but easily accessible location. Cats don't like to eliminate in busy locations.

In natural circumstances, different cats seldom use the same latrine site. If you have a multiple-cat household, set up two or more litter boxes.

## Types of cat litter

### CLAY

Gray, pink, or white, clay is the most popular type of litter, absorbing urine and moisture from feces. Clumps are easily removed from the litter box. Do not flush clay down the toilet even if the label says it is safe to do so.

### WOOD- AND FIBER-BASED LITTER

A by-product of the pulp and paper industry, pelleted litter expands as it absorbs moisture and is biodegradable. Fiber-based products, made from substances like coconut fiber or dried grass, are very absorbent and need frequent changing. Fiber- and wood-based litters often have added odor eliminators that may be offensive to a cat.

### NONABSORBENT LITTER

Sometimes made of pelleted corncob coated in paraffin wax or polystyrene, this litter is used in a special box with a urine-collecting unit below. Urine drains through. Feces are removed and disposed of. The litter is washable for reuse.

### EARTH AND SAND

These natural substances are a cat's favorite litter materials. Because they are bulky and not biodegradable, they are not suitable for urban use. Fortunately, young cats are willing to use other substances when introduced at an early age.

### Litter boxes

The choice of open, covered, manual, or automatic litter box is yours. Remember that your kitten should be introduced to your preferred receptacle as early as possible in order to avoid a rejection later on. For example, cats that are familiar with open boxes may be apprehensive about using an enclosed model. The variety of self-cleaning litter boxes is enormous. Many are practical and effective, especially those that help clean the cat's paws after use.

**A scoop makes the removal** of stools and clumps of urine much easier. Likewise, lining the box with a plastic bag facilitates a quick litter change.

### Litter-box deodorizers

Deodorizers for litter boxes come in granules, powders, and sprays. It is wise to avoid scented products—they may drive your cat away from the box. The best deodorizers use enzymes to break down odor molecules.

If a cat has urinated elsewhere, the carpet, underlay, and even the floor beneath should be treated with any odor-eliminating product. White vinegar and water is good for removing stains from carpets.

### Indoor elimination problems

A cat may refuse to use its litter box if it does not like the location of the box or the texture of the litter underfoot. It is also possible that you may not be cleaning the box regularly enough or, curiously, that you may be cleaning it so fastidiously that you are leaving cleanser smells in it rather than natural ones. A cat may also avoid a litter box used by another household cat.

Loss of litter training may also be a sign of medical problems. Pain when

**There are several reasons** why your cat may refuse to use its box, including its location. There may also be reasons of a medical nature.

**Spraying urine** is the way a cat marks its home territory. Although the main culprits are usually unneutered males, all cats may display this behavioral trait when threatened by a new arrival.

defecating—for example, from blocked anal sacs—will be associated in your cat's mind with its litter box. It may continue to urinate in the box but defecate outside it.

Similarly, pain when urinating may induce a cat to urinate elsewhere while continuing to defecate in the box. Painful urination is caused by crystal formation in the urine, bladder or urethra infection (bacterial cystitis), or even emotion (interstitial cystitis). Affected cats often urinate in unusual locations, such as sinks or bathtubs. Your vet will need a urine sample to help determine the cause of the problem.

### Spraying urine

A cat marks its home territory by spraying urine. Unneutered males mark more than others, but unneutered females increase urine-marking when calling, and all cats, neutered or entire, may urine-spray when they feel threatened by a new cat in the family,

by seeing a cat in the yard, or even when human stress levels in the household increase.

Determining the cause is vital for eliminating the problem. Until you know and eliminate the cause, keep your cat in a contained environment—a dog crate, for example—large enough for food, water, a bed, and a litter box. Clean up wherever urine has been sprayed with an enzymatic odor eliminator. Place food or water bowls near where urine was sprayed and, if you catch your cat backing up to the wall with a quivering tail, calmly push the tail back down and distract your cat with play.

### Collecting a urine sample

When your vet needs a urine sample from your cat, empty its litter box of its normal absorbable cat litter and refill it with nonabsorbent litter. If this is not readily available, use thoroughly washed fine gravel or polystyrene beads. Collect the urine immediately in a clean container.

# An indoor life

- Cats adapt well to life indoors
- Cater to your cat's needs
- Expect natural cat activities

For a lone hunter there is nothing more unnatural than a life permanently indoors, deprived of the physical and sensory challenges of the outdoor world. Yet most cats enjoy a hedonistic life indoors, cared for by human slaves. By understanding a cat's natural needs, it is simple to prepare your home for permanent indoor feline residents.

**Although cats** are the ultimate lone hunters, built to thrive in the wild, few complain about spending their lives indoors, cared for by humans.

## Adaptable to indoor life

The degree and type of mental and physical activity needed by an indoor cat varies with its own personality and its early experience. Indoor neutered cats retain more kitten behaviors, including the need to play. Left to their own ingenuity, cats are adept at creating their own amusement. What your cat sees as an exciting project—climbing the curtains, scratching furniture, or knocking food off shelves—can be annoying, expensive, and even dangerous to us. Use a little ingenuity and forward planning to prevent feline boredom and its associated problems (see pp.190–95).

## The importance of play

Playful activity might seem a waste of time and energy. Some cats get so reckless when they play, they run the risk of injuring themselves.

### How to play with your cat

Both young and adult cats enjoy grab-and-hold games. These are really capture-and-release activities that are played with suitable toys rather than helpless small animals.

A fluffy, light object on the end of a string is ideal for grab-and-hold. Dangle and move the object in front of your cat. Be even more creative. If you have stairs, dangle the toy on one side of the stair rails while your cat moves up and down the stairs, reaching with its paw through the rails at the tantalizing toy. This type of play provides stimulation that an outdoor cat gets from climbing fences and grabbing at butterflies.

Yet play is very important for cats, more so for those who live indoors. It is a way to learn about the home environment, and it also releases the pent-up energy needed by outdoor cats for successfully stalking and capturing their food. Channel your cat's inherent predatory abilities into constructive games.

## Bursts of feline energy

Outdoor life involves quiet periods of solitude interspersed with episodes of stalking, chasing, or being chased. Indoor cats create their own variations of this episodic behavior. Some owners call their cat's actions "the mad half hour," although the indoor cat's surge of activity seldom lasts that long.

A variation of this creative play is the "wall of death." Your cat suddenly bursts into the room, circles it at such velocity that it runs off the floor and onto the walls, then, just as abruptly, darts out of the room. If you follow it, you might find your feline companion sitting inscrutably, as if nothing happened, calmly grooming itself. This is creative self-amusement, a normal activity of any indoor cat.

## Cat claws

Deprived of real hunting opportunities, and in the absence of our channeling their behavior into non-damaging play, indoor cats can behave in ways that we feel are unacceptable. One of the thrills of life for a cat is clawing and climbing.

Claws are used to grasp and to cling, but also to scratch items, leaving visible territorial markers.

These natural needs may become problematic. My personal feeling is that, if you choose to live with a cat, you choose to live with its natural behaviors, including scratching and climbing. From the time you acquire a cat, provide it with a scratching post and climbing frame. Clip the ten front nails routinely, at least every three weeks, to keep them short and blunt.

**A climbing frame** with a dangling toy provides your indoor cat with mental stimulation, exercise, and a great scratching post!

# Toys and accessories

- Choose creative toys
- Anticipate your cat's needs
- Good accessories satisfy both of you

Cats create their toys out of anything small and lightweight they chance upon, from balls of string to butterfly wings. Indoor cats have the same urges as those that have access to the outdoors. Creative toys, from simple dangling items on "fishing rods" to full-fledged cat "gymnasiums," satisfy these needs.

## Toys are satisfying

A cat needs to satisfy its natural urges to sharpen its nails and leave scratch marks on its territory, stalk, climb, view its turf from a height, chase and pounce, bite and bat at objects, or simply respond to any small movement as if it were catching its own food. The following toys fulfill some of these needs.

### Suitable toys

A selection of small, lightweight toys (feathers, balls, felt mice) will help recreate the excitement of the outdoors for your housebound cat.

- **Scratching posts:** Provide a scratching post for your cat at as early an age as possible and place it in the middle of the room. Always play with your cat beside the post, using it for games. Reward use of the post with food treats. With time you can move the post to a less obtrusive location.
- **Wall-mounted accessories:** Wall-mounting keeps scratchers and climbers secure. Wall-mounted sisal scratching posts with carpet borders are ideal for most cats. This gives a choice of two textures to scratch.
- **Cat trees:** A cat tree with different materials—such as bare wood, sisal, and carpet for scratching, carpeted platforms for lounging, and a covered retreat for secure relaxing—is cat heaven. It satisfies most of the needs of indoor cats.
- **Cat hammocks:** Cats are heat-seekers. Introduce your cat to a hammock hung on a radiator, especially in a sunny position. This reduces the amount of unwanted hair on your furniture.
- **Fishing lures:** Cats of all ages enjoy batting, grabbing, or running after fluffy and mobile items dangled from poles. Play for short periods and reward good behavior with petting and food treats.
- **Pounce games:** Table-tennis balls are inexpensive, lightweight, very mobile, and excellent for swatting or pouncing games. Wrap cotton string or wool

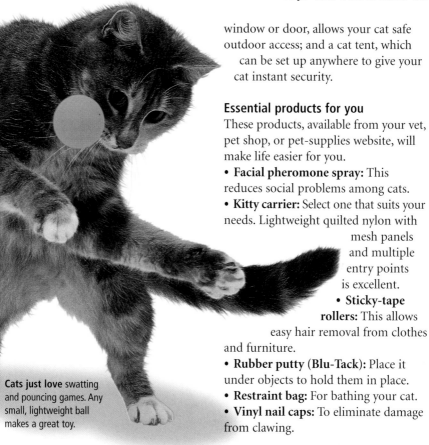

**Cats just love** swatting and pouncing games. Any small, lightweight ball makes a great toy.

window or door, allows your cat safe outdoor access; and a cat tent, which can be set up anywhere to give your cat instant security.

## Essential products for you

These products, available from your vet, pet shop, or pet-supplies website, will make life easier for you.

- **Facial pheromone spray:** This reduces social problems among cats.
- **Kitty carrier:** Select one that suits your needs. Lightweight quilted nylon with mesh panels and multiple entry points is excellent.
- **Sticky-tape rollers:** This allows easy hair removal from clothes and furniture.
- **Rubber putty (Blu-Tack):** Place it under objects to hold them in place.
- **Restraint bag:** For bathing your cat.
- **Vinyl nail caps:** To eliminate damage from clawing.

around the ball, so that, when batted by the cat, the ball will go in unexpected directions. Take care that your cat does not eat the wool or string.

- **Cat gymnasiums:** Consider investing in a cat gym if you have two kittens and want to provide them with a play area that allows climbing and jumping. Placing food treats on the platforms stimulates climbing to investigate.

## More cat-friendly products

Other products I find beneficial for cats include edible cat grass and catnip (you can either grow your own or get them from garden centers); a cat enclosure kit, which, when erected outside a

### Safety accessories

If you live in a high-rise, cat-proof your windows with security locks that prevent even the smallest cat from getting through. Falls from five to eight floors are usually fatal for cats, but lightweight cats sometimes survive falls from greater heights because they have sufficient time to relax.

# The indoor–outdoor cat

- Outdoors is natural
- Outdoors can be dangerous
- Good planning is essential

If your cat goes outdoors, safety is your prime consideration. Is the outdoor area safe from road traffic? Are there dangers from heights or open water? Are there natural cat predators in your vicinity? Let your cat outdoors only when you have determined that it is safe to do so.

### Introduce your cat to the yard

If you have recently moved to a new home, give your cat a few weeks to adjust to its new indoor environment. Once it feels secure inside, allow access to the yard, just before a mealtime. The lure of food is likely to bring it back in.

Your yard may already be "owned" by a local cat. Initially, accompany your cat, armed with a water pistol—most thugs hate squirts in the face. If you think your cat may run away while in the yard, train it to wear a harness before taking it outdoors *(see pp.188–9).*

### Cat-flaps

Indoor–outdoor felines need their own exit and entry facilities. The best option is a cat-flap, especially one activated by a magnet on your cat's collar.

Show your cat how a flap works. Hold it fully open to allow ease of access, letting it just touch your cat's body.

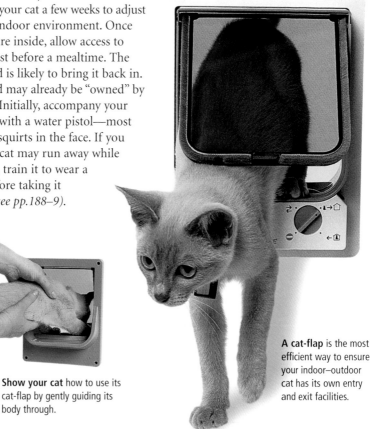

**Show your cat** how to use its cat-flap by gently guiding its body through.

**A cat-flap** is the most efficient way to ensure your indoor–outdoor cat has its own entry and exit facilities.

# OurHarvest

## We bring the farmers market to you

OurHarvest is the rapidly-growing online farmers market and grocery store that connects you to real food, straight from local farmers and producers. Our wide selection of products includes:

- Organic seasonal produce
- Premium grass-fed meats
- Pasture-raised poultry and dairy products
- Sustainably-caught fish
- Clean-label pantry items

Fresh, delicious, and convenient – OurHarvest will change the way you eat.

### How it works

1. Visit ourharvest.com
2. Schedule your convenient home delivery
3. Shop our selection of farm-fresh groceries
4. Enter the code **KIDS** for 25% off your first order

### Eat well, Do good

- For every order above $25, we proudly donate a meal to a local food bank or pantry.
- Every time you shop, the Sea Cliff Elementary School PCA earns a percentage of what you spend!

**ourharvest.com**       @OurHarvest f 🐦 📷 P

**Keep your planting** dense year-round. Your cat will appreciate grassy or large-leafed plants that provide a natural jungle for it to wander through.

Have a reward ready on the other side. Graduate to partially opening the flap, stimulating your cat to use its own body to keep the flap open.

## Outdoor toilets
Provide a "toilet" exactly where you want it, in an area where toddlers have no access but that is easy for you to reach for routine cleaning.

Dig a small sandbox and scent it with litter from your cat's litter box. Sift the site regularly, but do not dispose of your cat's waste on a compost heap. Intestinal parasites can survive there. Bury or dry and burn the feces, or flush them down the toilet.

## Create a cat-friendly yard
The more cat-friendly your yard is, the more likely your cat will spend its time there, rather than in your neighbor's. Shrubs provide cool shade in the heat of the day, while smooth wood, stone, or brick surfaces provide warm areas for soaking up the sun. Wooden posts are ideal as vantage points to oversee the territory and as scratching posts.

Avoid bare soil because it is attractive for elimination. If your cat persistently messes the soil, lay strips of chicken wire, plastic mesh, or gravel between and under plants.

## Check local laws
Some places have laws restricting the free movement of cats to protect local bird populations. If there are restrictions where you live, but you still want your cat to be exposed to the outdoors, try enclosures for windows, decks, patios, or balconies. Patios are easiest to enclose, using glass, wooden fencing, and linked wire for cover. Climbing vines can be used to prettify the linked-wire cover.

### Plan ahead
Cats are easily frightened outdoors and, if frightened, they are likely to hide rather than return home. Do not rely solely on an ID tag or microchip: train your cat to meow when it hears its name being called. This is an effective way of finding a frightened or injured cat *(see pp.185–6)*. If your cat goes outdoors in areas accessible to other animals, make sure it is protected against disease and parasites. Life-threatening viral infections can be transmitted in cat bites *(see pp.214–17)*.

# Outdoor concerns

- Be a considerate neighbor
- Cat-proof your yard
- Survey for possible dangers

Cats thrive on the adrenaline surges that come from outdoor access. Responsible owners should anticipate outdoor problems, assess where the risks are, and reduce those risks as much as possible.

## Traffic is lethal

Never expect your cat to develop road sense. Some do, but only through trial and error—a hazardous method! If your cat goes outdoors, equip it with a reflective collar to reduce nighttime risks. This gives drivers a greater chance of seeing your cat either by the roadside or on the road itself.

A human territory marker, such as a fence, is often completely irrelevant to a cat, but it may adopt it as its own boundary perimeter.

## Reduce urban hunting

While hungry cats kill to eat, well-fed cats kill for the excitement of the hunt. Make sure your cat causes as little harm as possible. Attach a bell or two to its collar. Do not set up a bird feeder in your yard! There are commercial devices available for use in your garden to deter birds from landing.

## Control social encounters

Cats have demarcation disputes that lead to fights. Fights mean bites, and bites mean more opportunity for viruses such as FIV (feline immunodeficiency virus) and FeLV (feline leukemia virus) to be transmitted *(see p.215)*.

Reduce the risk of fights by having your cat neutered. Neutered cats need smaller territories than entire cats. It may be difficult to prevent unneutered feral tomcats from entering your yard or even invading your home through your cat-flap. If this is a problem, install a magnet-operated cat-flap and arm yourself with a noise-maker or high-powered water pistol to use when social encounters become problems.

## Prevent slash and grab

Even the best-fed feline finds it hard to resist a slash-and-grab attack on plastic garbage bags. Keep your garbage in securely lidded cans. If your cat raids your neighbor's garbage, invest in cat-proof cans for their use.

**Cats warn one another** by staring, hissing, and spitting. However, when these noncontact warnings prove ineffectual, fighting might ensue.

## Avoid garden chemicals

If your cat has walked in any chemical products *(see pp.232–3)* and licked its paws, do not induce vomiting. It will only cause more damage. ***Seek immediate veterinary attention.***

## Maintain good neighborly relations

Before any problems even arise, tell your neighbors that neutered cats like yours do not produce pungent, foul-smelling urine, nor do they leave their droppings unburied as territory markers. Urine and droppings are produced by unneutered, often unowned, territory-owning feral tomcats. If your neighbors do not enjoy seeing your cat relaxing in their yard, respect their rights.

Suggest that they can keep cats out of their yard by spraying diluted rubbing alcohol on fences, spraying eucalyptus and citrus smells on flower beds and vegetable patches, and watering last thing at night. Cats dislike wet soil.

### Prevent sun damage

The ears and nose on white cats, and other felines without thick protective hair, are at risk from sunburn, even cancer, if exposed to strong sunshine. Like some humans, cats are sun worshippers. If your light-colored cat goes outdoors in the sun, routinely use a sunblock product with SPF 30 UVA/UVB protection.

# Basic training

- Cats can be trained
- Have realistic expectations
- Channel your cat's natural behavior

Contrary to popular belief, cats are open and responsive to training, as long as you remember your cat is not a dog in disguise. It thinks differently and needs a different approach if training is to be successful. The essence of effective cat training is understanding how a cat thinks. Its world is far less social than a dog's and more three dimensional.

### Unwitting training

You might not realize it, but your cat already responds to your unplanned training. Does it gallop into the kitchen when it hears the sound of a can opener? If it does, it has learned that that sound is usually followed by a reward, food.

In the early 20th century, Ivan Pavlov, a Russian physiologist, studied behavior in dogs and found that, by pairing the sound of a bell with food, he could train a dog to salivate when the bell rang.

### Reward and punishment

In the 1930s, American psychologist B.F. Skinner explained how, by using rewards, an animal can be trained to perform a desired behavior, like coming when called. He called rewards "positive reinforcement," and mild punishment "negative reinforcement."

A negative reinforcer is used to stop a cat from doing what it planned to do. A sharp squirt from a water pistol or a soft tap on the head are forms of mild punishment.

### Using rewards and discipline

Cats respond to rewards and discipline because both are components of life in the real outdoor world. Patience while stalking prey earns a food reward. Similarly, a soft paw on your face

**Combine a form** of mild punishment, like a soft tap on the cat's head, with a vocal "No!" Eventually, just a sharp "No!" becomes effective punishment.

**A cat learns** through adverse experiences, so mild punishments like a sharp squirt of water are naturally effective.

at dawn will be followed by a tap, then a thump, and, if you still do not get up to feed your feline, maybe a punch. Persistence is rewarded.

Early in life, kittens learn to interpret the meanings of difference sounds. Cats are very articulate, from the calming purr sound, through the demanding meow, to the menacing hiss and spit. They have little difficulty learning to understand our sounds, too, from rewarding murmurs to disciplinary shouts. You can associate a mild punishment, like a squirt of water, with a firm "No!" and eventually use words alone to discipline your cat.

### How to begin

Active shorthaired cats tend to learn a little faster than more reserved longhairs. Young kittens do not have the necessary concentration, and older cats do not have the interest. Cats from around four months of age onward are the most open to training, but only cats

that are used to routine handling are likely to take to it. A one- or two-minute lesson is perfect for most cats. Five minutes is too long.

### Clicker training and name training

Training with a clicker is a popular form of positive-reinforcement training. The "click" sound is paired with a food

---

**Basic training rules**

Follow these rules when training your cat:

1 Train just before meals, when your cat is at its hungriest.

2 Train in a quiet area. Indoors is best.

3 Use tasty treats. Change them if your cat is getting bored.

4 Associate these treats with words.

5 Train only a few minutes at a time.

6 Have patience. Your cat will learn only if it is having a good time.

reward and acts as a marker signal that gives a cat instant feedback about what behavior is desired.

Accurate timing is the essence of effective clicker training. Give a food reward and, as it is taken, click the clicker. After frequently repeating this, you should be able just to click the clicker and have your cat's attention. Shaking a container of tasty vitamin tablets is another alternative. Your cat hears the shake as it gets a food reward.

You can try saying your cat's name as you give it a reward. Soon, just calling its name will get its attention.

### Have equipment at hand
If using a clicker, carefully read the instructions so you know exactly how and when to use it. Timing is vital.

### Training your cat to sit

This is basic training for almost anything else. Teaching your cat to sit after it has come to you in response to its name or the sound of the clicker is the first part of training your cat to do pretty much any other sequence of behaviors.

Hungry cats will usually respond to this training within 10 attempts. Finish the training session with "Okay," which indicates to your cat that training is over, and some dinner. Train again just before the next meal.

1 Start this exercise just before your cat's mealtime. Place your hungry cat on the middle of a table. If it naturally sits down, pet its rump to trigger its instinctive "rump-in-the-air" response.

2 Hold a tasty food treat 1–2 in (2.5–5 cm) in front of its nose. (If using a clicker, have it in your other hand.)

3 When your cat shows interest in the food, slowly move it up and over its head, keeping it 1–2 in (2.5–5 cm) away until it is between its ears. Keeping its eye on the food, the cat will sit. As it does so, say its name, followed by "Sit."

4 At the instant your cat sits, say "Good sit" and give the food reward. If using a clicker, click fractionally before you give the treat. If giving the treat on a spoon, allow only a couple of licks.

Clicking a little too soon or too late makes training much more difficult.

Have your food treats at hand. Use what your cat loves most, from crispy liver bits to succulent shrimp. Tasty, meaty baby food is good because you can use the spoon to trigger "high-fives" or other paw training.

## High-five training

This is really touch training—simple and enjoyable for most cats. You need a teaser toy, such as a small feather on a short string attached to a stick. The aim is for you and your cat to exchange a high five.

Start with your cat—using Felix as an example—in the "sit" position. Dangle the teaser toy just over its head and, when it raises a paw to touch it, say "Felix, high five." As your cat touches the toy, say "Good high five" and give it a food reward. If using a clicker, click and give the food reward.

When Felix learns that raising his paw gets a reward, he will do it more willingly when you just say "High five." Gradually stop using the teaser toy, replacing it with the flat palm of your hand.

### Kiss me quick

Try this trick only if you do not have any hygiene hangups about getting licked by your cat. You will need a volunteer assistant and something gooey and tasty. A family member makes a good volunteer, while fish or meat pâté works well, as do many meaty baby foods.

1. Smear the gooey food on the part of your volunteer to be kissed, usually the tip of the nose.

2. Get your hungry cat in the "sit" position and place your volunteer 1–2 ft (30–65 cm) directly in front of it.

3. Have your volunteer lean forward, then back.

4. As your cat moves forwards to lick your volunteer's nose, say "Felix, kiss."

5. As your cat kisses, offer it an alternative, tastier treat.

6. Over days and weeks, increase the distance between your cat and your volunteer, and decrease the amount of "face food" while maintaining the amount of handheld food.

Eventually, upon hearing the command "Felix, kiss," your cat will kiss a clean face even in the absence of face food. Once it does this, the volunteer holds the food reward. Felix will now kiss almost anyone who gives a food treat. Being kissed by your cat is a fascinating (if slightly disgusting!) experience.

### Meeting other cats involves training

Littermates form relationships with each other early in life. They too, unwittingly, use rewards and discipline to create relationships that develop within the family group. It is unnatural for adult cats to willingly play with unrelated cats. They think other cats are potential intruders. The basis for successful social integration of several cats in your home is for you to control their meetings and reward calm behavior.

## Training for vet visits

If the cat carrier is used only for trips to the vet or the kennel, your cat will associate it with unpleasant sensations. Use positive reinforcement to train your cat to enjoy the comfort and enclosure of its travel basket. Cats naturally enjoy the security of confined spaces. Do not pack the cat carrier away. Leave it open, in a warm place, and with an enticing food treat inside. Use it at home as a feline safe haven. Your cat will learn to naturally retreat to it and treat it as a personal den. It will feel less frightened and insecure when you use the basket to take it to the vet for its annual health checkups.

**Kitten are easiest** to train when it comes to walking on a harness and leash. Success, however, depends on the individual.

## Walking on a leash

Training to walk on a harness and leash is practical for the active, inquisitive cat. Success depends on the individual cat's personality, and on how well it takes to wearing a harness.

## Your cat is not a dog

Unlike a dog, your cat is not going to do what you want it to simply to please you. Cats do what they do to please themselves. Your role is to channel what your cat wants to do into the way you want it to behave.

A cat on a leash needs time to stop, look, listen, sniff, and, after it is sure of itself, to walk where it wants to go. Be prepared for a little sun-lounging, dust-rolling, grass eating, or simple contemplation of nature. You may take a dog for a walk, but a cat takes you!

## A nonthreatening harness

Get your cat used to a soft, lightweight harness by leaving it on the floor for a few days where it can be sniffed and investigated. After the cat is used to it, slip it over its head for a few seconds, without tightening it.

Give praise and treats for acceptance. If the cat rejects it, go back to play and try later. Never force it to wear the harness. Repeat this exercise over days, even weeks, until it accepts the buckled harness without becoming upset.

## Adding the leash

Once your cat is comfortable with the harness, attach the leash, letting it drag behind it. When it is comfortable with that, pick up the leash and follow it around the house. This process can take days or weeks.

Your cat is now ready for you to kneel in front of it with a treat and, as it comes forward to it,

**Once your cat** is comfortable with the harness, attach the lead and let the cat drag it around.

give the command "Come." As with all obedience training, use only rewards, never discipline (not even verbal discipline), during training.

## Moving outdoors

Early morning or evening are quiet times to venture out into the yard for the first time. Stay a little ahead and to the side of the cat as it chooses where to walk. If it goes where you do not want it to, let the leash get taut enough to stop it, but do not pull. Give voice commands the cat already knows—like "No!"—when it heads where you do not want it to head. Be still and silent when the cat becomes intense and concentrated.

**The first time** you venture out with your cat on a leash should be stress free. An early-morning walk in the yard is a good start.

# Behavior problems

- All cats develop behavior problems
- Prevention is easier than cure
- Be realistic about the causes

Even within the comfort of a home environment, cats do what cats need to do: climb, mark territory, hunt, and find their own food. Stealing food, climbing the curtains, or attacking our ankles is fun for cats, but problematic for us.

## It is not a problem to your cat

You may think that your cat is creating problems, but what is a problem to you may be perfectly natural for a cat.

Cats lead three-dimensional lives: They climb; they keep their weapons sharp; they use substances in constant supply—urine and feces—to mark territory; they eat vegetation; they stalk and chase small things that move quickly. These are natural cat activities. Climbing curtains, scratching sofas, spraying urine, eating houseplants, stalking your ankles—none of these activities is wrong in a cat's mind. Unfortunately, most of us find them unpleasant and unacceptable. Fortunately, there are a few simple remedies.

## Clawing the furniture

Cats claw items to mark territory, leave signature scent, shed old nails, or express anxiety. To prevent damage to your furniture, provide your cat with its own furniture, like a scratching post.

Do not hide the scratching post in a corner or a distant room. One of the functions of scratching is to leave a visible mark of a cat's presence. Initially, place the scratching post in the middle of your cat's favorite room. Reward your cat with food treats for using it. Once your cat is using it, move it slowly, a small amount per day, into a less obtrusive position. Eventually position the scratching post near your cat's favorite sleeping area.

**Give your cat a** sturdy, stable, tall scratching post. Cover it in sisal and cut, non-looped carpet, two textures that are especially attractive to cats.

Catnip rubbed on the post, verbal praise and petting, and food rewards when the post is scratched all promote further use of it.

If your cat is already scratching your furniture, cover the damaged area with heavy plastic or double-sided tape to make the surface texture unappealing. If you catch your cat scratching, shout "No!" or make a sudden noise—for example, by dropping a bunch of keys.

## Climbing the curtains

Satisfy your cat's need to climb by providing an acceptable indoor location for this natural activity.

Use mild forms of indirect punishment to retrain cats that climb where you do not want them to. Indirect punishment means that your cat does not know it is being reprimanded by you. For example, as your cat starts to climb in a no-go area, make a loud noise by dropping a bunch of keys or squirt it with a water pistol. Sensible cats soon associate their activity with mildly unpleasant consequences.

Of course, provide suitable rewards when your cat climbs where you want it to climb.

**If your cat** climbs where it is not allowed to, retrain it with mild indirect punishments.

## Stalking your ankles

Ankle-stalking can be painful. Your cat ambushing your ankles from a hiding spot can be either redirected play or a sex attack (even if your cat is spayed or neutered).

One remedy is to get your cat another cat with which it can interact. Discuss this with your vet before doing so.

Alternatively, channel your cat's need to stalk by providing well-designed toys to pounce on. There are many battery-powered toys that stimulate stalking, capturing, and holding prey. Dangling items on "fishing rods," wool wrapped around a table-tennis ball, and glove toys all are excellent for channeling natural predatory activity.

If your cat still stalks your ankles, arm yourself with your water pistol and shoot when you see the glint in your cat's eyes! An alternative is to always carry a pounce toy and throw it to your cat before you get pounced on.

## Eating houseplants

Cats that go outdoors often graze on grass, to help digestion and for the satisfaction of chewing on items with fiber. Provide your housebound cat

**Some houseplants** are poisonous to your cat. Indulge its desire for fiber by growing or buying your own kitty grass.

with its own grass to chew on. You can grow it from seed or buy it at pet shops. Any fast-growing thin grass is suitable.

Check out all your houseplants to ensure you do not have any that are potentially dangerous if chewed, such as dumb cane. If your cat is attracted to your existing houseplants, put them out of reach or temporarily surround them with double-sided tape. Cats do not like the sticky feel underfoot. Alternatively, after testing on a small area to ensure it is not damaging, spray the exposed area of plants with safe but bitter-tasting spray.

**If your cat stalks** your ankles, always carry a toy with you to rechannel its pouncing instinct.

**Cover the soil** in your favorite plant pot with gravel, marbles, or anything else your cat dislikes.

close the doors to that area. If this is not a practical option, you can use heat or movement sensors, available from hardware or security stores. These sensors are inexpensive and great for training an indoor cat in your absence. A cat crossing the beam of the small sensor activates a high-pitched sound, scaring it off.

## Predawn alarm calls

The simplest way to avoid a silk brick landing on your midsection at 5 o'clock in the morning is to keep the bedroom door closed. If your cat meows constantly, wear earplugs for a week (and preemptively give boxes of chocolates to your nearest neighbors). If this is not practical (either physically or psychologically), do not respond in any way to your cat's pestering. Even a verbal reprimand is rewarding. Stop giving morning meals or anything else first thing in the morning that your cat looks forward to you doing when you get up.

## Digging in plant pots

Keep your cat away from the plants. If this is not practical, cover the soil with gravel or other material, such as marbles, that cats get no satisfaction out of digging in.

## No-go areas

Cats assume they are permitted anywhere. If you want to prevent your cat from visiting particular locations— for example, your bedroom—simply

## Jumping on tables or counters

Cats like to survey their manors from a good height. Kitchen counters and tables are also ideal for hunting for food. Satisfy your cat's need for high viewing locations by providing a climbing frame from which it can easily see outdoors.

To break the habit of jumping on a counter or table, block off all tempting locations but one, applying lots of double-sided tape in this clear location. This form of aversion therapy works well in your presence or absence.

**Feeding your cat** away from your own eating area should help prevent it from begging for table scraps.

## Begging food

Keep your cat out of the room while you eat. Feed it in another room so that it associates that room with food.

## Living with other cats

If two outdoor cats do not like each other, one bullies the other until it leaves. Since this is impossible for indoor cats, a result is not just tension between the individuals but also behaviors such as urine-marking and increased irritability.

If you want a multicat household, acquire two kittens at the same time or, if your cat has kittens, keep one to increase the resident cat population with minimal risk of serious cat fights.

If one of your cats is bullying others, see your vet to eliminate any possible medical causes, such as chronic pain.

### Retraining rules

1 Satisfy your cat's natural needs by creating acceptable outlets for natural behavior.

2 Eliminate the satisfaction your cat gets from its unacceptable behavior. Use bitter spray, Tabasco sauce, or other safe but disagreeable tastes to prevent chewing where you do not want chewing. Use inexpensive vibration-sensitive alarms for windows, beds, or the sofa if you do not want your cat jumping on these in your absence. Use double-sided tape or rubber putty (like Blu-Tack) to prevent scratching. If you are at home and see your cat doing something you do not want it to do, a squirt from your ever-ready water pistol or a clunk on the floor with a bunch of keys works wonders.

3 Persevere. Do not expect overnight miracles.

4 If you are unsure or if aggression is involved, get professional help.

Watch your cats' behavior and step in if you see the dipped-head, arched-back scenario developing. Restore order by feeding the feuders in separate rooms.

Use facial pheromone spray liberally. In my experience, this on its own is effective in perhaps half of all instances of bullying and urine-spraying related to territorial problems.

## Exits outdoors

Any cat with the slightest curiosity is interested in going outdoors and might bolt past you when you open the door. If this is a risk, associate the open door with something mildly unpleasant, such as a water pistol. Give your cat a food treat or favorite toy before you leave, so it is distracted from your departure.

### Cat intelligence testing

It can be fun, although not necessarily scientifically accurate, to compare intelligence in cats. Rank your cat on the following points.

**My cat:**
• Is alert and curious;
• Tries to manipulate me;
• Is independent of me;
• Is sensitive to my moods;
• Is easily trainable;
• Is confident with strangers;
• Responds to its name;
• Is manually dexterous.

Score your cat as follows for each question:

| True? | Score |
|---|---|
| Absolutely not | 1–2 |
| Sort of no | 3–4 |
| Sometimes | 5–6 |
| Sort of yes | 7–8 |
| Absolutely yes | 9–10 |

**Results**
**0–34 points:** Lovable but dim;
**35–49:** Average cat;
**50–64:** Smarty cat;
**65–80:** Master cat.

### Where to get help

If your cat starts to display any serious behavior problems—either of the types illustrated in these pages or of a different nature—a qualified cat trainer or cat behaviorist should be able to help. Speak to your vet about your needs; he or she can give you the names of recommended trainers.

## Lovebites or petting aggression

Unexpectedly, while your cat lies there in a reverie as you pet it, it bites. Petting aggression occurs because your cat has mixed emotions about your touching it. On one hand, petting is comforting and reminiscent of mother's licks; on the other, unrelated adult cats never touch each other except when fighting or during sex. With these mixed signals, most cats eventually feel uneasy. Some just mouth you, putting their mouths around your hand, but not biting. Others clamp down.

Follow your cat's lead and do not pet to excess. This is a primitive conflict, hard to overcome without diminishing the relationship your cat has with you.

**With petting aggression,** your cat is telling you that it wants to be in control. It may like sitting on your lap, but no more than that.

# Body maintenance

- Train kittens to accept grooming
- Develop a grooming routine
- Report any abnormalities to your vet

Cats are magnificent self-groomers, typically spending from eight to 15 percent of their waking hours cleaning themselves. Even so, your cat needs your help with body maintenance. Routine brushing keeps the skin and coat in excellent condition and, at the same time, trains you to notice when anything out of the ordinary develops. Cats of any age benefit from your caring for their nails, teeth, ears, and eyes.

### Self-cleaning is vital for survival

In the wild, catching, killing, and eating small mammals is a messy business. The cat's fur becomes contaminated with dirt, debris, and bits of that particular meal. Left unattended, this leads to a variety of smells, drawing unwelcome attention from cat-eating predators. Efficient grooming removes food, dirt, debris, and, most importantly, smell from a cat's coat.

There is more. Cats evolved in a hot climate where regulating body temperature can be a matter of life and death. Grooming keeps the coat free from dead hair and tangles. When properly maintained, there is an insulating layer of air "captured" in the coat; this protects the cat from overheating.

Finally, on hot days, the evaporating saliva left from licking has an even greater cooling effect on the body.

## Cat bathing

Dry shampoos are available that mimic natural dust baths. Occasionally there are instances when your vet may ask you to give your cat a full bath. These are the guidelines for bathing your cat.

**1** Brush your cat before bathing to remove mats and tangles.

**2** Use a restraint bag if you have one. Alternatively, suspend a rope above the tub—your cat will instinctively grasp it while you bathe it. Place a nonslip rubber mat in the tub to prevent slipping.

**3** Ensure the water is not too hot. Run it first to get the right temperature.

**4** Use shampoo recommended by your vet. Take great care not to get shampoo in the eyes.

**5** Use a handheld shower to wet and rinse your cat. If your bathroom is not equipped with one, get an inexpensive rubber one that fits on the faucet.

**6** Towel-dry your cat and congratulate yourself on what you have done.

## Coat brushing

A smooth, short coat is the easiest to care for. Use a rubber, bristle, or slicker brush, or even a hound glove or chamois, once weekly.

A medium coat needs to be slicker- and bristle-brushed more frequently, preferably for short periods daily, to get your cat used to this type of attention. You will also need a wide-toothed comb for combing through the longest hair.

A longhaired cat needs daily combing and slicker-brushing to remove dead hair, prevent mats, and reduce hairballs (*see The problem with long hair, p.157*).

**Get your cat** used to being brushed from a young age. This will make it easier for you to handle it and easier for the vet to examine it.

## The rest of the body

Routine body maintenance keeps your cat in good physical condition and saves you avoidable veterinary expenses. By regularly examining these areas, you notice problems before they become serious. You also make life a whole lot easier for your vet. Cats that are used to letting their owners carry out routine maintenance are far easier to examine and treat when necessary.

## Mats of hair

All medium- or longhaired individuals are prone to hair matting, especially behind the ears, behind the elbows, and on the belly and hind legs. Tease out mats as you feel them. If your cat resents the pulling needed to tease

**Matted hair is most common** in medium- and longhaired cats, usually in those areas they can barely reach when grooming.

## Grooming at the vet's

Sometimes mats are so thick and so close to the skin that the only alternative is to shave them off. This takes a lot more time than you might think and, for a cat's sake, it is best done under general anesthesia. Generally speaking, all hair is removed except the hair on the face. This allows uniform regrowth. Good hair cover is back in a month and a full coat in less than three months.

them out, cut them off—but be very careful. It is extremely easy to accidentally cut the thin skin while cutting out a mat of hair.

## Checking anal sacs

There is a scent sac under the skin on either side of your cat's anus, at the 3 and 9 o'clock positions. In older cats, the substance in the anal sacs, normally almost watery, can become tenacious and tarry. Blockage causes irritation and exaggerated grooming of the anal region, as well as of the belly and inner thighs.

Check the sacs if your cat is licking excessively. Wearing a disposable glove for protection, squeeze this area,

## Nail cutting

Use a guillotine-type clipper. This gives a cleaner cut with less pressure. While the sharp tip of the nail consists only of keratin, the rest contains the quick, which is living, sensitive tissue. If you cut the quick, it hurts. In a cat's translucent nails it is easy to see the quick *(see Retractable claws, p.27)*. Cut each claw well in front of the pink quick.

starting at the 4 and 8 o'clock positions and completing the examination at 3 and 9 o'clock.

## Preventing bad breath

Bad breath usually means a tooth-and-gum problem, the most common reason cats are taken to the vet. Train your cat from kittenhood that tooth brushing is simply part of life's routine.

**If your cat obsessively** licks and grooms its anal region, examine its anal sacs, which may be blocked.

**Sharing your toothpaste?**

Do not share your toothpaste with your cat. Most cats do not like it, and it is meant to be spat out, not swallowed. Use palatable toothpaste formulated especially for cats and safe to swallow.

Using a child's toothbrush, begin by gently brushing up and down for only a few seconds. Apply something tasty, like pâté, to the toothbrush. If the cat does not squirm, give it an immediate food reward. Repeat this exercise daily, each time increasing the time and the area of teeth covered until, after about two weeks of training, you are brushing all the teeth, top and bottom as well as front and back.

### Ear inspections

Check your cat's ears routinely for discharge or gritty wax. Dry discharge usually indicates common ear mites. Use an ear-mite treatment for at least three weeks, available from your veterinarian. *If you see a moist discharge, contact your vet.*

**It is important to** check your cat's ears regularly for discharge or a buildup of wax. A moist discharge should be further examined by a vet.

### Eye checks

Flat-faced cats often have a tear overflow. Overnight this can dry into a crust and stick in the hair in the fold of skin below the eye. Soften it with a cotton ball dipped in body-temperature water. *If the eyes and the skin around them do not look normal, see your vet.*

**Some cats,** especially flat-faced ones, are prone to a tear overflow that results in a crusty buildup below the eye. Clean the eyes with damp cotton balls.

### Grooming checklist

1 Grooming a cat can make or break friendships.

2 Start grooming your cat from a young age.

3 Introduce grooming to a kitten while it is still with its mother.

4 Be brief with grooming sessions.

5 Once your cat is used to short sessions, you can start working up to longer sessions.

6 Learn your cat's grooming limitations.

7 Watch your cat's body language. Tail-lashing means your cat has had enough.

8 Give rewards for good behavior. In most cases, they are well deserved.

# Good nutrition

- Cats have special dietary needs
- Needs change with age
- Obesity is a common problem

Your cat is an "obligate carnivore." Unable to convert vegetable fat and protein into the amino acids and fatty acids it needs, it will die without meat.

## What food really is

Food is energy, and energy comes from protein, fat, and carbohydrate.

Protein is broken down into its constituent parts, amino acids, which help body parts grow and repair.

Fat is broken down into its basic units, fatty acids, essential for healthy cells and an efficient immune system.

Some carbohydrates, in the form of fiber, are insoluble, while soluble carbohydrates are converted to sugar, providing immediate energy. Energy is measured in kilocalories, often just called calories. Once your cat has finished growing, the number of calories consumed each day should be no greater than the number of calories spent each day as energy in activity.

## Cats have unique needs

Cats can manufacture most amino acids from the protein they eat, but they cannot manufacture the amino acid taurine, which can be acquired only by eating meat. Taurine deficiency causes blindness and heart disease.

Animal fat contains essential fatty acids such as arachidonic acid and linoleic acid. The former is vital for blood clotting, efficient reproduction, and coat condition, while the latter is necessary for body growth, wound healing, and liver function.

Cats cannot manufacture vitamin A, which maintains good eye health, and must eat parts of animals high in natural vitamin A, such as fish oil and liver.

## The value of fiber

Fiber is an important and natural part of a cat's diet. Soluble fiber slows down digestion, while insoluble fiber stimulates bowel activity.

Fiber also helps in treating excess fat in the bloodstream and inflammatory bowel disease and helps control obesity.

## Vitamins are important

Vitamin D, calcium, and phosphorus are needed for bone development, while vitamin K, which the cat manufactures, is necessary for blood clotting.

**Fiber is eaten** indirectly when a cat consumes the fur, feathers, and viscera of its prey. Insoluble fiber stimulates bowel activity and is therefore invaluable for treating constipation.

Recently, deficiency in the B vitamin folic acid has been implicated as a factor in human heart disease. The same may be true with cats.

### Healthy micronutrients

Vitamin E assists in fat metabolism. As an antioxidant, it cleans up those chemicals, called free radicals, that damage cell membranes.

The water-soluble vitamins include the B group and vitamin C. Cats manufacture the latter, so be careful with supplements. Excess vitamin C is excreted in the urine as a substance called oxalate. In the last 20 years there has been an increase in the incidence of oxalate bladder stones in cats *(see p.263)*. B-group vitamins have diverse roles to play in good health and metabolism.

Calcium and phosphorus are vital to build bone as well as for cell membrane and nerve function. Meat is low in calcium. A meat-only diet may lead to serious bone and joint conditions, while feeding excess calcium supplement may trigger a zinc deficiency. Iron is vital for red-blood-cell production.

Selenium, a mineral essential for a healthy enzyme system, is another natural antioxidant. It may also play a role in the immune system.

Sodium helps to transport nutrients across cell membranes.

**Your indoor cat** is dependent on you to provide it with balanced nutrition for a healthy life.

## Feeding your cat

The simplest and most reliable way to feed your cat is with a variety of foods that meet your cat's unique needs. While some experts say a diet should be consistent, my hunch is that cats enjoy variety. Make changes gradually. This gives the bacteria in the gut time to modify to new digestion demands.

## What is good cat food?

The best cat-food manufacturers use foods fit for human consumption, and their premium products are made to fixed formulas. The ingredients are always the same.

At the next price level down, foods are manufactured from a varying supply of ingredients to set nutritional and quality standards. While the nutritional value of these foods remains constant, the ingredients vary. This is important to know if your cat has a sensitive stomach or fixed taste preferences.

## Dry cat food

All-in-one dry food is convenient, though not necessarily the best for your cat. These foods are cooked under pressure, then dried. Fat is sprayed on for palatability, but since heat, humidity, light, and even oxygen can spoil fat, dry foods need a preservative. Antioxidants are excellent preservatives, and because they destroy free radicals, they are good for cats as well as good for preserving food. Vitamin C (ascorbic acid) and vitamin E (tocopherol) are commonly used antioxidants.

## Reading a food label

Cat-food makers list a guaranteed analysis on the label, stating the protein, fat, fiber, and moisture levels. To compare the levels of anything in food, convert the label information to a "dry-matter" basis—that is, what is there once the moisture has been removed. Here is how you do it.

A typical canned food label might read:

| | |
|---|---|
| Crude protein | 8% |
| Crude fat | 6% |
| Fiber | 1% |
| Moisture | 78% |

This food is 78 percent moisture so it is 22 percent dry matter.

Compare the true levels of the nutrients (protein and fat) using this formula.

$$\text{Dry-matter nutrient content} = \frac{\text{The label's nutrient percentage x 100}}{\text{Dry-matter content percentage}}$$

Therefore, for protein:

$$\frac{8 \times 100}{22} = 36.4\%$$

This is the only accurate way to compare basic protein and fat contents of one food with another. Reliable pet-food manufacturers will give you this information via their helplines.

The quality or "digestibility" of protein becomes increasingly important in older cats. Calorie content is rarely stated on a label. As a guideline, a 7-oz (200-g) pouch or can of cat food contains 150–200 calories.

**Your cat** probably loves canned food, but relying too heavily on it may compromise your cat's oral health.

## Canned cat food

Heat sterilization and vacuum sealing prevent spoilage of canned or vacuum-packed foods, so no preservative is needed. Canned food, although tasty, provides no exercise for the teeth and gums and is prone to contamination if it is not eaten immediately.

## Home cooking

Avoid raw meat that can harbor the parasite *Toxoplasma gondii*, for which the cat is the intermediate host and to which we are also susceptible.

Avoid single-protein diets. A diet restricted only to tuna may cause severe liver problems. A muscle-meat-only diet will lead to decalcification of the bones.

When selecting ingredients for your cat's diet, always use products fit for human consumption.

### A balanced home-cooked diet

This recipe uses medium-fat chicken. For greater control of your cat's weight, try using lean chicken instead.

- Chicken          5 oz (140 g)
- Liver            1 oz (30 g)
- Uncooked rice    2½ oz (70 g)
- Sterilized bone meal  ⅓ oz (10 g)
- Iodized salt     a pinch (2 g)
- Sunflower or corn oil  1 tsp (5 ml)

Cook the rice, bone meal, salt and oil in twice the volume of water for 20 minutes. Add the chicken and liver, simmering for another ten minutes. Blend thoroughly.

This recipe produces approximately 800 calories, which is enough to feed a typical house cat for three days.

### What about bones?

If introduced early in life, bone, such as in well-cooked chicken necks, is an excellent and satisfying source of nourishment, but it can be dangerous both for cats that never learned how to eat bones and for cats that wolf down their food in a doglike fashion.

Avoid giving your cat uncooked bones. They may be contaminated with harmful salmonella bacteria.

**Dry foods** come in a variety of shapes and flavors to appeal to all feline tastes. Owners find dry food most convenient.

## Needs vary through life

Your cat's energy needs increase with activity and in cold weather, and decrease in the senior years. Older cats benefit from better quality, easier-to-digest protein and from increased levels of vitamins and minerals. High levels of antioxidants reduce tissue damage, more common in the senior years.

## Changes in eating habits

A healthy cat's appetite is constant. For housebound cats with little mental or physical activity, an increased appetite may simply be a sign of boredom. However, if this happens without weight gain, it may indicate illness— for example, diabetes or an overactive thyroid gland (hyperthyroidism).

If your cat is eating less or is picking at its food, this is often a greater cause for concern. Picking may indicate gum or tooth disease, and diminished taste or smell. It is an important sign for a variety of underlying illnesses. *If your cat starts eating less, seek veterinary advice immediately.*

After an illness, encourage your cat to eat once more by warming the food to about 95° F (35° C). This releases natural aromas, the best trigger to appetite.

## Food addictions

Varying your cat's diet eliminates the possibility of your cat's becoming addicted to a single-ingredient food, a considerable problem if that food is not nutritionally complete.

## Tackling fat

Sex hormones affect metabolism. When these hormones are reduced, through neutering or advancing years, many cats gain weight. This can be prevented.

After your cat is neutered, increased activity increases energy consumption and halts excessive weight gain.

**Cats can become picky eaters,** willing to avoid perfectly good food for days while waiting for you to feed them what they want.

Alternatively, over three weeks, gradually reduce the quantity of food you are offering by 20 percent or switch to a low-calorie diet. Your cat will probably retain its pre-surgical weight. If it is losing weight, return to its usual diet.

You may be harassed for more food by your cat, but do not give in to feline psychological warfare. Talk to your vet for reassurance.

### Specialty diets for health problems

Manufacturers such as Iams, Waltham, Hill's, and Purina produce ranges of foods, available through vets, to nourish cats with kidney, bladder, heart, liver, bowel, skin, or allergic conditions. These companies also provide a variety of tasty diets for debilitated cats or for those that have had surgery.

### Diet and lower urinary tract problems

Some cats produce a sticky substance in their urine that is associated with lower urinary tract complications. Capturing urinary crystals, this substance forms a partial or complete blockage to passing urine. Affected cats benefit from eating wet food. This dilutes the urine.

### Milk and cream

Dairy products may upset digestion in some adult cats, causing diarrhea. This happens because adult cats do not have enough bacteria in their intestines that produce an enzyme to digest lactose, the sugar in milk. Feeding lactose-free milk, available at supermarkets for lactose-sensitive children and also as "cat milk," overcomes this problem for cats that have a lifelong love of dairy.

### Hairballs

Frequent grooming by you reduces, but does not eliminate, hair swallowed when a cat grooms itself. All major cat-food makers produce "hairball diets," in which added fiber, acting like a plunger, pushes hair through the stomach and prevents it from accumulating in the digestive tract.

An effective alternative is a malt-flavored petrolatum laxative. Some cats, however, are disinclined to take this form of medicine.

### Water is life

Some pet cats, especially those fed on wet foods, may seldom drink, giving the impression that they do not need water. But, of course, water is essential for all forms of life. Water absorbs the water-soluble vitamins and is absorbed by fiber to add beneficial bulk to your cat's diet.

# New experiences

- Plan ahead for a baby's arrival
- Have travel plans for your cat
- Do not panic if your cat is missing

During your cat's lifetime, you will possibly move, certainly take vacations, and need to find someone to take care of your cat in your absence. People and other pets will come and go. How will your cat react to these changes?

### A new baby in the home

Invest in simple netting to place over the crib or carriage. Make necessary changes to any sleeping arrangements before your baby arrives. When the baby comes home, let your cat smell it, but try not to change any of its routines. Continue giving the cat the attention it deserves. Do not leave baby and cat together unattended until you trust they are both mature enough.

### A new dog or cat

When bringing a new cat or dog into your home, restrict it to one room and let the resident cat go where it wishes.

If your newcomer is a kitten or pup, let your cat inspect and sniff it while it is sleeping. If the pup awakens and your cat hisses and spits, perfect. You want your dog to respect your cat. Let your resident feline make all the first moves.

Do not introduce a new pet to your cat by putting them nose to nose on first meeting.

### Car travel with your cat

Never leave your cat to roam freely in your vehicle while you are driving. Your

**Give your cat** and a new pup time to get to know each other. They will not become best friends just because you want them to!

cat should travel safe and secure in its travel basket or carrier. On long trips, stop every two hours to let your cat out of its carrier for a walk inside your car. Take a litter box with you, though it is unlikely your cat will use it. Carry a water bowl and a bottle of water. If travel sickness is a problem, discuss suitable medication with your vet.

Never, ever leave your cat in your car in hot weather or direct sunshine. Heatstroke in hot cars is one of the most common causes of death in pets.

## Vacation care

Caring for your cat is a big responsibility. Develop reciprocal relations with your friends and family so you look after each other's pet when you are away.

Professional pet-sitters are an expensive alternative. If you plan to use a boarding kennel, always visit, inspect, and ask questions. The most conscientious kennel owners provide comfortable beds, tasty food, and the freedom to remain indoors or spend time in enclosed outdoor facilities. The best kennels are booked up months before busy seasons, especially Christmas and New Year's Eve.

**The best kennel owners** provide "home away from home" facilities, with freedom to roam within an outdoor enclosure or snooze indoors.

## Air, rail, and sea travel

Your cat's traveling container should be secure, the right size, and meet the carrier's regulations. Your cat should have visible ID. When flying, avoid hot, sunny weather. Fatal heatstroke accidents have occurred because of runway delays. Whenever possible, book direct flights. Avoid tranquilizers. Giving one makes you feel better, but increases your cat's risk of accidents. Many airlines allow your cat to accompany you in the passenger cabin as long as the cat carrier fits under the seat in front of you.

## What to do if your cat is missing

① Do not panic. Think sensibly about where your cat may go or hide if separated from you.

② Carry out an immediate search, asking people if they have seen your cat.

③ Contact the police, the humane society, your vet, and all local vets, giving them a description of your cat and his microchip ID number. Give these people at least two contact numbers for you, ideally your cellular and home phone or e-mail. Keep a phone-number list of everyone you contact.

④ Photocopy and post notices where your cat disappeared, with LOST and REWARD in large letters. A reward is always an effective inducement. Include a picture of your cat on the notices.

⑤ When the cat is safely returned, always contact the people on your phone list to give them the good news and to thank them for their help.

# CHAPTER FIVE

# Health
# concerns

Cats are naturally curious, and curiosity leads to risk.
You can significantly reduce health hazards through
simple and practical disease and accident-risk
prevention. Make sure your cat is vaccinated against
contagious diseases and protected from common
parasites. Only let your cat outdoors where it is safe to
do so. Know what to do when accidents do happen.
Be familiar with what is potentially dangerous and the
clinical signs of general illness. If you think there is
any reason for concern, see your vet sooner rather
than later. Early diagnosis virtually always makes
treatment easier and more successful.

# Choosing a vet

- Ask around, visit, and check out the practice
- Qualifications and experience vary
- It pays to be insured

Veterinarians are qualified to care for all animals, wild or domesticated. In urban and suburban areas, vets see mostly companion animals, such as dogs and cats. Even within a rural practice, where vets attend primarily to livestock, there is often one vet who focuses on pets. Some companion-animal vets have cat-only clinics. These vets are not necessarily "specialists" in the medical sense of the word, but rather individuals who feel most comfortable with cats. Facilities are cat-friendly and quieter than typical dog-and-cat animal clinics.

## Different facilities

All veterinary practices should have the basic equipment necessary to cope with urgent cases: X-ray and emergency operating facilities, basic laboratory apparatus, and a post-anesthesia recovery room. Better facilities often depend on the workload seen, on the location, and on what local pet owners are capable of paying for veterinary care.

## Location and cost

The issues of location and cost are interlinked. Urban practices charge more than rural ones because items such as rent, taxes, and salaries are more costly in highly populated areas. Costs also reflect a vet's investment in diagnostic and treatment facilities. In most, but not all, circumstances, a vet's charges reflect his or her costs.

## Visit and ask questions

Other cat owners are your best source of recommendations. Before committing yourself and your cat to a practice, arrange to meet with veterinarians and see their medical facilities. If you are interested in holistic care, ask whether complementary treatments are ever used. Find out how many vets work at the practice and how likely it is that you will see the same one most of the time. Ask what their referral policy is.

Even where space is tight, a vet should be willing to show you the operating area, diagnostic facilities, and cat accommodations. The practice may seem a little chaotic, but the premises should still be clean and well organized.

**Cat-owning friends and family,** who have first-hand experience, are the best source of information when looking for a vet.

## Round-the-clock emergency care

Every veterinarian should provide 24-hour emergency cover. Find out how this is offered—for example, is there a special telephone number to call? Does emergency cover rotate through different practices? Is there an emergency and critical-care facility used by your vet? If there is, will they be able to access your cat's medical records or speak to your vet when they need to?

## Specialists

A specialist is someone who has taken courses and passed exams in his or her special area of interest. In North America this qualifies for membership in an American College of Veterinary Medicine and adds a selection of initials after the vet's graduate degree initials, DVM (Doctor of Veterinary Medicine) or VMD. The more letters you see after a vet's name, the more qualified he or she is in a specific area.

Specialties presently recognized include: Anesthesiology (ACVA); Behavior (ACVB); Dermatology (ACVD); Emergency and Critical Care (ACVECC); Internal Medicine

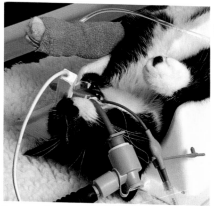

**Emergencies can happen** at any time, day or night. Make sure you choose a veterinary practice that provides 24-hour emergency cover.

(ACVIM); Nutrition (ACVN); Ophthalmology (ACVO); Preventive Medicine (ACVPM); Radiology (ACVR); Surgery (ACVS); Dentistry (AVDC); and General Practice (ABVP).

## Insurance

Prepare for unexpected veterinary bills by insuring the health of your pet. Pet health insurance is available from many different companies. Your vet can recommend an experienced insurance provider. Premiums are $100–$200 per year, depending on the type of cover you want and where you live.

Alternatively, you can act as your own insurer. For each of your cats, invest a sum equal to an insurance premium in a secure investment. Insurance-company figures show that claims are high in the first year, then drop until cats are about ten years old, when claims start to climb as the years advance. If your cat is typical, by the time he or she is a senior citizen, you will have a nest egg tucked away for unexpected veterinary bills.

### Ethical policies

Do you have strong opinions about how animals should be treated? Most of us do. For example, I will not declaw a cat. Personally, I feel that a cat should be able to do what cats evolved to do, which is mark with their claws. It is up to us to provide scratching posts and train our cats to use them rather than our furniture. People who feel I am introducing my own moral judgments into their private decisions will feel more comfortable elsewhere. At some time, you and your vet will have to make agonizing, possibly life-and-death decisions on your cat's behalf. If you understand each other and where each of you is coming from, those decisions will be easier to make.

# Examining your cat

■ Train your cat to be examined
■ Carry out routine examinations at home
■ Keep accurate records of your cat's weight

Training your cat to be examined means that you can carry out some home diagnoses. Routine home exams reveal problems early, when they are easiest to treat. It is also much easier and faster for a vet to make a diagnosis on a cat that allows itself to be examined. Do not try to do all of the following in a single session. Examine one area, then reward your cat with games, petting, and treats.

## Weight, mobility, and appearance

Weigh yourself on your bathroom scale while carrying your cat, then subtract your own weight to get your cat's. A change of 8 oz (225 g) may not be visibly noticed but is often of medical significance, so your scales should be very accurate.

Your cat's general appearance is a fine indicator of its health. Its coat should retain its natural sparkle. Increased dullness and lack of sheen is often an outward sign of an internal problem.

Any of the following symptoms warrants seeing your vet the same day:
• Sudden difficulty getting up, down, or comfortable;
• Staggering, falling over, or walking in circles;
• Overreacting to light, sound, or touch;
• Holding one side of the head down;
• Unexpected restlessness;
• Bloated belly;
• Unusual chest movements;
• Muscle spasms;
• Any acute body swelling;
• Crying, moaning, or wailing.

## How to take your cat's temperature

A cat's normal temperature ranges between 100.5°F (38°C) and 102°F (39°C). Nervous excitement or fear can increase a cat's temperature.

If using a glass, mercury-filled thermometer, shake it down and lubricate it with water-soluble jelly. Gently insert the thermometer about 1 in (2.5 cm) into your cat's rectum, holding it in position for 90 seconds. Remove, wipe clean, and read.

Digital rectal or ear thermometers are simple to use and easier to read.

Never try to take a cat's temperature by mouth or if the cat resents it.

### What your cat's temperature means

| °F | °C | CAUSE AND ACTION |
|----|-----|------------------|
| 106+ | 41+ | Heatstroke. Cool down immediately—get urgent veterinary attention. |
| 105 | 40.6 | Dangerous. Seek same-day veterinary attention. |
| 104 | 40.0 | High fever. Seek same-day veterinary advice. |
| 103 | 39.4 | Moderate fever. Telephone veterinarian for advice. |
| 102 | 38.9 | Normal. |
| 101 | 38.3 | Normal. |
| 100 | 37.8 | Normal. |
| 99 | 37.2 | Subnormal. Seek same-day veterinary advice. |
| 98– | 36.7– | Hypothermia. Keep your cat warm and get urgent veterinary attention. |

## Eye, ear, and mouth examination

① Check your cat's eyes for redness, discharge, cloudiness, or obvious injuries. Dilated pupils in bright light mean fear, pain, excitement, or shock.

② Look in the ears for inflammation, discharge, excess wax, or physical damage. Check the skin on the ear flaps for swelling or bite injuries. The nose should be clean and wet, with no sign of discharge.

③ Examine the chin and lips. There should be no swelling, inflammation, or unpleasant odor. Open your cat's mouth. The gums should be a healthy pink. Check inside. It is easy for bones, especially soft chicken bones, to get caught between your cat's back teeth. You may need to use the flat end of a spoon to get the bone off the teeth.

## Body, skin, and coat examination

① Run a hand over your cat's head, cheeks, jaws, and throat, feeling for heat, swelling, or signs of bite abscesses. Resistance by the cat could indicate pain.

② Feel down your cat's neck, over its back, sides, and chest. Any stickiness might indicate a site of self-inflicted skin damage or a penetrating injury—for example, from a bite.

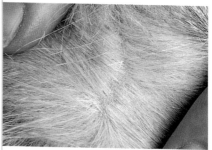

③ Part the hair to examine the skin, which should look "quiet" (without inflammation or excessive flaking dandruff). Black, shiny dust means that fleas are in residence.

④ Run your hands over the hips, around the groin, and down each limb, feeling for swelling or excess heat. Flex the joints and watch for signs of pain. Examine both hind legs or both forelegs together. The muscles and joints should feel perfectly symmetrical. Examine the feet, checking the pads for damage, between the pads for injury, and the claws for length. Older cats commonly suffer from ingrown claws.

⑤ Feel along the length of the tail and gently lift it to inspect the anus, which should be perfectly clean and odor-free. There should be no discharge from a female cat's vulva or a male's penis sheath.

### A dull coat means a sick cat

Most shorthaired cats normally have lustrous coats that lie flat on the body. When a cat is sick, its coat is often immediately affected. It becomes "staring": this means it looks duller than normal, with patches standing up slightly, away from the body. If your cat's coat suddenly looks staring and if its eating habits are anything other than normal, make an appointment to see your vet.

# Practical prevention

- Inoculate against infectious diseases
- Be aware of adverse reactions
- Give boosters according to local risks

Preventing problems is better and cheaper than seeing your veterinarian when problems happen. By "problems," I mean infectious diseases, internal and external parasites, physical accidents, unwanted pregnancies, and diseases that might spread from your cat to you, or even vice versa.

The subject of annual inoculations against infectious diseases has rightly become a topic of intense discussion. My advice is to read the following, then—with your vet's help—develop an inoculation timetable that is appropriate for the vaccine your vet uses, where you live, and the type of lifestyle your cat leads.

### Feline infectious diseases

Cats harbor the most enigmatic and serious infectious diseases, not all of which can be vaccinated against. Prevention and treatment of these conditions is often both complicated and problematic.

Some of these diseases are insidious, lying latent for years before causing clinical illness; others may be treated with apparent success, only to return when the cat is older or physically or emotionally stressed.

### Feline infectious enteritis (FIE)

Despite being highly contagious, FIE, also known as feline panleukopenia or feline parvovirus, is a preventable disease. However, it can be fatal if it is not treated.

Signs of FIE include:
- Severe vomiting and diarrhea, possibly with blood;
- Lethargy and listlessness;
- Dehydration.

### Upper respiratory tract (URT) infections

The following are just some of the causes of upper respiratory tract infections. All are extremely contagious.

Reovirus often only causes a little eye inflammation, while chlamydia, a bacterium-like organism, causes significant inflammation that responds to antibiotic eye-drops.

Calicivirus and rhinotracheitis virus cause the most severe signs of URT infection. A cat may recover from calici

**Your veterinarian will help** you develop a vaccination program for your cat. This should reflect where you live and your cat's lifestyle.

or rhinotracheitis infection but become a "silent carrier," appearing healthy while still infecting other cats.

Rhinotracheitis is a herpesvirus. This means that, when your cat is under physical or emotional stress, the virus may reactivate, causing renewed clinical infection.

Calici and rhinotracheitis signs include:

- Sneezing often, with a thick nasal discharge;
- Sticky or runny eyes;
- Ulcers and open sores in the mouth;
- Fever;
- Loss of appetite associated with loss of smell;
- Eye ulcers (caused by rhinotracheitis virus);
- Lameness and swollen joints in kittens (caused by calicivirus).

## Feline leukemia virus (FeLV)

Feline leukemia virus has a long incubation period—often years—and usually leads to serious, and eventually fatal, disease.

Signs of FeLV are unpredictable. They include:

- Development of white blood cell cancers, such as lymphoma;
- Secondary infections from a variety of agents (because of the suppression of the immune system);
- Anemia (associated with bone-marrow suppression).

## Feline immunodeficiency virus (FIV)

FIV is not as aggressive as FeLV and is not normally associated with tumors. However, with its long incubation period, it too is an eventual killer disease.

Like FeLV, signs for FIV are also unpredictable. They include:

- Secondary infections from a variety of agents (because of the suppression of the immune system);
- Anemia (associated with bone-marrow suppression).

## Highly recommended vaccinations

| DISEASE | KITTEN SHOTS | ADULT BOOSTERS |
|---------|--------------|----------------|
| Feline infectious enteritis (FIE), or feline panleukopenia | Two injections starting as early as eight weeks old. Given behind the shoulders. | At 15 months, then every three years. |
| Cat flu = feline rhinotracheitis virus or feline calicivirus | Two injections starting as early as eight weeks old. Given with the above shot behind the shoulders. | At 15 months, then every year. Inoculation does not provide immunity, it merely lessens the severity of illness. Not all strains of calicivirus are protected against. |
| Rabies | Over three months old. Given low on the right hind leg. | According to manufacturer. Non-adjuvanated vaccine is available. |

## Other vaccinations

| | | |
|---------|--------------|----------------|
| Feline leukemia virus (FeLV) | Two injections at over ten weeks old. Do not vaccinate cats at little or no risk of being exposed to saliva of infected cats. Given low on the left hind leg. | Every year. |
| Feline chlamydia | Use only in exceptional circumstances. Treat disease when it occurs with appropriate antibiotics. | |
| Feline infectious peritonitis (FIP) | Many experts question the value of this vaccine. Not recommended at this time. | |

## Feline infectious peritonitis (FIP)

Young kittens are most susceptible to feline infectious peritonitis, which is a mutation of feline coronavirus. Clinical disease is usually lethal.

FIP is divided into "wet" and "dry" forms. Signs are unpredictable.
Wet FIP may cause:
- Fluid buildup in the chest, causing breathing difficulties;
- Fluid buildup in the abdomen, causing swelling and distension;
- Fever, vomiting, diarrhea, and loss of weight.

Dry FIP may cause almost any signs, including:
- Kidney failure;
- Gastrointestinal disturbances;
- Respiratory conditions;
- Seizures;
- Liver disease;
- Lameness.

## Rabies

Rabies is invariably fatal and highly contagious to people.

The signs of rabies include:
- Lameness;
- Difficulty swallowing;
- Seizures;
- Increased aggression or, rarely, docility;
- Other behavioral changes.

## Vaccination concerns

Sensible vaccination eliminates concern about a variety of infections. However, any medical procedure involves risk, so what you have to ask your vet is how the risk from vaccination compares to the risk of not being vaccinated.

Risk-analysis is the basis for vaccine recommendations that have been formulated in the United States and Canada by the American Association of Feline Practitioners (AAFP) and the Academy of Feline Medicine (AFM).

With the exception of the combined flu and enteritis vaccine, the AAFP and AFM discourage the use of polyvalent vaccines—that is, single injections that contain vaccines against many diseases. They say that combination vaccines "may force practitioners to administer vaccine antigens not needed by the patient."

In North America in the 1990s there was an increase in reports of skin tumors at the site of injections. This did not happen in Europe. The best evidence available shows that these tumors occur more frequently where leukemia and rabies vaccines are injected, specifically with vaccines containing an adjuvant—a substance that enhances the potency of the vaccine. Injection-site sarcomas (see p.273) are extremely rare with the flu and enteritis vaccine.

## Biological vaccines

A biological vaccine is made by altering an infectious agent so that it does not cause serious illness. The infectious agent may be live or dead. If it is live, it will be modified through growth in tissue culture so that it no longer causes illness.

In some circumstances, the specific parts of infectious agents that stimulate the immune system to produce antibodies can be manufactured by bacteria through genetic engineering. In the resulting vaccine there are no infectious agents whatsoever, either live or dead.

When the vaccine is introduced into a cat by injection, by nasal spray, or even by eye-drops, it stimulates the cat's immune system to produce antibody protection to the specific infectious agent it contains.

The antibodies produced by the immune system survive for a variable period of time, which depends upon the infectious agent itself and the quality of the vaccine. Some vaccines offer longer protection than others.

## Using homeopathy

Homeopathy is based on the principle that "like cures like." For example, a skin irritation may be treated with Rhus tox, prepared from irritating poison ivy. Practitioners believe that the more diluted the substance, the more effective it is.

A homeopathic nosode is a remedy made from tissues, excretions, or secretions from a cat that has that a specific infection. For example, a cat-flu nosode is made from discharges from a cat that has cat flu. These discharges are diluted, usually in alcohol and distilled water, until they are one part discharge per million or more diluent. Drops of this dilution are added to lactose tablets, which absorb the remedy.

## Homeopathy vs. biological vaccines

Cats given homeopathic nosodes do not produce antibodies to the infection from which the nosode was produced. Some homeopaths say that nosodes offer protection by triggering other forms of defense.

There are acknowledged potential dangers from biological vaccines and these should be taken into account when planning a vaccination routine for your cat.

All evidence, however, suggests that the immune system of a cat that has been treated with a homeopathic nosode is not prepared for the challenge of infection. Therefore, the cat would be unable to respond to the infection as well as it would had it been exposed to a good-quality biological vaccine.

### Preparing homeopathic remedies

Homeopathic remedies are made from plant, animal, and mineral extracts. The extract is chopped or ground and soaked in a mix of 90 percent alcohol and 10 percent distilled water. The mixture is shaken from time to time to dissolve the material.

① The mixture stands for two to four weeks, until it becomes infused. It is strained into a dark glass bottle and is then known as the mother tincture.

② One drop of the tincture is diluted in 99 drops of alcohol, then shaken rapidly—a process called succussion. Dilution and succussion are repeated.

③ After dilution and succussion have resulted in the required potency, a few drops are added to lactose tablets, which absorb the remedy.

# Parasite control

■ Use effective, licensed products
■ Treat your cat's home environment
■ Some alternative treatments work well

Many feline parasites are seasonal, increasing in numbers during warm weather. Routine examination of your cat is the best way to remain vigilant for external parasites. Even the tapeworm, the most common internal parasite, leaves its dried segments around an affected cat's bottom. Cats are not usually bothered by most parasites. Itchiness occurs when there is an allergic reaction to their saliva. Some parasites—such as ticks, fleas, and ear mites—are visible, while others— including other mites, yeast, and fungi—are invisible to the eye.

## Preventing external parasites

Cats can carry a variety of external parasites. Advances in parasite control mean there is no reason for any cat to suffer from them. Yet parasitic skin conditions are still common. Parasites may cause head-shaking and scratching, a dull, dandruffy coat, and itchiness with or without inflammation or hair loss.

## Ear mites are common

Many kittens and feral cats catch ear mites from their mothers or neighbors. Eradicating mites takes time. They are highly contagious, so if one cat has them,

## External parasites

| PARASITE | HOW CATS ARE INFECTED | DIAGNOSIS AND TREATMENT |
|---|---|---|
| Fleas | Fleas are activated by body heat, vibration, and cat odors. Dormant larvae come alive, mature into fleas, then hop on your cat for a blood meal. They spend the rest of the time making baby fleas. Fleas are picked up from the environment and from other animals. | Fleas do not necessarily cause itchiness. Look for fleas or flea dirt—shiny black specks on the skin—especially over the rump. Prevent or treat with effective, safe medications. Always treat the home environment as well as all pets. Use products that prevent the flea life cycle from completing, safe sprays, or spot treatments that kill fleas. |
| Mites | Ear mites are contracted from another cat, usually a kitten's mother. They are most active at night, causing ear and skin itch. | Cats with ear mites produce wax and debris in their itchy ears. Treat with a proprietary veterinary eardrop or lotion. |
| | *Cheyletiella* mites are most commonly a kitten problem, inherited from the mother. | These mites cause dandruff over the back, often with no itchiness. They are easily killed with antiflea treatments. |
| | Sarcoptic mites (scabies), common in dogs, are rare in cats. | Diagnosed by a skin scraping. Treat with selamectin (Revolution). |
| Ticks | Ticks wait in long grass. A shadow, vibration, or even a minute change in temperature tells it a meal has arrived. The tick attaches to the cat, burrows its mouth into the skin, and sucks a meal until it bloats with blood and drops off. | Ticks swell enormously and are easily seen when engorged. Apply alcohol to the tick to kill it. Then, using tweezers, twist it at its root in the skin to corkscrew it out. Avoid squeezing ticks. This releases more "poison" into the cat. |
| Lice | Rare in cats. | Lice or eggs visible in hair. Treat with fipronil (Frontline). |
| Ringworm | Technically not a parasite, but common and transmissible to other cats and to us. | *See Skin and coat conditions, pp.234–7.* |

## Internal parasites

| TYPE | HOW CATS ARE INFECTED | DIAGNOSIS AND TREATMENT |
|---|---|---|
| Roundworms (common) | Usually mothers pass these worms to their kittens before they are born; sometimes kittens are infected from suckling on the mother's contaminated skin. | Kittens are pot-bellied and vomit worms. Mothers are wormed routinely during pregnancy and kittens are wormed from 14 days of age using products such as fenbendazole (Panacur). |
| Tapeworms (common) | The most common tapeworm (*Dipylidium caninum*) is picked up by eating an infected flea. | Tapeworms rarely cause signs of disease in cats. The most common sign of infection is dried tapeworm segments, which look like grains of rice in the hair around the anus. Worm with praziquantel. |
| *Giardia* (increasingly common) | A microscopic, single-celled parasite picked up from contaminated water. This is an underdiagnosed cause of diarrhea in cats. | Diarrhea, possibly with blood. Treat with fenbendazole (Panacur) or whichever drug your veterinarian recommends. |
| Heartworms (rare) | Eggs are passed on to a cat by mosquito bites. These mature into large worms that reside in the heart. | Coughing and debility do not occur until the disease is well advanced. Cats outdoors are more at risk than indoor cats. Prevent, using selamectin (Revolution), or treat following your veterinarian's advice. |
| Toxoplasmosis | Contracted from eating contaminated wildlife. | No clinical signs but a public health hazard. *See below.* |

treat all your cats and dogs. Ear mites are easy to eliminate with ear-mite drops or a drop of selamectin (Revolution) on the skin of the neck. Dripping mineral oil in the ears smothers most ear mites but does not get rid of the stragglers outside the ear canal. Continue topical treatment for at least two weeks.

## Defleaing your cat and home
• **Flea birth control:** Using lufenuron (the flea contraceptive Program) will sterilize any flea that has a meal off it. Adults die off and your cat and home are cleansed of fleas. This is an excellent product to use on cats that do not have an itchy allergic reaction to flea saliva.
• **Flea repellent:** Apply selamectin, fipronil, or imidacloprid (the "spot treatments" Revolution, Frontline, or Advantage respectively) monthly on the skin of your cat's neck. Revolution also kills ear mites, roundworms, and scabies. Frontline kills ticks as well as fleas. These products can be used in conjunction with a household biological spray that prevents flea eggs from hatching.

• **Cleaning the carpets:** Fleas leave their eggs and larvae in your carpets. Professional carpet treatment with sodium borate, tetraborate, or polyborate destroys flea eggs and usually comes with a one-year guarantee. Do not use laundry-grade borax. It may cause eye, respiratory, and kidney problems.

## Internal parasites
Internal parasites seldom cause signs of disease. The exception is *Giardia*, an increasingly common cause of chronic diarrhea in cats. *(see table, above.)*

### Dangers to us from toxoplasmosis
*Toxoplasma* is a parasite that seldom causes problems to a cat. For a few weeks after their first—and only their first—exposure to *Toxoplasma*, cats pass infectious particles in their feces. It is through these contaminated feces that *Toxoplasma* can be transmitted to us. There is no simple treatment.

Pregnant women and immune-compromised individuals are most at risk. An infected human fetus may develop serious problems. Pregnant women should wear rubber gloves when cleaning litter boxes and when gardening or handling raw meat. Undercooked meat should be avoided. It is the most common way people contract toxoplasmosis.

# Responsible ownership

■ Prevent unwanted pregnancies
■ Make all efforts to avoid diseases transmissible to us
■ Aim to prevent traumatic accidents

We all must behave responsibly toward our cats, ourselves, and our communities. We can avoid road accidents by keeping cats away from roads, and we can reduce unwanted pregnancies and the problems that accompany sex-hormone-induced behavior simply by neutering our pets.

### Prevent unwanted pregnancies

The number of unwanted cats rises as uncontrolled breeding continues. For an indoor cat, breeding is out of the question, but lack of sexual fulfillment can lead to unpleasant behaviors, like spraying or "calling." Neutering makes life more congenial for indoor cats and eliminates the risk of unwanted matings for those that go outdoors.

### Potential problems

Neutering has few potential problems, regardless of the age of the cat. Some individuals gain weight after neutering, but this can be controlled through diet. When your cat is neutered, assume it will gain weight and reduce its calorie intake by about 20 percent. Routinely

weigh your cat over the following weeks and, if you notice weight loss, increase the number of calories offered.

### The right time to neuter

Neuter a female cat just before her first season. Neutered females live, on average, over a year longer than unneutered females. Males can be neutered at any age. Neutering after puberty allows secondary sex characteristics, such as thick jowls, to develop, but it also means that you are likely to contend with the pungent aroma of mature cat urine.

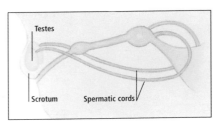

**Neutering a male cat** involves removing its testicles through a small incision in the scrotum. The spermatic cords are then tied.

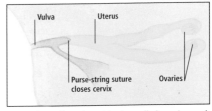

**Neutering a female cat** is also called spaying and involves major abdominal surgery. The uterus, down to the cervix, and ovaries are removed.

## Safe play and safe return

Only let your cat outdoors where you know it is safe to do so. This is the only way to avoid traffic accidents. Make sure your cat is wearing some form of ID. As well as ID on a quick-release collar that opens if it tangles in branches, make sure the cat has been microchipped: if it does get lost, you want to ensure that the people who find it will know who to contact.

Neutering a male reduces fighting and, therefore, the risk of saliva-transmitted infectious diseases like FIV and FeLV from other cats.

## Zoonoses

There is a limited range of diseases that cats can transmit to humans; these are known as zoonoses. They are always of concern, but almost all of them are rare.

• **Toxoplasmosis (toxo):** The most common small-animal zoonosis is not contracted by direct contact with a cat. It is most often contracted by eating raw or undercooked meat. Cats contract usually hard-to-detect toxo from prey they eat. The first time, and only the first time, this happens, they pass toxo eggs in their feces for a few days to a few weeks. These can contaminate soil or litter boxes. Pregnant women should wear rubber gloves when gardening or emptying a litter box to reduce the health risks to the unborn child.

• **Cat-scratch fever:** Most cats in the United States have been exposed to *Bartonella*-species bacteria. *Bartonella henselae* can cause cat-scratch fever, especially in children and young adults. If you have been scratched or had a wound licked and you have a fever, malaise, and headaches, contact your doctor for appropriate antibiotics.

• **Ringworm:** Ringworm is a fungal infection that affects livestock, pets, and humans. Cats, especially Persians, are the most common pet carriers. Cats and humans are treated with topical antifungal medication and oral antibiotics for at least four weeks.

• **Rabies:** Where rabies exists, we are at risk when bitten by any outdoor cat not vaccinated against the disease. Once the disease develops, there is no cure.

• **Gastrointestinal diseases:** Several gastrointestinal microorganisms can be transmitted from cats to us. All are rare. The most common may be *Giardia*, which causes mild diarrhea; others include campylobacter and salmonella, which cause fever, headache, abdominal cramp, and watery to bloody diarrhea. These problems are usually caused by contaminated water or meat but, in a few instances, can be traced back to cats. If anyone in your family is diagnosed with a gastroenteric infection, have your pet examined to see if it is a carrier.

### Cat bites and cat allergy

Not truly zoonoses, bites and allergies are by far the most common conditions we suffer from as a result of contact with cats. Bites are usually on the hands, arms, and face. Because they are small, deep wounds, difficult to irrigate, many lead to infection. Allergy to cat dandruff is a serious problem for some people and is described in detail on page 271.

**This cat is ready** to scratch and bite. Small cat-inflicted wounds to humans can lead to infections.

# Giving medicines

- Be fast and efficient
- Use bribery when possible
- Always complete the full course of treatment

Bribery is the best method for giving medicine to cats. Whenever possible, try to hide the medicine in something tasty. Of course, the problem with bribery is that cats are too clever for it to succeed. They smell and taste what we are trying to do. That means there is often no choice but to give pills to your cat. Few cats willingly accept being forced to swallow medicines. Be firm but gentle. Always reward your cat afterward with soothing words and strokes.

### Hiding drugs in food

When possible, hide pills in food, such as a ball of meat. Alternatively, if it is tasteless, powder it and mix it in food. Mix liquid medicines thoroughly in your cat's favorite food. Note: some drugs should not be given with certain types of food, so check with your vet first.

## Giving pills

## A difficult task

Some cats can be extremely difficult to give oral medicines to. However, it is important to complete a full course of prescribed medicines. If you have any difficulties administering drugs, contact your vet. *If you are severely scratched or bitten, always seek medical advice.*

1 While speaking soothingly to your cat, hold it firmly to prevent it from scratching you or escaping. Gently wrap it in a large towel if necessary.

2 Place the forefinger and thumb of one of your hands behind the upper canine teeth, turn the head up, and use your free hand to draw the lower jaw down.

3 Squeeze in gently so that the mouth remains open, then, again using your free hand, drop the pill as far back over the tongue as possible.

4 Close the cat's mouth immediately and rub its throat until you see it swallow.

5 Open the mouth and check that the pill has been swallowed. Cats are magnificent at hiding pills.

## Giving ear medicines

To be effective, ear medicines should reach right down to the eardrum. Most bottles and tubes come with applicator nozzles large enough to fit the ear, but not so large that they cause damage.

①  Place your cat on a table, speak soothingly, and wrap it in a towel if necessary. Wipe away visible debris from the ear opening.

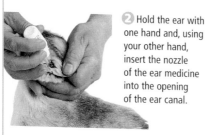

②  Hold the ear with one hand and, using your other hand, insert the nozzle of the ear medicine into the opening of the ear canal.

③  Squeeze drops or ointment into the ear canal.

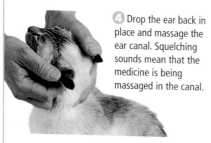

④  Drop the ear back in place and massage the ear canal. Squelching sounds mean that the medicine is being massaged in the canal.

⑤  After massaging, a cat usually shakes its head. Use paper towel, tissue, or cotton balls to prevent earwax and debris from flying everywhere during the head-shaking.

⑥  Praise good behavior and give the cat a reward.

### Caution!
Never use proprietary wax removers if there is a risk that the eardrum has been ruptured.

## Giving liquids

①  Hold the upper jaw as you would for giving a pill, but keep the head level, not tilted upward.

②  Tip or squirt the medicine into the side of the mouth. Do not squirt it into the back of the mouth—it might go down the windpipe.

③  Close the mouth and rub the throat until the cat swallows, then praise it for good behavior.

## Applying eye ointment and drops

①  Put your cat on a table, speak calmly, and wrap it in a towel if necessary.

②  Using dampened cotton balls, gently remove any eye discharge.

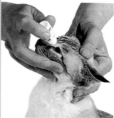

③  Support the hand holding the ointment tube or dropper against the cat's head to prevent the container from coming in contact with the eye if the cat moves abruptly.

④  Apply a line of ointment or a drop directly to the eye. Close it to allow body heat to soften and disperse the medication. Ointment runs smoother when the tube is first warmed in your hands.

⑤  Praise good behavior and give a reward.

### Caution!
Make sure that the medicine container NEVER comes in contact with the eye.

## Administering injections

Insulin injections are often needed to treat sugar diabetes. In other circumstances, your vet might provide you with life-saving medicine to give by injection if your cat is known to go into anaphylactic shock when bitten by wasps or insects. Giving injections sounds daunting, but it is quite simple, simpler in many ways than giving oral medicines.

①  Draw the medicine into the syringe.

②  Tap the syringe until the air bubbles rise to the top, then expel them until the first drop of medicine emerges from the needle.

③  Hold your cat on a table and, while speaking calmly to it, grasp a fold of skin on the neck between the shoulder blades (this is relatively insensitive skin).

④  With a steady hand, insert the needle through the skin into the tissue under the skin and above the underlying muscle, then squeeze the contents of the syringe. (Your vet may show you how to give some life-saving drugs directly into muscles.)

⑤  Praise your cat and give it a reward.

# When accidents happen

- Stay calm
- Protect yourself before approaching the cat
- Monitor the cat's vital signs

Fortunately, the likelihood of your ever needing to use lifesaving skills on your cat is low. That does not mean we have no need for these skills. Lifesaving first aid is logical. Assess the dangers, making sure you do not put yourself in danger, restrain your cat, check its heart and breathing, look for signs of shock, and, if all of these systems are in order, arrange for the care of physical injuries such as puncture wounds or broken bones.

Shock—the failure of blood to be transported throughout the body in necessary quantities—is a hidden lethal danger. A cat may appear normal after an accident but have potentially life-threatening internal injuries. ***Always have a vet examine the cat as soon as possible.***

## Accident procedures

When accidents happen, follow these steps.

1. Calmly approach the cat. Try not to frighten it into attempting an escape. Talk to it reassuringly and avoid intimidating eye contact.

2. While still talking, check the cat's expression to determine its degree of pain or fear. Wrap it in a large towel or any other soft material. Lift the cat away from further danger.

3. If the cat is calm, gently but firmly hold its head under the chin. Apply light pressure against the cat's body with the elbow of your free hand while you carry out your examination with that hand.

4. For a frightened cat, ensure that the towel, blanket, folded sheet, or other available material is wrapped under it, so the cat cannot lash out with teeth or claws.

5. Gently unwrap the cat's head while keeping the rest of its body safely cocooned. Hold the material around the cat's neck to prevent it from unraveling.

6. Carry out your examination only when your cat is calm.

**A frightened cat** can be a dangerous cat, so approach with caution, even if you are the owner. Calm the cat down with gentle speech patterns.

## Monitor the cat's breathing

Cats breathe in and out about 30 times a minute. This rate increases with pain, shock, and lung and heart problems. Calculate breathing by counting a cat's chest movements for 15 seconds and multiplying by four.

Breathing and panting are different. Panting occurs with anxiety or pain, or to get rid of excess heat. If your cat is unconscious and there is no breathing at all, artificial respiration is necessary.

### Cat-scratch disease

Cat-scratch disease, or cat-scratch fever (see p.221), is a rare infection caused by a bacterium called *Bartonella henselae.*

The disease is transmitted to people through cat bites and scratches. Fleas are the probable mode of transmission between cats, and possibly to us, too. This is a good reason for effective flea prevention.

While cat-scratch disease seldom causes clinical illness in cats, it may cause a fever, headaches, and tender, swollen lymph nodes in susceptible people, especially children and immune-suppressed individuals. Cat-scratch disease responds to antibiotic treatment.

### Taking your cat's pulse

Your cat's resting pulse rate is about 120 beats per minute, increasing to 200 when frightened. A kitten's heart may beat over 200 times a minute.

Your cat's heart rate will increase with fever, pain, heart conditions, and in the first stages of shock. To monitor your cat's heart, grasp the chest on both sides, just behind the elbows, and squeeze gently until you feel heartbeats. This may be difficult to do on very fat cats.

Alternatively, feel the pulse by placing your fingers where the hind leg meets the groin. A large artery, the femoral artery, passes through here, close to the surface of the skin. Move your fingers around until you can pick up the pulse. Count for 15 seconds, then multiply by four to calculate the heart rate. If your cat is unconscious and the heart is not beating, heart massage becomes your priority.

1 To check your cat's heart rate, start by holding its head under the chin. This should be done gently but firmly, and will prevent the cat from biting.

Femoral artery passes where hind leg meets groin

2 Place your fingers on the point where the hind leg meets the groin, and move them around until you can feel the pulse.

# Lifesaving first aid

- Never underestimate shock
- Think ABC: "airway–breathing–circulation"
- Give first aid and get professional help

A cat may look fine after an accident but then die a few hours later of clinical shock. Controlling shock takes precedence over first aid for other injuries, such as broken bones.

The color of your cat's gums gives a firm clue to shock. Normal gums are a healthy pink; during shock they become dull pink or even white.

In healthy cats, when you press your finger against the gums, blood is "squeezed out"—the gums whiten—but it returns as soon as you remove your finger. The more advanced the state of shock, the longer it takes for the gums' capillaries—microscopic blood vessels—to refill.

**Checking your cat's gums** helps you determine shock. Press your finger against the gums and remove it. The longer it takes for the blood to return to the gums, the greater the degree of shock.

## Know your ABC

In case of accidents, it's as easy as ABC to remember what you should check for in your cat.
**A** is for airway. Is the airway open? If not, clear any debris and pull the tongue forward.
**B** is for breathing. Is the cat breathing? If not, give artificial respiration *(see opposite)*.
**C** is for circulation. Is there a heartbeat or pulse? If not, give heart massage *(see p.228)*.

### Early-shock signs
The signs of early shock are:
- Faster-than-normal breathing, sometimes panting;
- Faster-than-normal, pounding heart rate;
- Pale gums;
- Anxiety or restlessness;
- Lethargy and weakness;
- Normal or subnormal rectal temperature;
- Slow capillary-refill time to the gums (more than two seconds).

### Late-shock signs
The signs of late shock are:
- Shallow, irregular breathing;
- Irregular heartbeat;
- Very pale or blue gums and dilated eyes;
- Extreme weakness or unconsciousness;
- Very cool body temperature, especially the paws, less than 98°F (36.7°C);
- Very slow capillary-refill time to the gums (more than four seconds).

*In such cases, heart failure and death are imminent.*

## Dealing with shock

If your cat shows signs of shock, do not let it wander around or give it anything to eat or drink. Do the following:

**1** Stop any bleeding and give the cat artificial respiration *(see below)* or heart massage *(see p.228)*.

**2** Place the cat on its side, with its head extended.

**3** Wrap the cat in a warm blanket to prevent further heat loss.

**4** Use pillows or towels to elevate the cat's hindquarters, therefore allowing more blood to travel to the brain.

**5** Keep the head extended and *transport the cat to the nearest vet immediately*.

## When and how to give artificial respiration

Only give artificial respiration if your cat has stopped breathing. Check the gums. If they are pink, it usually means that oxygen is being carried around the body. If they are blue or white, artificial respiration may be necessary.

If it is difficult to determine whether the cat is breathing, place a little piece of tissue in front of a nostril and see if it moves.

If your cat has stopped breathing, do the following:

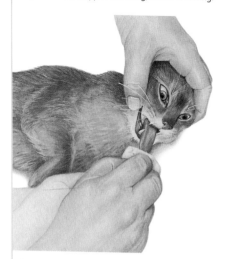

**1** Place the cat on its side, clear any debris from the nose and mouth, and pull its tongue forward.

## Ask the vet

**Q:** How do I know if an unconscious cat is breathing?

**A:** An unconscious cat sometimes breathes so gently it is difficult to see. If you are not sure whether your cat is breathing, hold a mirror close to the cat's nose and look for condensation, either fogging or tiny water droplets. If this is present, your cat is breathing. Alternatively, hold a small piece of tissue (or a cotton ball) in front of its nostrils; if the cat is breathing, the air coming from the nostrils will move the tissue.

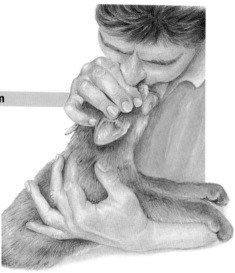

**2** Close the mouth and, with the neck in a straight line, place your mouth over the cat's nose and blow in until you see its chest expand. If you find this offensive, use your hand to form an airtight cylinder between your mouth and your cat's nose. Blow through this.

**3** Take your mouth away. The cat's lungs will naturally deflate. Repeat this procedure 10 to 20 times a minute until the cat breathes on its own.

**4** Check the pulse every 15 seconds to ensure that the cat's heart is still beating. If it stops, perform CPR, combining heart massage *(see p.228)* with artificial respiration.

**5** *Get emergency veterinary help as soon as possible.*

## When and how to give heart massage

Only give heart massage if your cat's heart is not beating. Check the eyes: they dilate when the heart stops. Feel for a heartbeat or pulse. Check the gums: if, when you press your finger against pink gums, they turn white then return to pink, the heart is still beating. If there is no pulse and the gums do not refill with blood, the heart has stopped.

## Heart massage for very obese cats

If your cat is very rotund, instead of laying it on its side, place it on its back with the head lower than the body. Put the heel of your hand on the cat's breastbone, pressing both down and forward to push blood to the brain. Continue with CPR *(see below)* until heart and breathing resume.

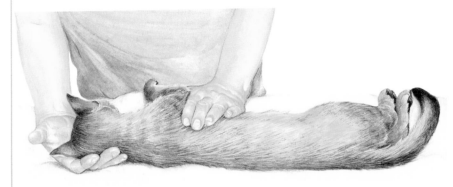

1 Place your cat on its side, if possible with the head lower than the rest of the body.

2 Grasp the chest, behind the elbows, between your fingers and thumb. Support the cat's back with your other hand.

3 Squeeze firmly, compressing the rib cage. Squeeze up toward the neck, repeating this action using quick, firm pumps 120 times a minute.

4 After 15 seconds of heart massage, give artificial respiration for 10 seconds.

5 Continue alternating until a pulse returns, then give artificial respiration alone.

6 *Get immediate emergency veterinary attention.*

## When more than one person is present

One person should give heart massage for five seconds, then the other should give a breath of artificial respiration. Alternate like this until it is safe for one (usually the person doing the heart massage) to leave to arrange transportation to the vet.

## Cardiopulmonary resuscitation (CPR)

Brain cells have an enormous need for oxygen, which is why 20 percent of the blood pumped by the heart goes to such a relatively small organ.

If brain cells are deprived of oxygen, even for a few minutes, they become damaged or die.

In emergencies, heart massage can restart a stopped heart while artificial respiration puts your exhaled oxygen in your cat's lungs, to be carried to its brain until it starts breathing again on its own.

The combination of heart massage and artificial respiration is called cardiopulmonary resuscitation, or CPR.

## When to use CPR

You may need to use CPR in the event of any of the following:
- Blood loss
- Choking
- Concussion
- Diabetic coma
- Electric shock
- Heart failure
- Near-drowning
- Poisoning
- Shock
- Smoke inhalation
- Severe allergic reactions.

## When bleeding occurs

Both heavy bleeding and lighter, slow, continuous bleeding will lead to dangerous clinical shock.

External bleeding can often be controlled by applying pressure.

Spurting blood means that an artery has been damaged. This is more difficult to stop because the blood pressure in arteries (carrying blood from the heart) is higher than in veins (carrying blood to the heart).

Watch for signs of shock, including: pale or white gums; rapid breathing; weak, rapid pulse; cold extremities; and general weakness.

### How to control bleeding

**1** If first-aid material is available, apply pressure with a nonstick gauze pad. If this is not available, use any clean, absorbent material, such as a paper towel, a pad of toilet paper or facial tissue, or a clean dish towel.

**2** Apply pressure for at least two minutes, adding more absorbent material if necessary.

**3** Keep the bleeding area above the heart if possible, but do not elevate a leg if there is a possible fracture.

**4** Do not remove the blood-soaked material—it helps with clotting. Leave the removal to your veterinary surgeon.

**5** *Get immediate veterinary attention.*

### Anaphylactic shock

An insect bite, some drugs, or even (rarely) food can cause a cat to go into anaphylactic shock.

Early signs are heavy breathing, wheezing, retching, vomiting, staggering, and sudden diarrhea.

Later signs are blue gums, gurgling lung sounds, and distressed breathing.

If you hear distressed gurgling sounds, suspend your cat by the hind legs for 10 seconds to try to clear the airway, and *see your vet immediately*.

**Swinging your cat** by its hind legs may seem like an unusual, even unpleasant, procedure, but it could save its life when it is going into anaphylactic shock. Hold your cat just above its knees and gently swing it from side to side.

# Penetrating injuries

- Never underestimate hidden damage
- Bandages protect but can also be dangerous
- Move an injured cat carefully

Injuries, especially penetrating injuries, can be deceptive in cats. When injured, a cat often tries to behave normally, so as not to draw attention to its vulnerability. Take care to cause as little discomfort as possible. Even the gentlest cat may bite and scratch when frightened and in pain. The two most common types of wound are closed, where the skin is not broken, and open, in which the skin is broken. There is a high risk of infection with open wounds. Fractures are also open or closed.

## Closed wounds

Never underestimate a closed wound. It may look like there is little damage, but there could be serious internal injuries, the full extent of which may not be apparent for days. *Even when wounds look minor, call your veterinarian and get professional advice.*

The signs of a closed wound are:
- Swelling;
- Pain;
- Discoloration (caused by bruising under the skin);
- Increased heat in a specific location;
- Superficial damage, such as scratches to the skin.

**Treatment:** Using a towel, carefully wrap the part of the body that has a closed wound in several layers of material. This immobilizes the injured area. Pin or tape the fabric so that it does not unravel during the trip to the vet.

### First aid for closed wounds

Apply a cool compress and seek veterinary attention. A bag of frozen peas wrapped in a dish towel makes an ideal compress, because it thaws faster than ice and wraps to the contour of the injured area.

## Punctures and other open wounds

Puncture wounds from fights, air rifles, or even guns, may not be immediately obvious, since there is often little or no bleeding. Because puncture wounds are exposed to dirt and bacteria, the risk of infection is high.

If you notice any of the following symptoms in your cat, look for a puncture wound:
- Increased licking to a specific area;
- A new scab on the skin;
- A skin puncture;
- A trace of blood or simply moist hair on the skin;
- Lameness.

*If you find a puncture wound, call your vet for advice.* If, in the meantime, you need to control bleeding, see Life-saving first aid, pages 226–9.

### First aid for minor open wounds

1 Flush any minor wounds with 3 percent hydrogen peroxide, tepid salt water, or clean bottled or tap water.

2 Using tweezers or fingers, remove obvious dirt, gravel, splinters, or other material from the wound.

3 Do not pull penetrating objects, like arrows or pieces of wood or metal, from any wounds. Uncontrollable bleeding may ensue.

4 If hair gets in the wound, apply water-soluble jelly to a pair of scissors, then cut the hair, which adheres to the jelly. Do not use petroleum jelly.

### General bandaging

1 Place a nonstick absorbent pad over the cleaned, dried, and disinfected wound.

2 Wrap with gauze so that the pad does not slip. Do not stretch the gauze tightly when wrapping an injury, since this cuts circulation to the area.

3 Apply a final stretchy or adhesive layer, placing two fingers under it as you start to wrap to prevent you from applying the tape too tightly. Wounds often swell. A seemingly well-applied bandage might be cutting circulation a few hours later. Never let a bandage get wet or leave it on for more than 24 hours unless instructed by your vet.

## A makeshift splint

Splinting a cat's broken leg is very hard. Do not try to straighten leg fractures. Splint them as they are, wrapping the leg in plenty of cotton batting (winding the roll around the leg) or torn strips of blanket or sheeting.

Wrapping rolled newspaper into the fabric adds rigidity, reducing pain and further injury on the way to the vet.

## The basics of bandaging

Bandages keep wounds dry and protect them from further injuries, including self-inflicted damage (biting, chewing, and licking). They also prevent wounds from becoming more contaminated and absorb seeping fluids. Bandaging provides constant mild pressure to control pain or bleeding, and prevents pockets of serum from building up under the skin. Bandaging a cat is usually difficult and best left to your vet.

## Tourniquets are dangerous

Bleeding from a limb can usually be controlled by hand pressure. Tourniquets can be dangerous. If your cat is bitten by a venomous snake, for example, a tourniquet will only increase inflammation. Instead, immobilize the bitten area and apply an ice pack to reduce the size of local blood vessels. *Seek urgent veterinary attention.*

## Moving an injured cat

When lifting and transporting an injured cat, avoid bending or twisting, which might cause further injuries. Wrap the cat in a bulky blanket and place it in a cardboard box for the journey to the vet.

**Fully conscious cats** are notoriously difficult to bandage. If your cat is no exception, you might want to leave this task to your vet.

# Poisoning

- Never use dog insecticides on cats
- Use painkillers only on veterinary advice
- Avoid potentially toxic flowers and plants

All too frequently, humans accidentally poison their cats by giving them human medicines, such as acetaminophen or aspirin, or by using on them insecticides licensed only for use on dogs. Chewing on some houseplants or flowers can also be fatal, as is eating a rodent killed by rodent bait.

It is highly unusual for cats to swallow poison, but they may do so inadvertently, by licking toxic or burning chemicals off their coats, for example.

### Cleaning a cat's coat

Cats can burn their mouths by licking toxic chemicals off their coats. When cleaning a cat's coat, never apply any substance to it, even if it is safe on us, unless you know it is safe for cats. Never apply laundry detergent, paint remover, denatured alcohol, or any similar product to clean a cat's coat.

- **Soft substances:** Wearing rubber gloves, rub plenty of vegetable oil into your cat's coat, then wash it off with soapy, fresh water. Baby shampoo is safe.
- **Hard substances:** If the substance has hardened, cut the fur away.
- **Extensive contamination:** Rub powdered starch or flour in with the vegetable oil to absorb the poison. Then remove the mixture with a wide-toothed comb.

If the coat is contaminated by something other than paint, tar, petroleum products, or motor oil, flush the area for at least five minutes with clean water. Concentrate on the cat's eyes, armpits, and groin.

### Canine flea-control products

Flea-control products for dogs may be toxic for felines. Never apply a flea- or tick-control product to your cat's skin unless the instructions explicitly state that it is safe for use on cats. Canine flea-control products are one of the most common causes of accidental poisoning in cats. Some—for example, concentrated dog insecticides—may cause neurological signs in cats, like twitching and salivating.

### Essential oils can be deadly

Do not dab even a drop of any essential oil on your cat's hair. A single drop of a concentrated product, even one such as tea tree oil (which, in very diluted form, may have therapeutic properties) can prove fatal for your cat.

## Acid, alkali, and petroleum poisoning

If an acid-, alkali-, or petroleum-based poison has been swallowed, do not induce vomiting.

**1** If acid, give egg white, bicarbonate of soda, charcoal powder, or vegetable oil by mouth. If alkali, give egg white or small amounts of citrus-fruit juice, milk, or vinegar. If petroleum, give plenty of water.

**2** Apply a paste of bicarbonate of soda to any burns in the mouth.

**3** Flush acid skin burns for at least 15 minutes with fresh water. Carefully apply diluted vinegar to alkali skin and mouth burns and **seek immediate veterinary help**.

Examples of acid-based products include:
• Rust remover;
• Descaler;
• Oven, toilet, and household cleaners.

Examples of alkali-based products include:
• Paint stripper (caustic soda).

Examples of petroleum-based products include:
• Wood cleaners and preservatives;
• Marble, brass, and paint-brush cleaners;
• Paraffin;
• Gasoline;
• Waterproofer.

## Other poisons

**1** If poison has been swallowed in the last two hours and *is not* acid-, alkali-, or petroleum-based, induce vomiting in the conscious cat by giving a large crystal of washing soda, concentrated salt, or 3 percent hydrogen peroxide. Give your cat one teaspoon every 15 minutes until vomiting occurs (*see Giving medicines, pp.222–3*).

**2** Call your veterinarian for advice. If vomiting has occurred, keep a sample to take to your vet.

**3** Call your vet or the Poison Control Center.

**4** *If the poison is unknown, see your vet as soon as possible.*

## Watch for shock

Signs of shock include: pale or white gums; rapid breathing; weak and rapid pulse; cold extremities; and general weakness.

## Breathing

If smoke or irritants, such as tear gas, have been inhaled, assume that the air passages have been inflamed. Do not put yourself at risk by entering an environment containing dangerous toxic fumes.

**1** For inhaled poisons, watch for signs of shock, keep the airway open, assist breathing, and give CPR if necessary (*see pp.227–8*).

**2** If the cat is convulsing, wrap it in a blanket and **seek immediate veterinary help**.

**3** Do not underestimate the damage caused by inhaling smoke or other irritant fumes. Serious and potentially fatal swelling may affect the air passages even hours later. *After any serious inhalation accident, seek veterinary help.*

## Plants and flowers can be deadly

Make sure you prevent your cat from playfully chewing on household plants or cut flowers. For example, eating just two lily leaves can prove fatal. The problem can be solved by a little monitoring and by providing your indoor cat with boxes of specially grown cat grass to chew on.

## Poisonous plants

Although cats are very careful about what they eat, their passion for grass may lead them to lethal mistakes. The following plants are very dangerous:
• Castor-oil plant
• Dumb cane
• Foxglove
• Lily of the valley
• Mistletoe
• Rhubarb (leaves)
• Stinging nettles
• Jimson weed
• Any type of flower bulbs.

The leaves and wood of the following trees or shrubs are also potentially fatal:
• Azalea
• Cherry laurel
• Hemlock
• Ivy
• Oleander
• Rhododendron
• Wisteria
• Yew.

**Ivy** can be poisonous to cats.

# Skin and coat conditions

- Fleas and ear mites are the most common problems
- The immune system is often involved
- Licking and chewing cause dramatic hair loss

Skin and coat problems account for around 40 percent of visits to the vet. If you notice something is happening to your cat's skin and hair, the cause is often obvious: parasites, particularly fleas and ear mites, are responsible for most irritating skin conditions.

You may never see it, but a single flea can lead to inflammation, scratching, licking, scaling, bleeding and crusting, erosions, ulcers, lumps, and hair loss.

Of course there are many other reasons for any of these visible skin changes. Your vet will carry out a thorough examination and use a number of methods to help diagnose the specific cause of skin disease.

## Making a diagnosis

The simplest way to make an accurate diagnosis is to see if a treatment works. Alternatively, your vet may want to examine your cat's skin with an ultraviolet light for ringworm, or take a smear or culture for bacteria or yeast, a scrape for parasites, or a biopsy for cellular changes. Skin and blood tests, diet, and environment changes are used to help diagnose allergic skin disorders.

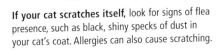

**If your cat scratches itself**, look for signs of flea presence, such as black, shiny specks of dust in your cat's coat. Allergies can also cause scratching.

## Signs of skin disease

Skin disease in cats may be indicated by scratching; hair loss; pigment changes; visible lumps; inflammation; scurfy, dry scales and crusts; or wet erosions and ulcers. Most forms of skin disease cause a multiplicity of these clinical signs.

### Diet and itchiness

An allergy to food might cause itchy skin disease. Feeding a unique "exclusion diet" that a cat has never had before—for example, capelin and tapioca for at least six weeks—is diagnostic of food allergy if itchiness diminishes. Commercially produced exclusion diets are also available; your veterinarian will be able to advise you.

## Common causes of itchy skin

| | |
|---|---|
| Parasites | Fleas; ear and skin mites; harvest mites; mosquito bites; lice; ticks; maggots; *Cheyletiella*. |
| Infections | Bacterial; fungal, especially ringworm; pox virus. |
| Allergies | Flea-allergy dermatitis; food-allergy dermatitis; atopic dermatitis; miliary eczema or eosinophilic granuloma complex; contact-allergy dermatitis; hives; drug eruptions. |

## Ask the vet

**Q:** Can humans be affected by cat parasites?
**A:** Yes, fleas and ticks are as much at home on us as they are on cats. Ringworm is highly contagious from cats to people, and vice versa. Longhaired cats, in particular, often carry ringworm without showing any clinical symptoms. The most common skin problem we get from our cats is allergy. If your eyes and nose run and your skin is itchy, you may be allergic to a protein in your cat's saliva and skin.

## Itchy skin

There is always a good reason for a cat's scratching, but since this can be hard to determine, sometimes the itch (pruritus) gets treated, rather than the cause.

Parasites and allergy are the most common triggers that make a cat scratch itself. Scratching may lead to secondary infection.

As well as scratching, cats respond to itchy skin by excessive licking and grooming. This can lead to hair loss and bleeding open wounds.

Itchy skin may also lead to changes in personality including loss of tolerance, irritability, and aggression.

## Pimples, scaling, and crusting skin

A pustule is a small, elevated, pus-filled pimple; a papule is a small, elevated pimple filled solidly with inflammatory cells. When they burst, they lead to an erosion of the skin. Allergy, not primary bacterial skin disease, is the most common cause of pustules and papules.

Scales are bits of the skin's surface layer that usually flake off as particles of dandruff. Scaling is sometimes associated with seborrhea, the increased activity of the skin's oil-producing glands.

A consequence of skin damage is crusts, which consist of serum, blood, and inflammatory cells.

## The perils of flea bites

The most common cause of scratching and hair loss is a simple flea bite. Some cats are irritated by the minute amount of anticoagulant saliva a flea leaves when it has a meal.

Excessive licking, especially on the back, causes hair loss and local red, crusty scabs. The skin can become broken and ulcerated. You and your vet may never see the flea that triggered the chain of events.

If your cat goes outdoors in warm weather, where other animals have access, assume it is in contact with fleas. Look for fleas by examining for flea dirt in the hair: it looks like black, shiny dust that turns mahogany red when dampened.

**Treatment**: If one of your pets has fleas, mites, or ticks, examine and treat all of your cats and dogs with an insecticide recommended by your vet. Treat your home, too, with an approved product to eliminate immature or resting parasites.

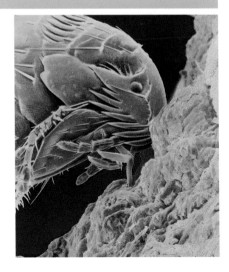

Scaling, crusting, and ulcerating diseases include:
- Ringworm;
- Feline acne;
- Ear mites;
- Bacterial skin infection (pyoderma);
- *Cheyletiella* mange;
- Leishmaniasis;
- Heat, chemical, or sunburns;
- Cancer;
- Immune-mediated disorders, such as pemphigus foliaceus;
- Pox virus;
- Eosinophilic granuloma complex (indolent, or rodent, ulcer).

### Ringworm
Ringworm is very contagious, especially to children. Isolate affected cats in a room in the house until it is cured.
**Treatment:** Bathe your cat in a miconazole-based shampoo. Small affected areas can sometimes be successfully treated by local shaving and topical application of an antifungal cream or lotion (miconazole or ketoconazole). More frequently a cat

**Shaving your cat** from head to tail is one of your lines of defense against the spreading of ringworm. A course of antibiotics is also necessary.

### Ringworm is common in cats
Ringworm is a fungal infection of hair and hair follicles, affecting any part of the body. It occurs more frequently in longhaired cats than in others. Cats can be symptomless carriers, spreading ringworm but not developing any clinical signs of infection. Ringworm does not usually cause itchiness, but it produces crusts with consequent licking and scratching.

needs oral antibiotics, usually griseofulvin, for at least one month, and head-to-tail shaving. Continue treatment until at least two weeks after signs have disappeared or two weeks after fungal culture is negative.

### Hair loss
Alopecia, or hair loss, is usually local or partial. It may occur because hair fails to grow, is scratched or licked out, or spontaneously falls out. The most common cause of hair loss in cats is excessive licking and scratching, which is triggered by itchiness.
Other causes include:
- Parasitic and fungal infection;
- Varieties of mange;
- Ringworm;
- Environmental or behavioral causes;
- Burns;
- Drug reaction;
- Injection-site reaction to corticosteroid or progesterone drug;
- Inherited or hormonal causes;
- Obsessive grooming, excessive licking;
- Overactive adrenal gland;
- Pattern baldness in the Sphynx breed.

### Skin lumps and bumps
The words used to describe skin lumps indicate the seriousness of the lump *(see chart, top right)*.

## Main types of skin lumps

| LUMP | DESCRIPTION | ACTION |
|---|---|---|
| Cyst | A simple, saclike cavity that develops within the skin. | Speak to your vet. |
| Abscess | A deep infection usually caused by a bite or deep scratch. It is usually walled off in a pocket of tissue under the skin. | See the vet within 24 hours. |
| Hematoma | An accumulation of blood under the skin, especially in the ear flaps. May be hot and red, but is rarely painful. | See the vet within 24 hours. |
| Granuloma | A connective tissue response to anything that penetrates the outer layer of the skin. | See the vet within 24 hours. |
| Injection-site sarcoma | A swelling at the site of an injection, usually an inoculation. | See the vet immediately. |
| Eosinophilic granuloma complex (indolent ulcer) | An allergic skin thickening to the lips or chin, often leading to ulceration. | See the vet on the same day. |
| Lipoma | A tumor of fat cells. It occurs anywhere on the body in older individuals. | See the vet within 24 hours. |
| Melanoma | A pigmented skin tumor (although there are also unpigmented melanomas). Almost always malignant. | See the vet immediately. |
| Histiocytoma | A buttonlike raised lump anywhere on the body. | See the vet within 24 hours. |
| Papilloma or wart | A cauliflower-like growth protruding from the skin. | Speak to your vet. |
| Mast cell, basal cell, or squamous cell tumor | Raised masses in the skin, often without distinct edges. | See the vet immediately. |

## Cat-bite wounds

A cat bite is the most common cause of skin swelling, usually around the face, neck, or tail. As with humans, males get into more fights than females. Severe cat-bite abscesses need surgical draining and cleansing and almost always respond well to antibiotics.

## Indolent ulcer or lip ulcer

While the exact cause of this non-itchy ulcer on one or both lips or the chin (eosinophilic granuloma complex) is unknown, the immune system seems to be involved. The condition usually responds to corticosteroids.

## Swollen foot pads

Plasma cell pododermatitis, an ulcerating condition on the foot pads, causes swelling, lameness, and increased licking. It involves the immune system and responds to corticosteroids.

**Unneutered male cats** tend to get into more fights than neutered males or females. Scratches usually heal themselves, but cat bites may lead to infections and abscesses, which require surgical draining.

### Shedding whiskers

Cats naturally drop and replace their vibrissae, their long facial whiskers. It is normal to find shed whiskers in your cat's environment. Frazzled whiskers usually mean that your cat has ventured too close to a source of heat, such as a fire.

# Respiratory disorders

■ Labored breathing is always a serious concern
■ Always check for signs of shock
■ The cause may be outside the respiratory system

Problems may occur anywhere in the respiratory system, from a nose tickle producing a sneeze, to trauma in the chest causing labored breathing and shock. Infections are usually restricted to either the upper or lower respiratory systems, but calicivirus flu infection may lead to secondary pneumonia, especially in kittens. Virtually all conditions of the respiratory system cause sneezing, a nasal discharge, or changes in your cat's regular breathing pattern.

## Sneezing

The most common cause of sneezing, with or without nasal discharge, is one of the cat flu viruses. Cat flu affects between 13 and 20 percent of all cats.

**A pollen-induced tickle** in the nose may cause a harmless sneeze, but do consult your vet if your cat's sneeze is accompanied by nasal discharge.

Allergy and environmental irritation are other common causes.

Although respiratory tract tumors are rare, when they do occur, about 75 percent of them are in the nose and cause sneezing. Cats with some white skin or hair are 13 times more likely to develop nasal tumors than other cats.

Intense sneezing may lead to a nosebleed. *If sneezing is accompanied by any type of discharge, see your vet within 24 hours.*

• **Cat flu:** This is caused by one of three different viruses or a mycobacterium called chlamydia. Reovirus usually causes only mild eye inflammation, while chlamydia causes serious eye inflammation that responds well to a two-week course of antibiotics.

Calicivirus and rhinotracheitis virus cause the most severe signs, including sneezing often, with a thick nasal discharge, sticky or runny eyes,

### Treating a nosebleed

1 Keep your cat quiet and confined.

2 Apply a cold compress (some frozen peas in plastic wrap) for five minutes to the top of the nose, between the eyes and nostrils. (This can be quite difficult to do.)

3 Lightly cover the bleeding nostril with some absorbent material.

4 Do not tilt the cat's head back or pack the bleeding nostril with anything. This will only stimulate sneezing.

and ulcers and open sores in the mouth. There can be fever, loss of smell and appetite, eye ulcers, and even joint swelling and lameness in kittens.

Cats can be protected from serious illness caused by these viruses, but the vaccine does not prevent mild infection.

A cat may recover from calici or rhinotracheitis infection but become a silent carrier, appearing healthy but infecting other cats. Under physical or emotional stress, the herpesvirus form of rhinotracheitis flu may recur when the virus reactivates.

• **Sinusitis:** Secondary bacterial or fungal infection to the sinuses can follow an episode of untreated viral cat flu. The discharge triggers paroxysms of sneezing accompanied by copious amounts of green-yellow material. There may also be eye inflammation (conjunctivitis).

An unusual form of sinusitis is caused by cryptococcus, a fungus found in bird droppings. Sometimes called "pigeon breeder's lung," cryptococcus is a serious health risk to immune-compromised individuals.

Sinusitis is difficult to control even with long-term antibiotic therapy.

## Coughing
Moist, productive coughing is rare in cats, whose cough is usually dry and nonproductive. It may be caused by allergy, pollution, infection, or foreign material in the air passages, but also by fluid in the chest cavity or airways, lung disease or injury, tumors, or parasites.

*If a cough lasts more than a day, or if it recurs, contact your vet for advice.*

## Breathing problems
A breathing problem may be caused by a physical obstruction, chest injury, pneumonia, tumor, trauma, heart failure, poisoning, allergic reaction, pain, smoke inhalation, heatstroke, collapsed lung, or a torn diaphragm. Changes in your cat's regular breathing pattern may also be caused by fear, pain, and shock.

Breathing problems associated with a fluid buildup in the chest or abdomen can develop insidiously. Fluid accumulates because of injury, heart or liver disease, or potentially lethal viral infection.

• **Rapid, shallow breathing:** Cats tend to breath fast after exercise, but also because of shock, poisoning,

**Breathing difficulties** can be seen when a cat hunches itself into an unnatural position, making an effort to inhale more air.

---

**Panting**

Hot, nervous, excited, or exhausted cats sometimes pant. Pain—urethra or bladder pain in cats with lower urinary tract disease, for example—may also induce panting, as may medications such as corticosteroids.

Panting is also associated with heatstroke, while some cats with heart disease have panting episodes.

*Contact your vet the same day if there is any inexplicable panting.*

heatstroke, or pain. *Contact your vet immediately if your cat's breathing rate has suddenly increased without any strenuous exercise.*

• **Labored breathing:** Difficult, labored breathing is always a significant symptom and is usually accompanied by rapid breathing. Causes include heart or airway disease; fluid in the chest cavity; lung disease (including a collapsed lung); trauma, such as a torn diaphragm; and tumors. *See your vet the same day.*

• **Noisy breathing:** In a cat, noisy breathing is always cause for concern.

Causes include fluid in the lungs and obstructions affecting the upper respiratory tract, such as foreign bodies or tumors. *Contact your vet the same day.*

## Respiratory disorders

Other words your veterinarian may use to describe your cat's respiratory disorders:

| | |
|---|---|
| Rhinitis | Inflammation to the nasal passages. Although usually caused by allergy or irritation, *Bordetella bronchiseptica*, the cause of canine kennel cough, is also a common cause of primary bacterial rhinitis in cats. |
| Bronchitis | Inflammation of the bronchi, the major air passages in the lungs. |
| Pleurisy or pleuritis | Inflammation of the lining of the chest cavity. |
| Pulmonary edema | Fluid buildup in the lungs. |
| Pleural effusion | Fluid around the lungs. |
| Pyothorax | Pus in the chest cavity. This infection is acquired either from puncture wounds or via the bloodstream. |
| Pneumothorax | Air in the chest cavity around one or both collapsed lungs. Usually caused by trauma from bites, bullets, arrows, serious falls, or road-traffic accidents. |
| Chylothorax | A milky fluid in the chest cavity, compressing the lungs. Chylothorax has many causes. |

• **Wheezing and asthma:** Wheezing is a sign of a lung problem, an inflammation to the air passages (bronchitis) usually associated with asthma.

Asthma may cause mild coughing and open-mouthed breathing as well as wheezing. Sometimes asthma can develop quickly, causing acute respiratory distress.

Asthma can be triggered by infection or inhaled irritants. It also develops as an immune-mediated allergic response. Siamese cats are more prone than other cats to asthma.

**Treatment:** The condition responds to corticosteroids. Bronchodilators are also used. *If your cat is wheezing or showing signs of an asthmatic attack, see your vet immediately.*

• **Heatstroke:** Cats are attracted to warm places. Always check your dryer before switching it on.

Never leave your cat alone in your car in hot weather, or even in cold sunny weather with the car heater on.

**Treatment:** If your cat has respiratory distress caused by heatstroke, put it in a sink or bath and run water over it, especially over its head, allowing water to fill the sink. Alternatively, place the cat in a pool of water or hose it thoroughly. A pack of frozen peas on the cat's head reduces heat to the brain. *See your vet immediately.*

## Choking

Gagging is caused by throat irritation. Choking occurs when, for any reason, the windpipe is blocked. It is an immediate emergency.

**Treatment:** If the cat is conscious, the first thing you should do—taking extreme care—is use your fingers to try to remove the cause of choking from

the throat. Be aware that a choking cat is in great distress and the risk of being bitten or scratched is enormous. *Seek immediate veterinary help.*
**Other causes:** Swallowing objects is not the only cause of choking. An allergic reaction to an insect bite or sting in the mouth may cause the tongue to swell. Physical injuries to the neck or throat may cause swelling and choking. A cat may choke on its own vomit. In such cases, *seek immediate veterinary help.*

## How to prevent choking

A variety of objects, from needles and thread to bones, may cause choking.

Bone may cause a problem if it gets stuck on the teeth at the back of the mouth. Prevent this by keeping your garbage, indoors or out, in covered cans.

Cats love playing with thread. Always clean up thoroughly after sewing. If you see thread hanging from your cat's mouth, pull gently on it. If it does not come out, do not pull more or cut it. The other end may be in the cat's esophagus, stomach, or even intestines. *See your vet the same day.*

---

### How to treat choking or gagging

If a cat makes choking sounds, has a blue tongue and staring, dilated eyes, and is greatly agitated, treat it at once.

#### CONSCIOUS AND CHOKING

1 Put your cat on its side and, with the palm of your hand, press firmly up and forward just behind the ribcage. This is a feline variation of the Heimlich maneuver.

2 Alternatively, place both hands on either side of the belly and squeeze firmly up and forward.

#### UNCONSCIOUS AND CHOKING

1 With the cat on its side, place the heel of your hand just behind its back ribs.

2 Press sharply to expel the blockage.

3 Carefully use your finger to sweep debris from the cat's mouth.

4 Give CPR if necessary *(see p.228).*

5 *If CPR is necessary, get immediate veterinary assistance.*

#### OBJECT IN MOUTH OF CONSCIOUS CAT

If your cat has unpleasant breath, is pawing at its mouth or rubbing its face on the ground, and is in mild distress, look for an object stuck in its mouth.

1 Wrap the cat in a bulky towel.

2 Open its mouth with one hand, grasping its upper jaw and pressing its upper lips over its upper teeth.

3 Open the cat's lower jaw with your other hand. Push the cat's cheeks between its teeth with the first hand.

4 Use a spoon handle to remove the object stuck on the cat's teeth or in the roof of the cat's mouth.

**Watch** what your cat chews.

# Blood and circulation

- Early treatment prolongs life-expectancy
- Some breeds are more at risk than others
- Clinical signs can mimic signs of natural aging

The most common form of heart disease causes a thickening (hypertrophy) of the bottom of the heart, the ventricles. This occurs more frequently in Persians, Maine coons, and domestic shorthairs.

The most common cause of blood-clotting failure is eating a rodent killed with an anticoagulant rodenticide.

FIV and FeLV infections are the most common causes of nonregenerative anemia (see Blood problems, p.39).

## Hypertrophic cardiomyopathy (HCM)

HCM is the most common form of heart disease, and it affects young to middle-aged cats. It is often undetectable.

Heart disease is usually discovered during a routine annual health checkup. Your vet might hear a faster heart rate and perhaps congestion sounds in the lungs. The pulse feels weak.

If left undiagnosed, the most common indication of HCM is pain, associated with blood-clot formation in the aorta (see below).

**Treatment:** Heart failure is treated with diuretics, such as furosemide, diltiazem, and nitroglycerine ointment. ACE inhibitors, used in canine and human heart disease, can be beneficial. Some cats respond to essential fatty acid (EFA) supplements and the antioxidants selenium and vitamin E. Ask your vet.

## Blood clots

Thromboembolism, a blood clot in the aorta, where the latter divides into the femoral arteries taking blood to the hind legs, is a painful sign of heart failure. Affected cats cry out and cannot use their hindlimbs, which are cool to touch. The prognosis is poor.

A condition called disseminated intravascular coagulation (DIC) causes small blood clots in the body. It is most likely triggered by a disease, such as feline infectious peritonitis (see p.216). DIC is more common than once thought.
**Treatment:** DIC is treated by finding and, if possible, eliminating the cause.

## Diagnostic aids

Diagnosing heart disease in cats improved dramatically with diagnostic aids. X-rays and electrocardiograms (ECGs) are useful, but the most effective tool is ultrasound, or echocardiography.

Doppler ultrasound visualizes blood flow. Ultrasound visualizes the thickened walls of the heart when the heart is not enlarged and there are no associated murmurs.

Blood pressure or culture and other blood tests may also be warranted.

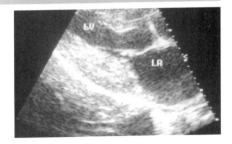

Q: Why is taurine important for heart function?
A: Cats do not naturally produce enough of this crystalline compound for their needs. Low taurine can lead to dilated cardiomyopathy (DCM), a form of heart disease, and is also associated with retinal conditions. Always feed your cat good-quality cat food that is supplemented with taurine, rather than dog food or home cooking, which may be lacking.

## Thyroid and heart disease

An overactive thyroid gland *(see Hyperthyroidism, pp.246–7)* increases the heart's rate and output. Eventually, the heart's chambers dilate and the blood pressure increases. Any cat with an overactive thyroid should be suspected of having heart disease.

**A remarkable weight loss** in your cat might indicate an overactive thyroid gland.

## Anemia

Anemia is a deficiency in red blood cells caused by a lack of production of blood cells, or their destruction. It causes lethargy and weakness.

Anemia results from obvious external bleeding, but also from internal bleeding from ulcers, tumors, parasites, or bowel disease.

The most common cause of anemia is FIV or FeLV infection. Some drugs, such as acetaminophen, and rodent baits are also a cause. A heavy flea infestation can cause severe anemia in kittens.
**Treatment:** The source of blood loss is found and further loss controlled. Blood transfusions are given when needed.

If feline blood is unavailable, a blood-replacer fluid may be used. Your vet will give you more details if necessary.

Rodenticide poisoning is treated with vitamin K injections.

### Feline infectious anemia (FIA)

FIA, or hemolytic anemia, is caused by the organism *Haemobartonella*. Signs include appetite and weight loss, fever, and depression. Most common in FeLV- and FIV-positive cats, FIA is probably spread by bloodsucking parasites.
**Treatment:** Antibiotics clear FIA—also called haemobartonellosis—but the cat remains a carrier, liable to relapse.

**The meaning of heart disease**

Heart disease denotes any abnormal heart condition. Cats may have heart disease but remain free from clinical signs of their condition. Some cats with heart disease never need any medical treatment. Heart disease, however, may lead to heart failure. Treatment is more effective when begun before there are signs of heart failure.

**Dangers from big cats**

*Cytauxzoon felis* is a protozoan blood parasite spread by ticks from subclinically infected bobcats to outdoor domestic cats in south-central and southeastern states. It causes bleeding and fatal anemia. It is not spread from cat to cat, only by ticks, and it is not dangerous to us. Drugs used to treat other protozoal diseases may be beneficial.

# Brain disorders

- Seizures vary from mild to severe
- A seizure can be mistaken for a heart condition
- Brain scans may reveal unexpected brain tumors

The brain, through its connections with the spinal cord and peripheral nerves, coordinates all your cat's activities, thoughts, senses, feelings, emotions, movements, and body functions. Brain damage can lead to behavior changes, seizures, loss of coordination, paralysis, or coma.

## Seizures or fits

A generalized seizure (also called a fit or a convulsion) involves a loss of consciousness accompanied by involuntary muscle contractions, paddling with the limbs, trembling, and face twitching. During a seizure cats frequently salivate, urinate, and defecate. The pupils are dilated. A partial seizure involves only some of these changes and does not necessarily include loss of consciousness.

Seizures may be mild, occur in clusters, or be prolonged, lasting more than five minutes. They may be triggered by a variety of causes, including brain injury, scar tissue on the brain, brain tumor, low circulating calcium, low circulating sugar, hydrocephalus (increased fluid in the brain), migrating intestinal worm larvae, or organophosphate and other poisons.

Epilepsy, the most common cause of a seizure in cats as well as in humans, is caused by an abnormal burst of electrical activity in the brain.

## Types of seizures in cats

A seizure may be stunningly dramatic, or so subtle that it is easily dismissed as a momentary loss of concentration.

Dramatic seizures, often called grand mal, include three stages:
- **Behavior changes:** These include restlessness, anxiety, and hiding.
- **The seizure itself:** This stage involves collapse and loss of consciousness, body rigidity followed by rhythmic jerking, or paddling of all legs, urinating, defecating, and salivating.
- **Return to consciousness:** Even at this point the cat is dazed, confused, and temporarily unable to stand.

**Treatment:** Phenobarbitone is the drug most commonly used to treat seizures. Phenobarbitone levels are monitored through blood samples.

### What to do if your cat has a seizure

1 Protect yourself. A cat may unintentionally bite.

2 Protect your cat. Pull it away from danger by the scruff of its neck. Place something soft, like cushions, around and under the cat's head.

3 For short seizures, comfort your cat with soothing words and soft touch.

4 For seizures over six minutes, comfort the cat, but *see your vet the same day*.

5 After a seizure, let your cat drink.

6 After a seizure, confine your cat to one room and stay with it, especially if it is disoriented.

7 Your touch and soothing words are vitally important for some individuals.

## Seizure, heart attack, or stroke?

If your cat collapses, it may be difficult to determine whether the collapse was caused by a seizure, a stroke, or heart failure. Strokes are not common in cats. Heart failure usually causes visible blanching of the gums. *Whatever the possible cause of collapse, your cat should be seen by a veterinarian as soon as possible.*

## Coma

Coma begins with confusion, evolves through a state of stupor, and leads to loss of consciousness.

It may be caused by a physical injury, such as concussion; heart, kidney, or liver failure; heatstroke or very high fever; high or low blood sugar; lack of oxygen to the brain; or infections, toxins, and other conditions.

*Get emergency veterinary attention.*

## Brain injuries

Often caused by traffic accidents, brain injuries—such as concussion or contusion—can also be caused by poisons, either natural, like snake venom, or man-made, such as insecticides. Meningitis (an inflammation of the tissue around the brain) and encephalitis (an inflammation of the brain itself) also cause brain injuries. Cats with brain injuries behave and move

**To ensure your cat** does not become the victim of a car accident, keep it off the roads. If that is not possible, try to control the times it goes outside.

## Hepatic encephalitis

If the liver does not cleanse the blood efficiently, toxic products remain in the circulation. Some of these can cause encephalitis, inflammation of the brain. Treating the primary liver condition cures the secondary brain disorder.

**The liver's blood-purification** process is vital in ensuring that no toxins that could potentially affect the cat's brain remain in the circulation.

differently. There may be seizures, stupor, coma, or paralysis.

**Treatment:** Treatment depends on the cause. Rabies, the most common cause of encephalitis, can be prevented by routine inoculation. *See your vet at once after any traffic accident.*

## Brain tumors

A very rare condition, brain tumors are reported in about one in 20,000 cats. However, the actual rate may be higher.

Clinical signs include behavior and temperament changes, seizures, circling, changes in movement and gait, altered mental abilities and senses, blindness, and loss of facial nerve control.

With the increasing availability of brain scans, tumors are successfully diagnosed more often.

**Treatment:** A vet aims to control symptoms and improve quality of life. This often includes using anticonvulsants and corticosteroids. To prolong a good quality of life, the vet may suggest radiation therapy, surgery, or both.

# Hormonal disorders

- An overactive thyroid is a geriatric condition
- Thyroid disease may initially benefit the kidneys
- Heart and thyroid disease are often interlinked

Until about 20 years ago, sugar diabetes was the only common feline hormonal disorder, but since then, an overactive thyroid gland, previously unheard of, has become common worldwide in older cats. The reason is unknown.

### Hyperthyroidism

Overproduction of thyroid hormone is now very common in mature cats and, unlike in dogs, it is rarely caused by a hormone-producing-thyroid tumor. What triggers the thyroid to produce too much hormone is still not understood. Theories include food preservatives or additives, environmental exposures to toxins, pollutants, constituents of cat litter, an as-yet-undiscovered viral infection, and even gene mutation. With hundreds of studies completed, there are still no common threads to explain the increased incidence of this condition.

### What an overactive thyroid does

Hyperthyroidism is classified as a geriatric disease in cats. It is rare under seven years of age, uncommon under nine, and most common at 11–13. While it occurs in any breed or sex, in indoor or outdoor cats, on all types of food, and regardless of treatment for parasites or inoculation against infectious diseases, the disease is uncommon in the Siamese and Himalayan. The disease is diagnosed by its clinical signs, a physical examination,

**The thyroids are located** in the neck. You can examine them by holding your cat's head firmly but gently in one hand and by feeling the throat with the thumb and forefinger of the other hand.

and a blood test for thyroid-hormone level. The most common signs are:

| Clinical sign | Frequency |
| --- | --- |
| Weight loss | 90% |
| Enlarged thyroid lobes | 90% |
| Behavior change | 80% |
| Increased appetite | 50% |
| Increased heart rate | 40% |
| Vomiting | 40% |
| Increased thirst | 35% |
| Increased activity | 35% |

An overactive thyroid may now be the most common cause of heart disease in cats. Hyperthyroidism can cause audible heart murmurs and an obviously increased heart rate, but it may also cause less easily diagnosed thickening of the heart muscle (see *Hypertrophic cardiomyopathy, p.242*) or increased blood pressure (hypertension).

**Treatment:** The whole cat, not just the hyperthyroid state, is treated. Depending on the cat, one or, more frequently, both thyroid glands may be surgically removed. Alternatively, drugs are used to suppress excess hormone production. Radioiodine is also effective. Its use involves hospitalizing your cat in a safe environment for a period of time.

### Hyperthyroidism and kidney disease
Early in the disease, the increased heart output in a hyperthyroid cat improves kidney function. This can mask age-related chronic kidney disease. Later, the increased blood pressure of hyperthyroidism accelerates kidney disease. Successful early treatment of the hyperthyroid may accelerate kidney failure in prone individuals. Always check kidney function before deciding on the course of action.

### Underactive thyroid
An underactive thyroid condition, common in dogs, is so rare in cats that textbooks do not even mention it. On the other hand hyperthyroidism, so common in cats, is very rare in dogs.

### Adrenal-gland disorders
The adrenal glands, located beside each kidney, produce cortisol and are vital for life-sustaining metabolic activities.
• **Overactive adrenal glands:** Also known as Cushing's disease, this is a rare condition in cats. Typically, an affected cat drinks and urinates excessively and is constantly hungry. It loses weight and becomes lethargic. Skin may tear easily.
**Treatment:** Cats with pituitary-associated Cushing's are treated "off-label" with mitotane. Alternatively, another drug, ketoconazole, may be used.

### Parathyroid-gland conditions
The paired parathyroid glands, one tiny gland beside each of the two thyroid glands, secrete parathyroid hormone (PTH), which increases blood calcium levels. A hormone called calcitonin, secreted from the thyroid, inhibits PTH production. Medical disease occurs when this balance is upset.

• **Underactive adrenal glands:** Addison's disease—an underactive adrenal gland—is also rare. An affected cat stops eating, loses weight, and vomits. The cat is weak and dehydrated.
**Treatment:** Typically, two types of cortisone, each with its own individual action, are given to treat underactive adrenal glands.

### Cortisone concerns
Many pet owners are concerned about their cats being given cortisone (or corticosteroids or steroids, as some call it) as a treatment for underactive adrenal glands. In excess, cortisone causes all the signs of an overactive adrenal gland. However, such concern is unwarranted when these drugs are used appropriately. Unlike most other drugs, corticosteroids are as close to naturally produced cortisol as medicine offers; this is what makes them so effective. They are most effective in two situations: when the immune system runs amok and needs suppression *(see Allergy, p.271)*, and when the body is in clinical shock. In both circumstances, corticosteroids are lifesavers.

### Sugar diabetes
A lack of insulin causes blood sugar to increase. This resulting condition, also called diabetes mellitus, is the most frequently reported endocrine disease in cats, estimated to affect about one in 200 cats.

# Muscles, bones, and joints

- Injuries are a common cause of problems
- Cats compensate and mask their discomfort
- Any loss of muscle mass is significant

Muscles are more often injured than diseased and are immensely capable of self-repair. Bone might seem inert, but it is living tissue, prone to disease just like other parts of the body. When it is physically damaged—for example, broken—bone has a dynamic ability to repair itself. Joints suffer from wear and tear, even in cats.

## Lameness and limping

Most bone, muscle, and joint disorders cause pain, which leads to lameness. By subtly shifting its weight, a cat hides its lameness—which is the most common sign of muscle, bone, or joint disease—until it can no longer compensate. As a result, bone and joint problems are often already chronic by the time a cat is examined by a vet. For causes of lameness, refer to the chart below.

**Treatment:** Keep outdoor cats in a confined indoor area where they cannot jump up or down until you see your vet.

## Diagnostic procedures

These include X-rays, blood tests, joint fluid analysis, MRI scans, biopsies, or a technique called nuclear scintigraphy to scan bone and surrounding tissue.

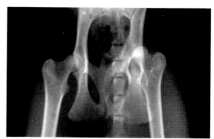

**Trauma is the most common cause** of bone fractures or joint dislocations. Treated immediately, this displaced femoral head can be repositioned.

## Identifying causes of lameness

| CONDITION | CLINICAL SIGNS |
|---|---|
| Cut pads | Licking may or may not occur. |
| Bite wounds and secondary infections | Licking wounds, swelling. Lameness worsens as swelling and infection increase. |
| Sprains and strains | Lameness is sudden, sometimes accompanied by swelling or bruising. May last days to weeks. |
| Osteoarthritis (arthritis) | In older cats. Worst upon awakening. Mostly in shoulders and elbows. |
| Inherited joint diseases | Mostly in Maine coons and Himalayans. Rare. Seldom associated swelling. Worsens over time. |
| Ligament tears | From trauma. Lameness is sudden. |
| Dislocations and fractures | Lameness is sudden. Pain is severe. Accompanied by swelling and inability to bear weight. |
| Bone tumors | Rare. Painful swelling felt through muscles. Worsens with time. Does not respond to rest. |
| Spinal-cord damage | Sudden and almost always caused by trauma. Lameness or paralysis. |

### Dietary supplements and osteoarthritis

There are many products marketed as joint-cartilage protectors (chondroprotectants). The most widely used are glucosamine and chondroitin. These are safe and may be beneficial. Feeding essential fatty acids (EFAs), found in marine fish oil or linseed oil, appears to reduce the need for licensed drugs to control joint pain in some individuals.

### Ask the vet

**Q:** Is acupuncture effective for cats?
**A:** The aim of medical treatments is to reduce physical and emotional stress. Acupuncture certainly reduces discomfort in many people and dogs. Consider this remedy only if you feel your cat will be relieved of stress both by the trips to the acupuncturist and the treatment itself.

## Arthritis

Osteoarthritis—often known simply as arthritis—occurs because the joint cartilage is unable to maintain a healthy state or to repair normally after damage.

Osteoarthritis develops insidiously and, because cats easily redistribute their weight from limb to limb—a trait that goes back to their wild roots, to hide signs of vulnerability—this painful condition can go unrecognized for a long time. You may observe increased irritability before lameness is noted.

**Treatment:** Your vet will determine the exact cause of osteoarthritis.

Fat cats should lose weight. Avoid any games or feeding routines that involve jumping up or down.

Pain control is vital but difficult, since many excellent drugs used for dogs are unsafe in cats. Always remember that aspirin and acetaminophen are dangerous for cats. Many of the newer nonsteroid antiinflammatories are safe, but only in short courses.

Follow veterinary advice to the letter.

### Specific breed conditions

Maine coons and Himalayans are more prone than other breeds to hip dysplasia, an inherited lameness caused by abnormal hip-joint development. Some Scottish folds inherit a painful joint disorder that produces a crouching gait. The Manx can be born with a spinal disorder causing lameness.

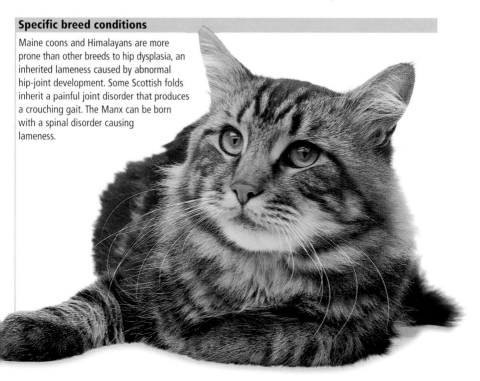

## Multiple inflamed joints

Polyarthritis (inflammation in many joints) is rarer in cats than in dogs. Calicivirus (cat flu) infection sometimes causes short-term polyarthritis in kittens. Rheumatoid arthritis, the most common cause of polyarthritis in humans, is extremely rare in cats.

## Joint injuries

Dislocations, or joint injuries, usually occur as a result of physical trauma, such as traffic accidents or falls.
**Treatment:** If seen shortly after an injury, dislocated bones can be manually replaced under general anesthesia. If left too long, a surgical repair is necessary.

## Osteomyelitis and septic arthritis

These are very rare bone and joint infections. Bacteria get in the joint or bone through bite wounds or via the bloodstream. Symptoms are fever, lethargy, loss of appetite and weight, and heat and swelling in the muscles around the site of the infection.
**Treatment:** Treat with antibiotics for at least six weeks.

## Broken bones

An open fracture is obvious. In a closed fracture, the break is not visible but causes pain and swelling. If it affects a long bone, that leg cannot bear weight. When falling from a great height, a cat may hit its chin on the ground and split the jawbone at the midline.
**Emergency treatment:** Treat shock before attending to broken bones. Remove the cat from danger and cover open wounds, preferably with sterile dressing. If that is not available, use a clean towel.

**Cats love to be in high places,** but falling from even a second-floor windowsill can cause dislocations of joints. Be vigilant.

Avoid movement at the site of the fracture. Heavy toweling usually provides sufficient support for traveling to the vet.

If splinting is necessary, do not try to straighten the break *(see p.231)*.
***See your vet as soon as possible.***

## Bone tumors

Although very rare in cats, bone tumors are almost always malignant. By the time of diagnosis, the tumor is likely to have spread.
**Treatment:** Amputation remains the treatment of choice for primary tumors in long bones.

Alternatively, limb-sparing techniques may also be used to control tumor-associated pain.

## Muscles

Strains, bruising, and tearing are the most common muscle problems, but they are difficult to see, especially in dense coats. They are caused by falling, car accidents, dog attacks, or abuse by people. Minor injuries produce local sensitivity and tenderness, while major damage causes swelling and greater pain. **Treatment:** Parting the hair may reveal reddening caused by muscle damage below. Treatment is cold packs and rest. The most vital treatment is rest (at least three weeks when damage is severe).

## Natural muscle wear and tear

Over time, your cat's muscles naturally shrink and lose their power. Metabolic disorders, especially kidney failure, may affect muscle mass by producing toxins that damage muscle fiber or by depleting the nutrients needed by the muscles.

Hyperthyroidism increases metabolic rate, leading to loss of muscle mass.

If your cat is losing muscle mass for no apparent reason, there is likely to be a medical problem somewhere.

## Spinal-cord damage

Damage to the spinal cord usually occurs after an accident. It can cause loss of voluntary muscle movement, changes in spinal reflexes and muscle tone, muscle shrinkage, and loss of touch and pain sensations. Damage is often irreparable.

## Paralysis

Complete paralysis affecting the hindquarters is not uncommon after severe back injury from traffic accidents, falling, and gunshot wounds. **Treatment:** Traumatic paralysis is treated intravenously with methylprednisolone. Surgery may be beneficial.

### How to handle a back injury

Cats with back injuries may have other life-threatening injuries. Check for these and for signs of shock, then do the following.

**1** Keep the back as straight as possible during the time you are handling the cat.

**2** Find a hard, flat object—such as a piece of plywood—that can be used as a stretcher. It should be small enough to fit in a vehicle. Place this along the back of the injured cat.

**3** With the help of others if they are available, speak soothingly and, grasping the cat by the skin over the hips and the shoulder blades, gently pull it onto the makeshift stretcher.

**4** Secure the cat to the stretcher using heavy-duty tape or similar material over the hips and shoulders. Prevent neck movement if there are neck injuries.

In the absence of hard material for a makeshift stretcher, fold over a large blanket so that it is thick and firm and pull the cat onto it. Secure the cat with tape and lift the blanket from both ends at the same time.

### Naming lameness

Your vet may use any of these words to describe the cause of your cat's lameness.

| | |
|---|---|
| **Strain** | Damage to muscle fibers and tendons. Strains are often accompanied by slight bleeding and bruising. |
| **Sprain** | An injury caused by overstretching a ligament. It causes lameness similar to a muscle strain. Sprains do not involve muscle. |
| **Cramp** | This occurs when muscle filaments, the components of muscle fibers, remain permanently contracted. |
| **Tear** | Ligaments, tendons, whole muscles, or parts of muscles can tear. |
| **Fracture** | The most common fractures cause two or more parts of broken bone to separate. These are called complete fractures. Less common fractures split or compress bone without separation. These are more difficult to diagnose. |
| **Dislocation, or luxation** | This is when a bone separates from its adjoining bone at a joint. Dislocations often involve ligament tears. A partial separation is a subluxation. |

# The mouth and teeth

- Gum disease eventually affects almost all cats
- Prevent problems by letting your cat chew
- Kidney failure can cause gum disease

The mouth and teeth are not only used to eat. They are also used for defense, grooming, exploring, playing, and much more. Consequently, they are vulnerable to a wide variety of potential problems.

## Mouth inflammation or infection

Viral infections, bone stuck between the teeth or in the gums, lack of chewing on natural foods, poor oral hygiene, and metabolic diseases such as kidney failure cause painful stomatitis, leading to bad breath and caution when eating.

**Chewing on skin and bone** massages the gums and scrapes the teeth. In the absence of these natural actions, calculus builds up on the teeth and infection ensues.

**Treatment:** Foreign objects—such as fish bones—are removed, and dental conditions corrected. Secondary bacterial infection is common, so your vet will almost always issue antibiotics.

Underlying metabolic disorders must be controlled to prevent recurrences.

## Foreign objects

Cats enjoy playing with thread, but this can wrap around the tongue. Foreign bodies—such as a needle on the end of thread—can lodge at the back of the throat or stomach. A cat with something in its throat gags, paws anxiously at its mouth, and may drool or vomit.

**Treatment:** If you see thread but cannot see where it ends, do not pull on it. **See your vet at once.** Give first aid if your cat is choking (see Choking, pp.240–41).

### Excessive dribbling

Cats are great dribblers. Anything that tastes unpleasant—such as medicines, some foods, or common household products—may produce a virtual Niagara Falls of saliva. Motion sickness will do the same to some cats. More seriously, poisons affecting the nervous system, mouth disorders, gastrointestinal ailments, and metabolic conditions such as kidney failure may cause excessive dribbling. **If your cat is drooling excessively and you do not know why, contact your vet at once.**

**Excessive** drooling.

## Mouth tumors

Oral tumors are not uncommon in older cats. They may occur in the jaw, on the tongue, or in the roof of the mouth. Jaw tumors must be differentiated from jawbone infection, which occurs as a result of untreated tooth-root infection.

*Any mouth swelling and bad breath should be checked by your vet immediately.*

## Gum disease

At some point, most cats will develop gum disease (gingivitis), brought on by poor dental hygiene and viral infections. Common signs are bad breath (halitosis) and a red line bordering the teeth. Early treatment prevents the development of more serious periodontal disease.

Severe mouth ulcers and gum disease may also be caused by kidney failure. In older cats, check kidney function before embarking on any dental treatment.
**Treatment:** The aims are to eliminate pain and infection, produce a healthy attachment between the gums and teeth, and prolong the use and function of the teeth. Teeth are scaled and polished. Those teeth with "neck lesions," the equivalent of cavities in humans, are best removed.

### Chewing is healthy

The best way for a cat to keep its teeth and gums in good condition is to use them to tear, gnaw, and chew. This is vitally important for young cats with gum inflammation and viral infections.

There are pros and cons to giving your cat bones to chew. In my experience, most cats are sensible and chew bones thoroughly. It is only the rare cat that wolfs down bones, doglike, and is at risk of a gastrointestinal impaction.

### Split hard palate

When a cat falls from a great height, its chin often hits the ground. The cat may seem fine, but look inside at the roof of the mouth. The force of landing frequently splits the hard palate down the middle. This injury usually needs a surgical repair.

## Tooth-root abscess

Upper premolars are most susceptible to abscesses. An abscess initially causes swelling under the eye. Eventually the abscess breaks through the skin. Pus and blood drain out, often lessening the pain.
**Treatment:** Usually the tooth is removed.

### Lip ulcers

An erosion on one or both upper lips (rodent ulcer or, more accurately, eosinophilic granuloma complex) is a surprisingly common immune-system condition. The chin may also be affected by swelling. The problem is treated with corticosteroids.

### Troubleshooting mouth and tooth problems

| PROBLEM | POSSIBLE CAUSES | SEE VET |
|---|---|---|
| Slow or selective eating | Any mouth condition that causes pain. | Within 24 hours |
| Eating with head tilted or dropping food then eating it | Pain on one side of the mouth. | Within 24 hours |
| Difficulty opening the mouth | Head, jaw, or neck injury; tumor; bite; abscess; or penetrating foreign body. | Same day |
| Drooling saliva | Most mouth and gum diseases; foreign object in the mouth; rabies; excess heat; tumor; saliva cyst; heat injury. | Same day |
| Gagging | Foreign object; tumor. | Immediately |
| Bad breath | Periodontal disease; foreign object; viral or metabolic disease. | Within 24 hours |

# Stomach problems

- Vomiting has causes inside and outside the stomach
- Withhold food and water from vomiting cats
- Hairballs are the most common cause of vomiting

The most common cause of stomach problems in cats is related to grooming, which can lead to swallowing hair and possible contaminants from the fur. Both can cause vomiting.

Playing with wool, needles, and thread can cause foreign-body complications associated with retching or vomiting.

If the cat's intestines are involved, diarrhea often accompanies vomiting.

**Eating grass** is a common cause of vomiting in cats. Often they will do this to help bring up hairballs.

### Vomiting

There are many reasons why a cat vomits. Some of the causes are minor, and others are life-threatening.

While simple vomiting is usually insignificant, persistent vomiting is more problematic *(see chart, right)*.

Some cats are extremely noisy when they vomit, howling or even shrieking loudly. Generally speaking, this is a feline trait and not necessarily associated with the severity of the problem.

• **Acute vomiting:** Cats naturally vomit up material that should not be in the stomach, such as hairballs and sometimes worms.

Acute vomiting preceded by dribbling may occur as a result of motion sickness.

**Treatment:** With cats that are otherwise healthy, simply withhold food and water for a couple of hours after a vomiting episode.

| Principal causes of vomiting | |
|---|---|
| **TYPE** | **UNDERLYING CAUSES** |
| Dietary causes | Eating grass; food intolerance; true allergy. |
| Gastric disorders | Inflammation (gastritis); parasites; ulcers; foreign bodies; tumors. |
| Intestinal disorders | Inflammation (inflammatory bowel disease, colitis); parasites; foreign bodies; tumors; infections (FIE); telescoping of intestines (intussusception); constipation. |
| Other abdominal disorders | Inflamed pancreas (pancreatitis); inflamed peritoneum (peritonitis); inflamed liver (hepatitis); abdominal tumors. |
| Metabolic and hormonal conditions | Kidney failure; liver diseases; diabetes; underactive adrenal gland (hypoadrenocorticism); overactive thyroid (hyperthyroidism); blood poisoning (septicemia, endotoxemia); electrolyte and acid-based upsets; anxiety and phobias. |
| Poisons and drugs | Aspirin; antifreeze (ethylene glycol); heart medications (digitalis); chemotherapy drugs; some antibiotics. |

## Drugs can cause problems

The antibiotic doxycycline can possibly cause a narrowing of the esophagus in cats, leading to regurgitation of food. Therefore, this medication, excellent for dogs, should be avoided in cats.

• **Intermittent vomiting:** This may be caused by a food allergy or by more serious conditions, such as metabolic diseases, ulcers, or tumors. *Consult your vet if intermittent vomiting occurs over several days.*

• **Persistent vomiting:** Repeated vomiting may be caused by a simple stomach irritation or a life-threatening obstruction. *It warrants an immediate visit to the vet.*

• **Projectile vomiting:** This is often caused by an obstruction preventing food from leaving the stomach. *See your vet the same day.*

• **Vomiting blood:** Vomiting blood suggests stomach or small-intestine ulceration, poisoning, foreign bodies, tumors, or a serious infection. *See your vet the same day.*

• **Vomiting only froth or bile:** This may be a mild form of allergic gastritis. Affected cats vomit bile or froth, often at the same time each day, but are otherwise healthy.
**Treatment:** Corticosteroids are given until a diet change is effective.

## Ask the vet

**Q:** Helicobacter bacteria cause stomach ulcers in people. Do they do the same in cats?
**A:** Helicobacter bacteria are certainly found in lots of healthy and unhealthy cats. The helicobacter species that causes stomach ulcers in us, *H. pylori*, has been found in pet cats, but never in feral cats. Pets probably pick it up from us rather than the other way around. In any case, to date there is no evidence that helicobacter is anything other than a rare opportunist cause of disease in cats.

## Treating vomiting

Withhold food for between four and 24 hours after vomiting, depending on the cause and severity of vomiting and the age and fitness of the cat. Give small amounts of water frequently. Powdered electrolyte solution mixed in drinking water is also beneficial.

When reintroducing food, give small, frequent portions of tasty, low-fat, low-protein soft food, which helps food leave the stomach and enter the intestines.

**After frequent vomiting** some cats are reluctant to eat or drink. Encourage intake by offering the cat a tasty liquid, such as chicken broth.

## Regurgitation

Different from vomiting, regurgitation occurs when food in the esophagus is almost effortlessly expelled back through the mouth. This can be mistaken for vomiting. Esophagus problems are rare in cats. When they do occur, they usually develop as a consequence of local damage from foreign objects, such as bone or even sewing needles, lodged in the esophagus.
**Treatment:** Cats are treated with frequent feeds of small, high-calorie diets provided on elevated platforms so that gravity assists the food through the esophagus. Drugs are sometimes used to stimulate the normal activity of the esophagus.

# Intestinal disorders

- Diarrhea may be trivial or life-threatening
- Bowel problems can originate outside the bowels
- The liver and pancreas are vital for digestion

The intestines are a vital part of the immune system, and some inflammatory bowel diseases and dietary allergies are really manifestations of immune disorders.

## Diarrhea

Damage to the digestive system may result in diarrhea. It may be painful, be accompanied by vomiting, or contain blood or mucus. It can be associated with an increase or loss of appetite, normal behavior, or severe lethargy. From its characteristics, one can reasonably accurately determine the causes of diarrhea, which include:
- Eating grass;

- Dietary allergy or sensitivity;
- Food poisoning;
- Parasites (such as *Giardia*);
- Viruses (FPV, FeLV, FIV, FCoV);
- Bacteria (such as *Campylobacter*);
- Drugs;
- Hyperthyroidism.

**Treatment:** Diarrhea is treated symptomatically. The known cause is eliminated. Withhold food for a few hours, but allow your cat to drink. Fluid therapy is essential when acute diarrhea is caused by FIE (feline infectious enteritis) infection (see p.214).

Many experts recommend feeding a cat its regular diet to provide the gut flora with familiar food. Antibiotics

## Identifying intestinal problems through stool analysis

| CHARACTERISTIC | CAUSE |
|---|---|
| **Consistency:** | |
| Watery | Rapid transit through gut |
| Covered in jelly (mucus) | Large-intestine condition (colitis) |
| Oily, greasy | Malabsorption condition (fat) |
| Bubbly | Gas-forming bacteria in intestines |
| **Colour:** | |
| Tarry, black | Bleeding from upper digestive tract |
| Clots or bright red | Bleeding from lower digestive tract or anus |
| Pasty, light | Lack of bile from liver |
| Yellow-green | Rapid transit through gut |
| **Frequency and quantity:** | |
| Small amounts very frequently | Irritation to colon |
| Large amounts 3–4 times daily | Digestion/malabsorption condition in small intestine |
| **Odor:** | |
| Normal | Rapid transit/malabsorption |
| Unpleasant | Bacterial action (fermentation), blood |
| **Other signs:** | |
| Vomiting | Gastroenteritis |
| Weight loss | Malabsorption, increased metabolism |
| No weight loss, good appetite | Large-intestine condition |

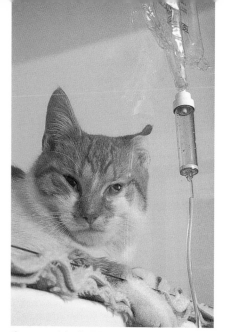

If your cat is badly dehydrated by persistent diarrhea or vomiting, it may need to be put temporarily on an intravenous drip.

are never used unless bacterial infection is suspected.

*Consult your vet at once if your cat is lethargic, has a fever, or passes blood.*

### Ask the vet

Q: Does milk cause diarrhea?
A: Any dietary change may cause diarrhea. Milk may cause it in cats that no longer produce sufficient amounts of the enzyme lactase, as they did as kittens. If your cat suffers from diarrhea when it drinks milk, feed it lactose-free milk for cats, available in supermarkets.

### Inflammatory bowel disease (IBD)

This is a group of increasingly diagnosed diseases related to the immune system. Affected cats, often middle-aged, usually have chronic vomiting and diarrhea, defecate more frequently, lose weight and litter training, and look malnourished.
**Treatment:** Your vet will start your cat on a hypoallergenic diet and prescribe

immune-suppressing drugs, such as corticosteroids.

Cats with IBD respond to dietary supplements. Antioxidants, such as zinc, selenium, and vitamins A and E, may improve the immune system. Bioflavonoids, such as proanthocyanidin, may work with vitamin C to support immune function and scavenge free radicals. N-acetyl glucosamine may reduce inflammation. Vitamins B12 and K and folate are also beneficial.

### Intestinal obstruction

The most common cause of this is a tumor invading the gastrointestinal system. Affected cats may vomit, have diarrhea, and lose weight. By then, your vet will probably be able to feel a lump in the abdomen. Surgically removing the mass and associated tissue is successful if it has not spread elsewhere.

### Constipation

Although not uncommon, constipation can be serious if the colon dilates into a megacolon and loses its function. In most cases the reason for megacolon is unknown, but it can be caused by diet, trauma, and neuromuscular disease. Affected cats vomit, appear depressed, stop eating, and strain to pass stools.

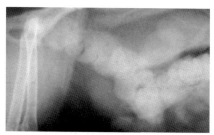

**Constipation is reasonably common** in older cats and may have any of several causes. This X-ray clearly shows unexpelled feces in the colon.

## Treatment for constipation

1 Mild cases are treated with enemas given by the vet. Do not do this at home. Given incorrectly, an enema can cause severe damage.

2 Soak dry food in equal parts of water and feed only when it is fully absorbed. This increases fluid consumption.

3 In multicat households make sure each cat has its own litter box and clean it regularly.

4 A little cow's milk, bran fiber, or psyllium (ask your pharmacist) added to a cat's diet may act as a laxative or increase the frequency of defecation.

5 Use a mild laxative, such as lactulose, as instructed by your veterinarian.

6 In the most serious instances, surgical removal of the colon is an option. Cat owners say their cat's personality and elimination habits return to normal.

## Anal-sac irritation

Anal-sac blockage or infection causes a cat to groom its bottom obsessively, so much so that it licks the hair off its hind legs and belly. Irritation from tapeworms causes similar, but less intense, licking. Infection causes a swelling on the affected side, to the left or right of the anus.

**Treatment:** Uncomplicated blocked anal sacs are emptied by squeezing by your vet. If the sac swells and bursts through the skin, producing a draining abscess, your veterinarian will prescribe antibiotics.

## Distended belly

Obesity is the most common cause of a distended abdomen. Other reasons are: tumors; accumulation of fluid (ascites), which develops most frequently as a result of feline infectious peritonitis (*see right*) or liver disease; and a general enlargement of organs as a result of, for example, womb infection (pyometra),

immune disorders (enlarged spleen), or an overactive adrenal gland (enlarged liver). *See your vet if your cat's abdomen is distended and you do not know why.*

## Feline coronavirus (FCoV) and feline infectious peritonitis (FIP)

Some strains of FCoV cause mild diarrhea. Others cause a serious, often fatal infection called feline infectious peritonitis (FIP). Shared litter boxes and mutual grooming are the ways these viruses spread in multicat households. FIP occurs in two different forms: dry, usually affecting the lungs, and wet, leading to fluid accumulation in the abdomen (ascites).

**Prevention and treatment:** One or two cats living in a home are at little risk. If more cats are introduced, however, they should be blood-tested for FCoV. Limit fecal contamination by cleaning the litter box daily and keeping the cats' food away from their litter box(es). The nasal vaccine is not recommended for routine use but could, in theory, be useful for vaccinating FCoV-negative cats before they enter FCoV-positive environments. Immune-suppressing drugs, such as corticosteroids, are at the heart of treatment. Unfortunately, once ascites develops, any form of treatment is unlikely to be successful.

## Anorexia

A loss of appetite (anorexia) can be caused by a range of problems inside or outside the digestive tract. They include pain, injury, disease, fear, stress, an unpalatable diet, and loss of the sense of smell. *You should always contact your vet if your cat stops eating.*

**Obesity in cats,** especially females, can lead to the common life-threatening condition hepatic lipidosis.

## Liver and pancreatic disorders

Small-bowel disease can ascend into the bile duct, which goes to the liver, and is also connected to the pancreas. Uniquely in cats, small-bowel disorders can lead to pancreas and liver disease. Also, many conditions cause hepatic lipidosis, the most common liver disorder in cats.

• **Hepatic lipidosis (HL):** HL occurs twice as often in females, especially fat females, as in males. It can be triggered by poor nutrition, obesity, other diseases, or simply not eating. Fat cells accumulate in the liver and affected cats lose their appetite, lose weight, and refuse to eat. **Treatment:** HL is life-threatening. Cats must eat, and the most effective way to ensure good hydration and nourishment is by surgically installing a stomach tube (gastrostomy) that remains in place for about a month.

• **Liver shunt:** After damage from chronic liver disease, blood vessels from the intestines may bypass the liver. Blood does not get purified of substances from the intestines, such as ammonia. These circulating substances cause brain inflammation. Affected cats dribble and stagger, act lethargic, experience seizures, or twitch. **Treatment:** This condition can be treated by diet management or surgery.

• **Drug-induced liver disease:** Some drugs, safe to humans and dogs, are toxic to cats, causing hepatitis. They include:
• Acetaminophen;
• Aspirin;
• Diazepam (Valium);
• Iron supplements;
• Glipizide (for diabetics);
• Ketoconazole (for ringworm);
• Methimazole (for hyperthyroidism).

## Pancreas problems

Chronic (ongoing) inflammation is the most common pancreatic disease in cats. Affected cats have nonspecific signs, like vomiting, diarrhea, lethargy, and weight loss. Diagnostic blood tests are not reliable in cats. A biopsy is needed for an accurate diagnosis. Chronic pancreatitis usually accompanies other liver and bowel diseases.

Cats rarely suffer acute (sudden) inflammation to the pancreas or exocrine pancreatic insufficiency, the most common pancreas disorders in dogs.

• **Diabetes mellitus:** Insulin, produced in the pancreas, helps body cells absorb glucose. A lack of insulin causes blood sugar to increase and leads to diabetes mellitus (sugar diabetes), which affects about one in 200–400 cats. High blood sugar alone is not diagnostic for diabetes. Even mild stress increases a cat's blood-sugar value. Diabetes typically causes increased drinking and urinating, combined with weight loss. The onset is slow and often missed by cat owners. **Treatment:** Diabetes is often treated with insulin injections and a high-protein, reduced-fat diet. Oral drugs to reduce blood sugar can be effective.

Once diabetes-induced cataracts develop, their progress is irreversible.

# Urinary tract disorders

■ Increased drinking is always significant
■ Pain accompanies many bladder problems
■ Chronic kidney disease is usually dangerous

Kidney failure occurs when more than three quarters of kidney function *(see pp.40–41)* has been lost. It may happen suddenly, but more often it is slow and is called chronic. Kidney failure may result from injury, disease, or immune disorder, but it is also an inevitable consequence of advancing years.

Lower urinary tract disease, involving the bladder and urethra, affects one in 100 cats and can be controlled by managing stress and altering the diet and acidity of the urine.

### Urine characteristics are important
The amount and quality of urine give clues to problems in the kidneys or lower urinary tract. Increased urinating can be caused by kidney failure, but also by:
- Diabetes mellitus *(see p.259);*
- Liver disease (hepatitis, *see p.259);*
- Womb infection (pyometra, *see p.264);*
- Overactive adrenal glands *(see p.247);*
- Underactive adrenal glands *(see p.247);*
- Drugs or diet;
- Pain, fever, or altered behavior;
- Pituitary, or antidiuretic-hormone-deficiency, diabetes—very rare in cats.

### Blood in the urine
If you notice blood in your cat's urine (hematuria), *see your vet the same day.* Medical reasons for hematuria include:
- Trauma;
- Severe inflammatory urinary tract disease;
- Bladder or kidney stones;
- Poisoning from coumarin rodenticide, such as warfarin.

### Acute kidney failure
This life-threatening condition is usually caused by a condition outside the urinary tract, like heart failure, shock, severe infection, or systemic diseases such as advanced tumors. Certain poisons—for example, ethylene glycol antifreeze—cause sudden kidney failure.

An affected cat may lose its appetite, become weak and lethargic, and collapse. There may be vomiting and diarrhea. Because acute kidney failure occurs so suddenly, increases in thirst and urination are not seen.
**Treatment:** Immediate intravenous fluid therapy is vital for survival. *Any cat showing the above signs should be seen by a vet as quickly as possible.*

**Ethylene glycol antifreeze** is tasty to some cats—and also toxic to their kidneys. Whenever possible, control your cat's activities.

## Chronic kidney failure

This is a slow, insidious disease, usually affecting older cats.

Early symptoms are increased drinking and urinating, a little slowing down and weight loss, and a poor coat. Listlessness increases and mild retching begins, followed by vomiting froth or meals. Mouth ulcers also develop. Body tremors or loss of fine balance develop and mild seizures start to occur.

**Treatment:** Diet management is the main treatment for chronic renal failure *(see right)*. As well as this, fluids are sometimes given, often under the skin (subcutaneously). Because many drugs are cleared from the body by the kidneys, the doses a cat receives should be reevaluated.

**One of the early signs** of chronic kidney failure is an increase in the amount of water your cat drinks. If you notice this, keep an eye open for the other symptoms, and see your vet if you are concerned.

### Ask the vet

**Q:** What is uremia?
**A:** Uremia is an accumulation of urine in the blood. It occurs at a late stage in kidney failure. The more advanced uremia is, the more grave the prognosis. Typical signs of uremia include:
• Excess thirst and drinking;
• Loss of appetite and weight;
• Lethargy and/or apathy;
• Ammonia breath;
• Pale gums and mouth ulcers;
• Vomiting and/or diarrhea.

### Chronic renal failure and anemia

The kidneys produce a hormone called erythropoietin, which stimulates bone marrow to produce red blood cells. Chronic kidney failure reduces erythropoietin production, leading to fewer red blood cells and anemia.

### Diet and kidney disease

Nutritionists say that a low-protein diet has minimal effect on kidney failure.

Uremia is managed by maintaining nitrogen balance, and this is done by reducing phosphorus in the diet. Because protein is a major source of phosphorus, feeding a low-phosphorus diet with moderate amounts of high-quality protein is recommended.

Supplementing the diet with Omega-6 polyunsaturated fatty acids (PUFA) appears to damage kidneys, while Omega-3 PUFA supplementation seems to protect the kidneys and possibly lower blood pressure. Omega-3 PUFA supplements or diets already containing these fatty acids may be an effective therapy for cats with kidney failure.

Free radicals damage kidney-cell membranes. Antioxidant dietary supplements, which are found in most specialty cat foods, scavenge free radicals, reducing kidney damage.

Introduce new food gradually, mixing the new with the old. Make the food palatable by adding a drop of hot water, or a little water from a can of unsalted tuna, before hand-feeding it to your cat.

### Polycystic kidney disease (PKD)

Over 40 percent of Persian cats have PKD, an inherited condition. It may cause clinical signs of kidney failure and is treated in the same way. Breeding Persians should be screened by ultrasound examination for PKD. Your vet will carry out an ultrasound examination or refer your cat for testing.

## Kidney-disease prevention

To reduce risk and increase early detection of kidney disease:

**1** Accurately weigh your mature cat every three months. Even a 8-oz (225-g) loss can be significant.

**2** Prevent gum disease *(see p.253)*. It could lead to bacteria in the blood damaging the kidneys.

**3** Have your vet routinely run a blood test to check your mature cat's kidney function.

**4** Examine breeding Persians and Persian crosses by ultrasound to detect any signs of polycystic kidney disease (PKD).

**Straining on the litter box** is often a sign that your cat is suffering from some form of lower urinary tract problem. It is always worth seeing your vet.

## Lower urinary tract disorders

Feline lower urinary tract disease (FLUTD) is a collection of conditions affecting the bladder and urethra. In any year, about 1 percent of the cat population suffers from a form of FLUTD. Some of these cats have painful, even life-threatening urinary tract obstructions, but the majority have nonobstructive FLUTD.

While FLUTD can cause nonobstructive cystitis in any cat, it is more likely to cause a serious, obstructive FLUTD in a neutered, overweight male who gets little exercise, eats dry food, uses an indoor litter box, and has no access to the outdoors.

## Pain or difficulty urinating

Dysuria, which is the technical term for pain or difficulty urinating, may cause your cat to:
• Strain;
• Squat longer on the litter box;
• Dig more obsessively in the litter;
• Lick the penis or vulva more frequently;
• Cry out;
• Resent being touched;
• Visit the box more frequently;
• Pass blood, sediment, or mucus.

## Nonobstructive FLUTD

About 65 percent of cats suffering from cystitis have a condition called idiopathic cystitis, with changes to the lining of the bladder. The bladder lining is a thin film of protective mucus (glycosaminoglycan, or GAG) that prevents microbes or crystals from sticking to the bladder wall.

Interaction between the nerve supply to the bladder lining and potentially noxious substances in the urine (such as crystals) leads to a bladder-wall inflammation and either a need to urinate more frequently or difficulty in urinating.

Most instances spontaneously resolve within five days, but some progress to complete blockage. All instances are painful.

## Obstructive FLUTD

Sand (crystals) or stones (uroliths) in the bladder account for about 10 percent of urinary tract obstructions. In 60 percent of cats, material leaks from the inflamed bladder wall, producing a substance that can accumulate in the urethra, forming a urethral plug.

If a cat is also producing some urinary crystals, these accumulate in

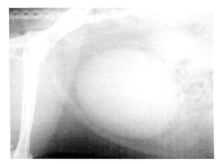

**Mineral sediment** in the urethra can prevent urine from leaving the bladder. The resulting distended bladder causes the cat great pain.

the plug, making it even more likely to cause a full obstruction.

Finding a few crystals in urine is not significant on its own unless there is associated disease or a history of previous disease. Equally, finding no crystals does not rule out a stone in the bladder. Some stones shed no crystals.
**Treatment:** This involves eliminating the underlying cause. This may be stress in some individuals (*see bottom right*), and stone formation in others.

Since infection is a rare cause, antibiotics are rarely needed, although some antibiotics have a pain-relieving, antispasmodic effect.

A cat with urinary tract obstruction is in obvious pain. Straining can sometimes be mistaken for constipation and straining to defecate. Using a catheter, your vet will try to push the blockage back into the bladder. If this is not possible, the distended bladder is reduced by drawing off retained urine via a needle inserted through the abdominal wall.

Urine pH is adjusted through diet and carefully monitored. This can be done daily at home with pH dipsticks. (Urine pH naturally goes up a few hours after each meal.)

### Types of FLUTD stones

Struvite (triple phosphate) is the most common stone, accounting for about 50 percent of problems. Some veterinary diets dissolve small struvite uroliths. Large stones should be surgically removed.

Calcium oxalate stones account for about 40 percent of uroliths. They cannot be dissolved by dietary means and may, if too large to pass through the urethra, require surgical removal.

Other stones, accounting for the remaining 10 percent of uroliths, are of varying types.

It is important to protect the layer of mucus that lines the bladder wall. In theory, this may be possible by adding GAG supplements such as N-acetyl glucosamine (cystease) to the diet. An alternative is pentosan polysulphate (cartrophen) injections.

### Diet and lower urinary tract disease

Major cat-food manufacturers make diets for cats with stone problems. Whatever the condition, treatment involves increasing water intake. This is most easily done for cats on dry food diets by switching to canned food, which is usually about 80 percent moisture.

### Ask the vet

**Q:** Does stress play a role?
**A:** Yes, it probably does. In one study several stress factors, such as diet changes and new pets, were found to be associated with idiopathic cystitis. The most prominent stress factor was living with another cat with which there was conflict. Reduce stress by avoiding or eliminating known causes. The antidepressant amitriptyline is beneficial in some circumstances.

# The reproductive tract

- Many conditions are life-threatening in females
- Infection is most likely to occur after ovulating
- Retained testicles are common in Persian cats

A womb infection is the most common reproductive disorder in intact females. If undiagnosed, it can be life-threatening.

Abortion in breeding queens can be triggered by almost all the common feline viruses.

Cancers in the male or female reproductive tracts are uncommon compared to in dogs or humans.

## Female medical conditions

The most common female reproductive disorders—womb infection and mammary cancer—are both life-threatening. Early neutering eliminates risk, which is why neutered females live considerably longer than intact females.

- **Womb infection (pyometra):** A womb infection often occurs within four weeks of calling, whether or not the cat has mated, although it is more likely after a cat has ovulated.

The earliest sign of impending womb problems is a mucus discharge (mucometra). The cat is clinically fine, but inside the womb mucus-producing cells have multiplied, creating a condition called cystic endometrial hyperplasia. This does not cause clinical illness, but mucus is an ideal environment for the multiplication of bacteria. Either in that season or the next, bacteria do multiply, turning the mucus to pus.

If the cervix remains open, as in about 60 percent of cases, pus escapes from the womb, through the vagina, and out of the vulva. This is an open pyometra. If the cervix has clamped shut, pus builds up in the womb. This is a closed pyometra, with faster developing clinical signs. A cat with pyometra:

- Has increased thirst;
- Urinates more frequently;
- Has a decreased appetite;
- Rests more;
- Has a distended abdomen;
- Often has a normal temperature;
- Has a pale green, creamy to bloody vaginal discharge if the cervix is open.

Left untreated, shock ensues. Signs of shock include:

- Vomiting;
- Rapid breathing;
- Racing pulse;
- Fever;
- Collapse.

**Treatment:** An emergency ovario-hysterectomy is the treatment of choice

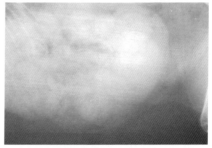

**The middle of this X-ray** shows the uterus. The absence of visible bones means that its enlargement is due to fluid buildup rather than pregnancy.

for all closed pyometras and most open ones. A breeding queen with an open pyometra may be treated with a natural prostaglandin (PGF 2alpha) and antibiotics. The natural prostaglandin affects many other tissues and appears to cause cats considerable distress.

• **Abortion:** Viral agents such as feline herpesvirus (rhinotracheitis), infectious enteritis (panleukopenia), infectious peritonitis (FIP), FIV, and FeLV are the most common causes of abortion.

Also, the rickettsia *Coxiella burnetti*, contracted from tick bites, may cause abortion. About 20 percent of outdoor cats are exposed to this agent. *C. burnetti* is transmissible to humans, causing Q fever, which can lead to heart infection.

While the risk is low, with outdoor cats exposed to ticks always wear gloves, and preferably a mask, when attending to an aborting cat or one that has a litter of stillbirths.

• **Mammary tumors:** While many mammary tumors appear as hard, mobile masses under the skin near teats in mammary tissue, the most aggressive ones cause rapid, painful swelling. Visually, it is not possible to differentiate this form of tumor from mastitis and, since it is often also infected by bacteria, antibiotics offer an initial reduction in swelling and pain.

**Prevention:** The risk of mammary tumors is negligible in cats spayed before their first season. Spaying after the first season still dramatically reduces risk. Subsequent seasons increase risk. Spaying after approximately six estrous cycles does not reduce risk.

**Treatment:** Removal and analysis is the only guaranteed way of diagnosing mammary tumors. Separate masses should be removed by regional (partial) mastectomy. Aggressive, inflamed tumors are particularly unpleasant and need wide excision. Most mammary tumors are malignant.

## Male medical conditions

Few medical conditions affecting the male cat's reproductive system are life-threatening. This is why early neutering of males does not increase their life-expectancy. The most common problem in males is retained testicles.

• **Undescended testicles:** In the fetus, testicles develop inside the abdomen, near the kidneys. As the fetus develops, they migrate down into the scrotum. Migration occurs by the time of birth or a few days after, but it is possible for one or neither testicle to migrate.

While only about 1 percent of all male cats have undescended or partly descended testicles, this is a problem in almost 30 percent of Persian toms. This condition is inherited, and such toms should not be used for breeding.

**Treatment:** Partly descended and abdominal testicles are removed.

**Male Persian cats** suffer an unusually high incidence of undescended testicles.

# Eye disorders

■ Minor eye problems can indicate major diseases
■ Eye ulcers can be caused by respiratory diseases
■ Blindness may result from diabetes or hypertension

Viral and chlamydial eye infections and fight wounds are the most common causes of eye disorders. An inflammation to the iris (uveitis) is often an indication of systemic disease, such as generalized viral infection or cancer.

## Understanding the signs

Eye disorders are among the easiest to recognize: many involve inflammation to the conjunctiva, the membrane that covers the cornea. Check with your vet if you see any of the following—they may indicate a primary eye disorder; a secondary one, such as FIV, FeLV, or FIP infection; or even cancer:

• Squinting;
• Discharge;
• Cloudiness;
• Redness or inflammation;
• Visible third eyelid;
• Tear overflow;
• Bulging or sunken eye;
• Crust or inflammation around the eye;
• Deterioration or loss of vision;
• Increased irritability associated with pain.

### Ask the vet

Q: What does it mean when my cat's third eyelids are visible?
A: While this may indicate an eye problem, it is more likely to suggest a generalized condition often affecting the gastrointestinal system. Certain chemicals and drugs cause the third eyelids to become visible.

### Causes of eye discharge

The color and consistency of the eye discharge give good clues to the cause.

| | |
|---|---|
| **Watery** | A clear, colorless discharge usually indicates physical or allergic irritation. |
| **Jellylike mucus** | Irritation or infection triggers increased protective-mucus production. |
| **Yellow-green** | This is pus. Bacterial infection is present and must be treated. |
| **Staining to the hair below the eyes** | Tears overflow when tear drainage is blocked. This is called epiphora and is most common in flat-faced Persians. |

**Confident cats** have head-to-head cat fights. Injuries, particularly to the conjunctiva and third eyelid, are not uncommon.

## Corneal injuries

Damage to the corneas, known as
ulcerative keratitis, can be caused either
by infection or during fights. Local
swelling occurs, causing a cloudy
appearance. Abrasions can develop into
ulcers. Viral corneal damage is often
accompanied by sticky conjunctivitis
that can glue the eyelids together.
**Treatment:** Your vet will clean the eyes
and use appropriate antibiotics. Urgent
surgery may be needed to save the eye.

## Cataracts

A cataract is a loss of transparency in
part or all of the lens. A complete
cataract creates a crystalline white lens
with a slight yellow tint. Physical injury
is the most common cause of a single
cataract, while sugar diabetes is the most
common cause of bilateral cataracts.

Cataracts are only removed when
they cause complete blindness.

## Dislodged lenses

Known causes of either partial
(subluxation) or complete (luxation)
lens-position changes include trauma,
from cat fights to road-traffic accidents;
inflammation to the anterior chamber
of the eye; glaucoma; or simply aging.
Surgery is usually needed.

## The iris and anterior chamber

This region of the eye is affected by
several problems, but also by cancer
or infection elsewhere in the body. The
iris appears inflamed (uveitis) and the
pupils may constrict. Symptoms include
red eyes, squinting, avoidance of light,
and production of excess tears.
**Treatment:** Antibiotics and cortisone
may be used to treat uveitis, but the
primary problem must be attended to.

### Age changes the lenses

The lenses focus light onto the surface of the
retina. In youth they are flexible and crystal clear.
With aging they become hardened, hazy, and
blue-gray. This natural change, called sclerosis,
is seen in cats over nine years old. It does not
require any treatment.

## Glaucoma

In a healthy cat, there is a constant, slow
exchange of fluid from inside the eye
into the general circulation. Glaucoma
occurs when this fluid is produced faster
than it is removed, causing a buildup of
pressure in the eye. Symptoms include
squinting, excess tearing, avoidance of
light, and swelling to the eye.
**Treatment:** Surgical removal of the eye
may be necessary.

## Retinal disorders

Progressive retinal atrophy, an inherited
deterioration to the retina, is rare in cats,
but through trauma or disease the retina
may become detached. It can be "spot
welded" back in place by laser surgery.

## Blindness

Blindness can be caused by diabetes;
high blood pressure associated with
kidney, heart, or other systemic illness;
or by eye injuries.

How a cat handles blindness depends
on its personality and on its owners.
Only you, your cat, and your vet can
decide how to manage *your* blind cat.

### Something in the eye

If you see foreign material on your cat's eye, use
your thumb to retract the lid, and flush out any
nonpenetrating foreign objects using tepid water.
Alternatively, moisten a cotton swab and ease the
irritant out. If you can't remove the irritant, use a
bandage or Elizabethan collar to protect the eye
and *seek immediate veterinary attention*.

# Hearing disorders

■ Ear mites are common in young outdoor cats
■ Chronic ear inflammation increases the chances of ear tumors
■ Deafness is inherited in some blue-eyed white cats

Ear conditions are among the most common reasons cat owners visit vets. An affected cat will scratch and shake its head in discomfort. The shape of the ear canal encourages the accumulation of wax and debris that cannot easily be shaken out. Left unattended, a simple external-ear condition can lead to a far more serious inner-ear infection.

**It is normal** for your cat to scratch its ear now and then—it may have an itch. But see your vet if it becomes a frequent or obsessive habit.

## Signs of ear problems

Ear problems may be indicated by:
• Head and ear shaking;
• Scratching one or both ears;
• An unpleasant odor from the ears;
• Yellow, brown, or mahogany-colored ear discharge;
• Inflammation of the ear flap or ear-canal opening;
• Aggression when touched near ears;
• Head tilted to one side;
• Apparent loss of hearing;
• Swelling to an ear flap.

## Ear mites and ear infections

In young cats, otitis (or canker), an inflammation of the skin in the ear, is often caused by ear mites, which are the size of a pinhead, white, and move vigorously when light is shined on them. Some mites live outside the ears and are the source of frequent reinfestations.

Some bacteria take advantage of mite infestations or other causes of ear-canal inflammation. The yeast *Malassezia pachydermatis*, often present in healthy ears but more often seen in inflamed ears, may also be such an opportunist.

Untreated external-ear infection may lead to a ruptured eardrum and middle- or inner-ear infection with associated head tilt or loss of balance.

**Treatment:** Ear mites should be treated with an effective product for at least three weeks. Always treat all your cats (and dogs, rabbits, and ferrets, if you have any). Mites spread very easily.

### Types of ear discharge

Ear mites usually produce a dry, gritty, coffee granule–type substance in the ears. Malassezia wax is usually dark brown and soft. A moist, light yellow, fruity-smelling paste indicates a bacterial infection. Itchiness and redness to the ear flap without discharge is often a sign of allergic otitis.

Your vet will dispense medicine for other causes of ear infection. Take care when using standard ear medicines if the eardrum is ruptured. Certain drugs, such as the antibiotics gentamycin and neomycin, can cause ear-nerve damage.

## Ear tumors

Mature cats often develop gray-blue, blisterlike tumors, which are called ceruminomas, in the ear canal. These may develop after chronic inflammation and often become infected.

**Treatment:** A chronic ear problem may best be solved by surgically altering the ear canal to allow better aeration.

If the eardrum has been ruptured and a chronic middle-ear infection exists, it may be beneficial to remove the entire ear canal and drain the middle ear.

## Middle- or inner-ear infection

Inflammation of the middle or inner ear may lead to fever and loss of balance, along with poor coordination, loss of appetite, and vomiting. It can also lead to vestibular syndrome, which shows similar symptoms but with no fever. These signs—sometimes mistaken for a stroke—often diminish within a week and disappear within a month, but a residual head tilt is not uncommon.

**Treatment:** Symptomatic treatment is given to control nausea and prevent accidental injuries.

Inner-ear infection is treated with antibiotics or, sometimes, surgery.

## Deafness

About 20 percent of white cats, especially those with blue eyes, are born deaf. Deafness may also develop in older cats. For accurate diagnosis, a specialist can carry out a brain-stem auditory-evoked response (BAER) test.

**Handling deafness:** Do not let a deaf cat outdoors; the risks outweigh the benefits. Be patient. Be careful when approaching or waking the cat so it is not startled. Consider getting the cat a hearing companion, even a dog, as a buddy. The deaf cat understands what is happening by watching what the dog does.

| Ear-flap (pinna) conditions | |
|---|---|
| **CONDITION** | **SOLUTION** |
| Hematoma (blood blister) | A hot, soft, fluctuating swelling to the ear flap occurs when a blood vessel breaks and blood accumulates between the skin and the cartilage of the ear. The hematoma is drained and stitched to prevent the ear from refilling with blood. Corticosteroids may also be used. |
| Frostbite | The tips of the ears are most at risk of frostbite. If your cat has been exposed to prolonged cold, dab the ears with lukewarm water. Do not rub them—that will only make them itchier. |
| Sunburn | Cats with white coats are most prone to sunburn, especially in sunny regions. They are also susceptible to skin cancer on their ear tips. Apply a sunblock of SPF 30 or more before letting your cat out in direct sunlight for prolonged periods. |

**Blue-eyed white cats** are the individuals most likely to suffer from congenital deafness.

# Immune-system disorders

- The incidence of allergy appears to be increasing
- FIV and FeLV viruses suppress the immune system
- Vets can help turn the immune system on or off

The immune system, consisting of white blood cells, recognizes and destroys invading microbes and any renegade body cells that have become cancerous. Some feline viruses, such as FIV and FeLV, suppress the immune system's response to challenge. If the immune system is oversensitive or doesn't turn off properly, allergy or autoimmune disease ensue. Allergy is diagnosed with increasing frequency.

## Managing the immune system

Vets can manipulate the immune system through stimulation or suppression.
- Vaccination with a dead or modified germ stimulates the immune system to produce natural antibodies, immunizing against the dangerous variety of that specific germ.
- Vets also suppress the immune system, usually with corticosteroids, when it becomes overactive, as it does in allergic reactions or autoimmune conditions.

## What antibodies are

Antibodies are proteins manufactured by specialized white blood cells. They act like markers, or tags, identifying cells to be dealt with by other cells in the immune system. As temporary protection, mothers pass antibodies to their young in the first milk the kitten consumes (colostrum). Maternal antibodies drop to low levels after a kitten is about 12 weeks old; this is when a kitten needs its final inoculation. Vaccine given too early is nullified by maternal antibodies.

## A poor immune response

The immune system's ability to respond is diminished by the following factors:
- Damage from FIV or FeLV infection;
- The level of virulence of the infectious agent;
- The size of the dose of infectious agent;
- The presence of other illness;
- Poor nutrition;
- Harmful environmental conditions.

**Newborn kittens** are protected from disease by the colostrum (first milk) they get from their mother.

## Immune-complex diseases

For as-yet-unknown reasons, antibodies sometimes combine with antigens to produce "antigen-antibody complexes," or "immune complexes." These get deposited in sites such as joint capsules, the kidneys, or the walls of blood vessels. Affected cats suffer recurring fever, malaise, and loss of appetite, and are treated with corticosteroids.

## Allergy

Allergens provoke the immune system, mistakenly, to respond as it would to disease. In a cat, allergic reactions can occur on the upper lips and chin, causing itchiness; on the lining of the air passages, causing sneezing, coughing, wheezing, or difficulty breathing; or to the lining of the gastrointestinal system, causing vomiting or diarrhea.

Chemicals in insect bites (as in flea saliva), certain foods, drugs, plants and herbs, dust mites, plant pollens, fungal spores, and even our own shedding skin can set off an allergic reaction in your cat.

**Treatment:** Through intensive history-taking, allergy testing using skin tests or blood samples, altered or novel protein diets, or temporary removal of a cat from its normal environment, vets try

| Ask the vet |
| --- |
| **Q:** Do cats suffer from autoimmune disorders? **A:** While conditions such as pemphigus and systemic lupus erythematosus (SLE) have been reported in cats, they remain extremely rare and are not commonly part of a vet's routine initial differential diagnosis. |

to determine the causes of allergies and then recommend avoiding those causes. Finding specific causes is frustratingly difficult. For immediate relief from allergy, vets use drugs such as antihistamines and recommend frequent shampoos. Corticosteroids are often needed to bring immediate relief from asthma. Vets increasingly recommend high-dose essential fatty acid (EFA) supplements *(see pp.200–1)*.

## Is your cat allergic?

If the answer is yes to any of these questions, your cat may be allergic. Talk to your vet about possible solutions.

- Has the problem occurred before?
- Does it occur at certain times?
- Does it occur in a particular place?
- Are the upper lips, chin, or ears involved?
- Does the problem occur at mealtimes?
- Is there a history of allergy in your cat's immediate family?

| Allergic conditions | |
| --- | --- |
| Skin conditions | Contact dermatitis; inhalant allergic dermatitis; food allergy; hives (urticaria). |
| Respiratory conditions | Hay fever (allergic rhinitis); allergic bronchitis; allergic pneumonia; asthma. |
| Gastrointestinal conditions | Allergic gastritis; allergic enteritis; eosinophilic enteritis; allergic colitis. |

### Are you allergic to cats?

Every cat carries a protein called Fel C-1 on its flaking skin and, most particularly, in its saliva. It is this protein that makes allergic people sneeze and wheeze. Every time a cat grooms itself, it is covering itself in this allergen.

We are less likely to be allergic to cats that are damp-sponged twice daily. The damp-sponging reduces the concentration of Fel C-1 that is shed by the cat. Dry, flaky, or oily skin conditions, which are common as cats get older, increase the levels of Fel C-1 that are produced.

# Cancer

- Genetics plays a central role in cancer
- Some viruses are cancer-inducing
- Therapies are improving

Cancer is a common name given to a variety of unrelated diseases with different effects but with a similar and dangerous ability. Cancer cells are not detected by the body's protective DNA-policing enzymes; they can also "trick" the natural killer cells of the immune system into not attacking and destroying them. Having eluded the body's natural defenses, cancer cells embark upon an eternal life of producing countless generations of descendant cancer cells.

## Names are significant

Cancers are dangerous malignant tumors classified according to where they originate.

Carcinomas arise from the tissues that line the internal and external surfaces of a cat's skin and organs, while sarcomas arise from within tissues under the skin, such as muscles, blood vessels, and bones. Lymphomas develop from lymphoid tissue.

A benign tumor is usually, but not always, harmless; it depends where it is located or if it is hormone-producing.

## Genes are at the root of cancers

Some cats have specific cancer-producing genes. In others, the genetic link is more complicated. Individuals may inherit both a cancer-producing gene and a cancer-suppressing gene. It gets more complicated: some cats may also inherit a gene that suppresses the

### Common signs of cancer

The American Veterinary Cancer Society's ten most common signs of cancer are:

1. Abnormal swelling that persists or grows;
2. Sores that do not heal;
3. Weight loss;
4. Loss of appetite;
5. Bleeding or discharge from any body opening;
6. Offensive odor;
7. Difficulty eating or swallowing;
8. Hesitation to exercise, or lack of stamina;
9. Persistent lameness or stiffness;
10. Difficulty in breathing, urinating, or defecating.

cancer-suppressing gene! Regardless of which genes are inherited, they are turned on and off by environmental factors, including ultraviolet light, radiation, various chemicals, and viral infections such as FeLV. In some cats, the minor trauma of an injection may lead to development of a sarcoma at the injection site *(see opposite)*.

**This picture** shows white blood cells that have identified, attacked, and destroyed a renegade cancerous cell.

## Diagnosing cancer

For an accurate diagnosis of cancer, a sample of suspect tissue is necessary. Small tumors should be removed completely, while, for larger ones, your vet may either take a small piece of suspect tissue (a biopsy), or use a needle and syringe to withdraw a sample of cells (a fine-needle aspirate) from the tissue to send to a pathologist.

## Cancers develop later in life

Cancer is a potential problem for cats over seven years old, but some, such as injection-site sarcomas, can occur in younger felines. The earlier the diagnosis, the more promising the outcome. This is one important reason for yearly, preventive veterinary examinations.

## Cancer treatments

• **Surgery:** Surgery is usually the most effective cancer treatment.
• **Radiation therapy:** This is used on local, radiation-sensitive tumors if it has been impossible to remove the mass completely or if the mass is inoperable.
• **Chemotherapy:** Chemotherapy kills fast-multiplying cells, especially when they are spread throughout the body.
• **New treatments:** New chemotherapies include drugs called angiogenesis inhibitors that selectively cut off the blood supply to tumors.
  Immunotherapy stimulates the immune system to attack a tumor.

In gene therapy, a gene rides piggyback on virus particles into cancer cells.
• **Other treatments:** Don't forget two common treatments—pain control and euthanasia. Most vets feel that a cat should not suffer from its therapy. Sometimes the best treatment is simply to regain a good quality of life, even if it means a shorter life expectancy. This is an emotion-laden topic filled with ethical dilemmas. You and your vet must decide what is best for your cat; this may not be what is best for you.

## Preventing cancer

To reduce your cat's risk of cancer:
• Choose parents wisely;
• Protect against FeLV where risk exists;
• Do not overvaccinate against FeLV or rabies;
• Spay females early in life;
• Avoid exposure to known carcinogens;
• Feed a balanced diet with ingredients known to support the immune system;
• Don't let your cat get fat;
• Avoid excess exposure to direct sunlight in white cats;
• Physically examine your cat routinely for lumps and bumps;
• Have routine annual veterinary examinations.

**Injection-site sarcomas**

In some genetically predisposed individuals, the inflammatory response to an injection may evolve into a locally invasive, and very aggressive, tumor called a sarcoma. A sarcoma may occur after any type of skin penetration that causes inflammation, but it occurs most frequently after injection with "adjuvanated" rabies or leukemia vaccine.

In North America, vaccinal sarcomas occur in one to two cats of every 10,000 vaccinated. From an epidemiologist's viewpoint, this is a high incidence. "Non-adjuvanated" vaccine is available and lessens the risk of an injection-site sarcoma.

# Emotional disorders

- Emotion is chemically controlled
- Some vets feel unsure about how to approach problems
- Drugs alone are not sufficient

Feelings like anxiety or worry protect cats from threats and dangers. Anxiety acts like a chemical first-aid kit. The cortex of your cat's brain thinks there is stress, communicates through the limbic system (*see below*) with the rest of the brain, and triggers a series of chemical changes that affects the entire body. However, if these get triggered too easily or last too long, emotional disorders may ensue. When this happens to elderly cats, there is an Alzheimer's-like deterioration in brain function.

## Stress can be good or bad

There is no harm in a cat's experiencing short bouts of stress. However, if stress is prolonged, or if the stress response is constantly and needlessly triggered, this leads to chronic stress and the sustained release of damaging stress chemicals.

## The role of the limbic system

Mind and body meet in the brain's limbic system. This primitive spiderweb of interconnections orchestrates instincts and emotions.

Both the nervous and hormonal systems (*see pp.30–33*) are controlled by the limbic system through its production of chemical messengers (neurotransmitters). The role of neurotransmitters is vital. Serotonin, for example, is important for mood, and decreased levels can lead to depression. Research in dogs suggests confident dogs have good levels of serotonin; cats have yet to be tested.

Mood-altering drugs affect brain chemistry. In cats, playful interactions with people, novel activities, and exercise all affect neurotransmitter levels, behaviors, and emotions.

## General behavior problems

A phobia is an irrational fear. Cats develop rational fears—of veterinary clinics, for example—but also irrational fears of nonthreatening sights, sounds, or situations.

### Stress in indoor cats

Professor Tony Buffington of Ohio State University says we should constantly examine whether we are unwittingly inducing chronic stress in some cats simply by routinely housing them indoors as we do. Living in constant proximity to other cats or being unable to get outdoors and do catlike things can induce chronic and dangerous stress.

### Ask the vet

Q: Can emotional problems be diagnosed in cats?
A: A cat's phobias, anxieties, depression, and grieving have not been considered an integral part of conventional veterinary medicine until recently. As a result, many vets feel unsure about using these terms. We feel more certain about diagnoses when they can be backed up by laboratory tests or technology. Vets with advanced training in behavioral medicine exist both in veterinary schools and in general practice.

Anxiety, part of the natural fight-or-flight response, is normal in many instances but may become irrational—for example, when a possessive cat is anxious if its owner leaves the room.

Restriction or boredom leads to compulsive behavior in which a cat ritually performs a certain activity, such as pacing back and forth or grooming obsessively. An inability to relax or sleep is an extreme form of feline anxiety.

Depression is difficult to diagnose in cats. It may manifest itself in a decreased or, less frequently, increased appetite, clinging or remote behavior, irritability, or lethargy. Grieving, a combination of depression and sadness, occurs in cats when an important member of their family dies or leaves.
**Treatments:** Sedatives are commonly used to tranquilize anxious cats. The antianxiety drug diazepam is now used less frequently because it is known to be associated with liver problems.

Increasingly, feline emotional disorders are treated with a combination of environmental enrichment, training, and newer mood-altering drugs. Drugs such as buspirone and amitriptyline, developed to treat anxiety, depression, and obsessive-compulsive disorders in people, are commonly used. A typical drug may raise serotonin levels. This can have a profound and not always anticipated effect on a cat's behavior.

Note that behavioral therapy and environmental enrichment are also vital. Drugs alone do not cure emotional problems.

### Age-related behavior problems

Cats display the same signs of senile dementia as humans. A typical age-related change in cats is standing at the wrong place when they want to go in or out. Some cats seemingly forget why they are where they are, while others wail and meow plaintively. This can be associated with loss of litter training.
**Treatments:** Routine, daily mental stimulation is beneficial. Play with your cat with new toys. Hand-feed an elderly cat. Touch the cat if it wants touch.

If your cat is having senior moments, check its behavior with your vet to eliminate other medical explanations.

Some aspects of aging are irreversible, but others can be delayed, even reversed, with effective intervention on your part.

**As for many humans,** touch is an important part of coping with emotional disorders. Feeling loved and worthy of attention helps lift the cat's spirits.

# Geriatric conditions

- Each body cell has its own life expectancy
- Aging is a natural occurrence, not a disease
- Aging changes can be slowed, sometimes arrested

One in three cats is geriatric and, therefore, susceptible to age-related medical conditions. Old age brings with it a variety of medical conditions. It also brings many age-related changes that can be slowed down through your intervention.

Disease control, good nutrition, and successful veterinary work mean that more and more cats are living into their late teens. However, increased life expectancy and the consequent rise in the incidence of debilitating geriatric conditions raise difficult ethical issues. How far should we go in treating an inevitable age-related medical condition?

## The immune system is vital

Aging is not an illness. With increasing age, a cat's body simply does not work as well as it once did. As the clarity of vision or the acuity of hearing diminishes, so does the efficiency of the immune system. For instance, it may fail to detect a cell that duplicated incorrectly. This is why tumors, both

malignant and benign, tend to be age-related problems.

## A biological clock is at work

Every cell in your cat's body has a built-in biological clock that determines how long it will live.

Some cells—for example, those lining the intestines—are replaced at least once a week, but this ability to create new cells eventually falters and is no longer as efficient, fast, or accurate as it once was.

Other cells—for example, brain cells—do not replace themselves. A cat has its maximum allocation when it is young. As these cells die, they are not replaced.

Inefficient replacement and no replacement create most of the medical conditions that are associated with aging.

## The importance of preventive checkups

With any age-related condition, the earlier it is diagnosed, the easier and cheaper it is to treat. Annual health examinations by your vet are vital.

From 10 years of age, arrange for your cat to have annual, full, senior-citizen preventive checkups.

### Age conversion chart

| HUMAN YEARS | CAT YEARS |
|---|---|
| 1 | 12 |
| 2 | 20 |
| 3 | 28 |
| 4 | 36 |
| 5 | 40 |
| 6 | 44 |

and so on, in steps of four cat years per human year.

## Diminished sight and hearing

Every cat over 10 years old develops sclerosis to the lenses *(see p.267)*. This eventually leads to a cat's having trouble seeing a mouse in front of its nose, but it may be able to see movement, especially at a distance. Impaired hearing may also develop and full hearing loss may occur rapidly over a relatively short period.

Maintaining a constant environment and daily activity patterns is very helpful.

## Behavior changes

Older cats sleep more and take more time to remember who, what, when, and where, when they wake up. It's no surprise, then, that they hate changes to their routines. You can slow down brain deterioration in your cat by creating appealing mental activities.

**Older cats tend to** sleep longer hours and be slightly confused upon waking. At this time in their lives, a stable environment is essential.

## Dry, dandruffy coats

Older cats have more difficulty—or less enthusiasm for—grooming their coats than they did when they were younger. Make sure you groom your cat more frequently.

## Bad breath

Gum infections and associated bad breath are the most common problems in older cats. To prevent this, your vet might suggest you try giving your cat chicken necks or wings to chew on and increasing your cat's dental hygiene by brushing its teeth and gums.

## Poor kidney filtration

Kidney inefficiency is the most common metabolic failure in older cats, which drink and urinate more. A diet low in phosphorus (see your vet) will increase life expectancy by an average of a year.

## Constipation and gas

Older cats are more likely to become constipated or pass more wind.

Feeding a moist, balanced, high-fiber diet that promotes the growth of non-gas-forming bacteria may control these problems. Ensure your cat exercises and drinks plenty of water. *At the first sign of constipation, see your vet.*

## Painful joints

Medicine alone cannot cure painful degenerative joint disease; weight reduction is also vital.

Try to stop your cat from jumping, and add an essential fatty acid (EFA) supplement to its diet.

## Lack of strength

Many of the natural changes of aging cause less nourishment to reach the muscles. A highly digestible diet with added vitamins and antioxidants is vital. Talk to your vet about medicines that increase oxygen in the bloodstream.

## Loss of litter training

Older cats are more likely to avoid the litter box than younger ones. Always ensure that litter boxes are easily reached, and keep them clean and filled with your cat's favorite litter.

# The end of a cat's life

- We make decisions on their behalf
- It is normal to grieve
- A new cat will be happy to fill your emotional void

Youth has its appeal, but it is impossible not to develop deep respect for elderly cats. With their natural dignity and poise, they are wonderful role models for us in how we should approach our own advancing years. If an elderly cat fails an attempt to jump, it just picks itself up and gets on with life. Elderly cats do what you and I are told to do but find so difficult, if not impossible. They do not look back on what they once could do, but rather concentrate on what they are now capable of.

**The dignified older cat** will not waste time trying to get onto its favorite old couch if it can no longer jump: it will simply find a new place to snooze.

## A hard decision

Many, if not most, of you will eventually decide, with the help of your vet, what is in your elderly cat's best interests. Thirty years ago a New York vet, Dr. Bernard Hershhorn, suggested that dog owners ask themselves these questions. They are just as relevant to cat owners today.

- Is the condition prolonged, recurring, or worsening?
- Is the condition no longer responding to therapy?
- Is your cat in physical or mental pain?
- Is it no longer possible to alleviate that pain or suffering?
- If your cat recovers, is it likely to be chronically ill, invalid, or unable to care for itself?
- If your cat recovers, will there be severe personality changes?

If the answer to all these questions is yes, then euthanasia is the honest, simple, and humane option. However, if you answered no to several of those questions, ask yourself:

- Can I provide the necessary care?
- Will providing this care seriously interfere with, or create serious problems for, myself and my family?
- Will the cost of treatment be unbearably expensive?

Your cat is a member of your family and, as such, any decisions should be family decisions.

## A release from suffering

These are valid reasons for euthanasia:

- Overwhelming physical injury;
- Irreversible disease that has progressed to a point where distress or discomfort cannot be controlled;
- Old-age wear and tear that permanently affects the quality of life;

## Euthanasia

Euthanasia means voluntarily ending the life of an individual who is suffering from a terminal illness or other incurable condition. The word comes from the Greek *eu* (meaning "good") and *thanatos* ("death")—a good death.

- Physical injury, disease, or wear and tear resulting in permanent loss of control of body functions;
- The carrying of untreatable disease dangerous to humans.

### The process of euthanasia

The anesthetic drug phenobarb is the most commonly used euthanasia agent. It is given intravenously in a more concentrated form than is used for anesthesia. Within seconds the cat loses consciousness, and within another few seconds the heart stops. Depending on the circumstances, a sedative may be given before the barbiturate.

**Afterward:** While brain death occurs within seconds, there is continuing electrical activity in muscles for several minutes. This may cause muscle twitches. If the respiratory muscles are affected there can be a reflex gasp, as if a cat were still alive. Reflex muscle activity may occur up to ten minutes after death.

Where I practice, all bodies are routinely cremated unless owners prefer burial. Bodies are kept in cold storage until they are collected.

If you bury a cat, make sure it is enclosed in biodegradable, not synthetic, material. A grave should be deep enough so that wild animals cannot dig it up. This usually means about 3 ft (1 meter).

### Grieving is normal

Nonpet owners might find it difficult to understand how awful it can be when a cat with which you share your home dies. We can feel embarrassed that the death of a cat triggers such raw emotion, but feelings of bereavement when a cat dies are normal. Anger, denial, anxiety… all the emotions we experience when we lose a human friend are part of the grieving process.

Most vets have experienced all these feelings themselves when their own pets died. If you are an average cat owner, the stages of grief, from disbelief through to resolution, typically evolve for almost a year. And while the vet may have to cope with the initial emotionally charged stages of anger and denial, I think I speak for virtually all vets when I say I receive far more letters of thanks in a single year for ending lives properly than I have had in all my years in practice for saving lives.

### Should I get another cat?

Cat owners often say the loss of a feline companion is too hard to bear. Yet within a year, most decide that living without a cat just doesn't feel right.

The universal value of cats is that the qualities of our previous cat can be found in all others: dignity, beauty, independence, self-control, constancy, and companionship.

Each cat is unique, but when a feline gap opens in your home there are countless, often needy individuals capable, willing, and pleased to fill it.

**It is quite normal** to want another cat after a much-loved pet has passed away.

# Glossary

**Abscess** A localized pocket of infection in body tissues.

**Anemia** Reduced red blood cells or a reduction in oxygen-carrying pigment (hemoglobin), associated with blood loss, bone marrow suppression, parasites, or immune-mediated disease that destroys red blood cells.

**Anaphylactic shock** An exaggerated, life-threatening allergic response to foreign protein or other substances.

**Antibody** Protein produced by specialized white blood cells in response to certain antigens. Antibody binds to antigen, a fundamental act of immunity.

**Antigen** Any agent capable of inducing a specific immune response.

**Ascites** The accumulation or exudation of fluid in the abdominal cavity. *See also* Exudate.

**Ataxia** A lack of muscle coordination.

**Atopy** Allergy to external allergens such as pollens.

**Atrophy** Wasting.

**Autoimmune disease** Any condition in which the body's immune system erroneously attacks normal body parts.

**Aversion therapy** Treatment of a behavior problem involving the use of mild physical or mental discomfort.

**Benign tumor** A local tumor that does not spread.

**Caesarean section** The surgical opening of the uterus to deliver full-term kittens.

**Castration** Usually refers to the surgical removal of the testicles in males (in law it

may refer to the sterilization of both male and female).

**Clinical signs** What you observe your cat doing.

**Clinical symptoms** How your cat is feeling.

**Colostrum** The first milk produced just after birth, containing passive protection against a variety of infectious diseases.

**Concussion** An unconscious state, lasting from seconds to minutes, that kills brain cells.

**Congenital** A condition present at birth; congenital conditions may or may not be hereditary.

**Corticosteroid** Any of the hormones produced by the adrenal cortex (outer layer of the adrenal gland).

**Crepitus** Dry, grating sound when a joint extends or flexes.

**Cryosurgery** Destruction of cells through freezing.

**CT scan** Computed tomography using X-rays to scan the body.

**Cyanosis** Purple-blue color to mucous membranes, caused by lack of oxygen.

**Cystocentesis** Removal of a sample of urine via a fine needle inserted through the abdominal wall into the bladder.

**Cytology** Examination of body cells under a microscope.

**Dehydration** Loss of the natural level of liquid in body tissue.

**Diabetes insipidus** Deficiency in a pituitary hormone (antidiuretic hormone or ADH) that controls urine concentration in the kidneys.

**Diabetes mellitus, or sugar diabetes** High blood sugar, either because of a lack of insulin production or because body tissue cannot absorb circulating insulin.

**Dislocation** The separation of a bone from its adjoining bone at a joint, often involving ligament tears; may be complete (luxation) or partial (subluxation).

**Dyspnea** Difficulty breathing.

**Dystocia** Difficulty in labor.

**Dysuria** Difficulty urinating.

**Echocardiography** Imaging of the heart using sound waves bounced off the interior and exterior of the heart, then visualized on a monitor.

**Edema** Excessive accumulation of fluid in body tissue; swelling.

**Electrocardiogram (ECG)** Record of the electrical activity in the heart.

**ELISA testing** Enzyme-linked immunosorbent assay; a test used to detect or measure levels of an antigen or antibody.

**Emphysema** Pathological accumulation of air in tissues.

**Endocrine gland** A gland that manufactures hormones and secretes them directly into the bloodstream.

**Endorphin** Naturally occurring brain chemical that diminishes pain perception.

**Endoscope** An instrument for viewing the inside of an area of the body.

**Eosinophils** White blood cells that increase in the presence of internal parasites and allergy.

**Epilepsy** A disturbance in electrical activity in the brain that causes a seizure.

**Essential fatty acids** Fatty acids that cannot be synthesized by the body and that must be acquired from the diet.

**Estrous cycle** The female reproductive cycle.

**Euthanasia** The painless termination of life; may be active (by giving a substance that causes death) or passive (by withdrawing medical support that sustains life).

**Exclusion diet** A diet that excludes all components of any previous diet, usually consisting of novel sources of protein, fat, and carbohydrate.

**Exudate** Fluid that has escaped from blood vessels and deposited either in or on tissues.

**Feline immunodeficiency virus (FIV)** A relative of the HIV virus, which weakens the immune system, causing death. Highly contagious to other cats, but not to humans or other animals.

**Feline infectious peritonitis (FIP)** A viral disease that is usually fatal. Symptoms include fluid accumulation in the abdomen, jaundice, and anemia.

**Feline leukemia virus (FeLV)** A virus affecting the lymphatic system, suppressing immunity to disease.

**Free radicals** Naturally occurring atoms that destroy cells.

**Genetic disease** A medical condition known to be transmitted to an animal through a parent's genes.

**Gingivitis** Inflammation of the gums.

**Glaucoma** Increased fluid pressure inside the eye.

**Hematoma** A blood-filled swelling under the skin.

**Hematuria** Blood in urine.

**Hypersensitivity** An exaggerated immune response to a foreign agent.

**Hypoglycemia** Reduction in blood sugar.

**Idiopathic disease** A condition of which the cause is unknown.

**Immune-mediated disease** A condition caused by an overreaction of the immune system.

**Incubation period** The time between exposure to a disease-producing agent and the development of clinical signs of disease.

**-itis** An inflammation; for example, nephritis is an inflammation of the kidneys.

**Jacobson's organ** *See* Vomeronasal organ.

**Jaundice** A yellow pigmentation of the mucous membranes or skin, usually associated with liver disease.

**Keratoconjunctivitis** Inflamed cornea and conjunctiva.

**Ketoacidosis** Buildup of ketone bodies in the circulation as a result of kidney failure.

**Laparotomy** The surgical opening of the abdominal cavity.

**Laser** Light amplification by stimulated emission of radiation; a concentrated beam of light used as a tool in surgery.

**Lesion** A change to body tissue caused by disease or trauma.

**Limbic system** Brain system that is in control of the nervous and hormonal systems.

**Lipoma** A benign tumor of fat, particularly common in older, overweight large breeds.

**Luxation** *See* Dislocation.

**Macrophages** Large white blood cells that consume debris.

**Magnetic resonance imaging (MRI)** Diagnostic imaging showing detailed cross-sections of the internal anatomy of structures such as joints or the brain; particularly useful for brain scans.

**Malabsorption** A condition in which insufficient amounts of nutrients are absorbed into the circulation from the small intestines.

**Malignant tumor** A tumor that has the capacity either to invade the tissue that surrounds it or to spread via the blood or lymphatic circulation to other parts of the body, such as the lungs or the liver.

**Melena** Black, tarlike diarrhea containing old blood.

**Meninges** Protective membranes surrounding the brain.

**Metastasis** Spread of cancer cells from the area of origin to other parts of the body.

**Mucosa** Another name for the mucous membranes, which line the hollow body structures such as the mouth and the small intestines.

**Mucus** Clear, lubricating secretion produced by cells in mucous membranes.

**Myelogram** X-ray of the spinal cord after the injection of contrast material (a substance opaque to X-rays).

**Myocarditis** Inflammation of the heart muscle.

**Necrosis** Cell death.

**Neoplasia** Cancerous cell growth, which may be benign or malignant.

**Nephritis** Inflammation of the kidneys.

**Nictitating membrane** Third eyelid.

**NSAID** Nonsteroidal anti-inflammatory drug; this group of drugs includes carprofen and meloxicam.

**Off-label use of drugs** Therapeutic use of a drug in a species or for a purpose for which it is not licensed.

**Ovariohysterectomy** Removal of the ovaries and uterus, the normal spaying procedure.

**Oxalate** Mineral sediment of stones produced in the bladder, as in "calcium oxalate."

**Palliative treatment** Therapy that improves comfort but does not cure.

**Paresis** An incomplete form of paralysis.

**Perianal** Meaning "around the anus."

**Perineal** Referring to the area between the anus and the genitals.

**Periodontal** Around or near the tooth.

**Peritonitis** Inflammation of the lining of the abdominal cavity.

**Pica** An appetite for unnatural and potentially dangerous substances.

**Pinna** The ear flap.

**Pituitary gland** The "master gland" at the base of the brain, controlling all other hormone-producing glands and controlled by the hypothalamus (an area at the base of the brain).

**Pneumothorax** Loss of negative pressure in the chest cavity, causing the lungs to collapse.

**Polydactyly** Any number of toes above five on each paw.

**Polydypsia** Excessive thirst.

**Polyphagia** Excessive hunger.

**Polyuria** Excessive urinating.

**Prostaglandins** Naturally occurring fatty acid substances with varied functions, including regulation of acid secretion in the stomach and control of inflammation.

**Pyo-** Pus-related, as in "pyometra" (a pus-filled womb) or "pyoderma" (purulent skin disease).

**Queen** Unspayed female cat.

**Regurgitation** Backward flow: for example, regurgitated food comes from the esophagus (as distinct from vomit, which comes from the stomach); regurgitated blood flows back from the heart's ventricles to the atria.

**Rex** Term for any mutation causing a curly coat. Also referred to as rexing.

**Sebaceous gland** Oil-producing skin gland that adds water-proofing to the coat.

**Seborrhea** An increased activity of the skin's oil-producing sebaceous glands.

**Seizure** Abnormal electrical activity in the brain that causes unusual nervous responses; also known as a convulsion.

**Septicemia** Bacterial infection in the blood circulation.

**Shock** A life-threatening emergency in which the cardiovascular system fails, causing physical collapse, rapid pulse, and pale mucous membranes.

**Stenosis** The narrowing of a passageway, as in "windpipe stenosis."

**Stomatitis** Inflammation of the mucosa of the mouth.

**Struvite** A mineral sand or sediment, otherwise called triple phosphate or magnesium ammonium phosphate hexahydrate, found in the bladder.

**Subluxation** See Dislocation.

**Synovial fluid** Lubricating joint fluid.

**Testosterone** Male sex hormone.

**Thrombus** A blood clot.

**Thyroid gland** The largest endocrine glands in the cat's body, producing hormones vital for growth and metabolism.

**Tomcat** Unneutered male cat.

**Torsion** Twisting.

**Transudate** Fluid passed through a tissue membrane or extruded from tissue.

**Tumor** Also called a neoplasm, a lump or bump, caused by multiplying cells, that can be benign or malignant.

**Ulcer** A lesion where surface tissue has been lost through damage or disease.

**Uremia** Buildup of waste in the blood as a consequence of kidney failure.

**Uroliths** Stones in the bladder.

**Vomeronasal organ** A sensory organ in the nasal cavity that analyzes smells and tastes. Also known as Jacobson's organ.

**Zoonoses** Diseases transmissible between animals and humans.

# Useful contacts

### General Veterinary Associations

*These websites contain general information on both cat care and the practice of veterinary medicine*

**American Animal Hospital Association**
www.healthypet.com

**American Veterinary Medical Association**
Tel: (847) 925-8070; www.avma.org

**Canadian Veterinary Medical Association**
Tel: (613) 236 1162; www.cvma-acmv.org

### Specialty Veterinary Associations

**American Association of Feline Practitioners**
Tel: (615) 259-7788, (800) 204-3514
www.aafponline.org

**American Board of Veterinary Practitioners**
Tel: (615) 254-3687; www.abvp.com

**Veterinary Cancer Society**
Tel: (619) 460-2002; www.vetcancersociety.org

### Breed Registries in the US and Canada

**American Association of Cat Enthusiasts (AACE)**
Tel: (973) 335-6717; www.aaceinc.org

**American Cat Association (ACA)**
Tel: (818) 781-5656; Fax: (818) 781-5340

**American Cat Fanciers Association (ACFA)**
Tel: (417) 725-1530
www.acfacat.com

**Canadian Cat Association (CCA)**
Tel: (905) 459-1481; www.cca-afc.com

**Cat Fanciers' Association (CFA)**
Tel: (732) 528-9797
www.cfainc.org

**Cat Fanciers' Federation (CFF)**
Tel: (937) 787-9009; www.cffinc.org

**The International Cat Association (TICA)**
Tel: (956) 428-8046; www.tica.org

**Traditional Cat Association, Inc. (TCA)**
www.traditionalcats.com
www.siamesecats.org

**United Feline Organization (UFO)**
Tel: (941) 753-8637; Fax: (941) 753-0043
http://unitedfelineorganization.org/UFO.html

### Welfare, Research, and Special Interest

**Alley Cat Allies**
*A nonprofit-making organization promoting sterilization of feral cats, rather than euthanasia*
Tel: (202) 667-3630; www.alleycat.org

**AltVetMed**
*Dedicated to complementary, alternative, and holistic veterinary medicine*
www.altvetmed.com

**ASPCA—American Society for the Prevention of Cruelty to Animals**
Tel: (212) 876-7700; www.aspca.org

**Cats International**
*Free answers to all your cat-behavior questions*
www.catsinternational.org

**The Delta Society**
*Society that researches the effects of animals in human well-being*
Tel: (425) 226-7357; www.deltasociety.org

**The Humane Society of the United States**
www.hsus.org

**National Association of Professional Pet Sitters**
www.petsitters.org

**The Vaccine-Associated Feline Sarcoma Task Force**
*Facilitates investigation, treatment, and prevention of injection-site sarcomas*
www.avma.org/vafstf/default.asp

**The Winn Feline Foundation, Inc.**
*The health-research arm of the Cat Fanciers' Association*
www.winnfelinehealth.org

For cat information and links to other websites:
www.lib.uoguelph.ca/veterinary/vetfile

# Index

# Acknowledgments

## Author's acknowledgments

The speed of change in medical knowledge is great. Not only are treatments changing, so too are diseases. For example, only 25 years ago an overactive thyroid problem was unheard of in cats. Today this is the most common hormonal condition in felines. This rapid change means that us practicing vets need help from our peers to keep up with evolving conditions, diagnoses, treatments, nutrition, and methods of training. Many organizations help but three in particular—the Feline Advisory Bureau (FAB) in the UK, and the American College of Veterinary Internal Medicine (ACVIM) and American Association of Feline Practitioners (AAFP) in North America—provide people like me with the type of practical information we need. I'm grateful to the vets who speak at their meetings and write in the publications.

This book has been a pleasure to write, simply because the team at Sands Publishing Solutions has been so wonderful. Simon Murrell is a first-class designer, and David and Sylvia Tombesi-Walton are dream editors and knowledgeable cat owners, the perfect combination for a book such as this. Thanks team.

## Packager's acknowledgments

Sands Publishing Solutions would like to thank the following people for their participation in this project: Hilary Bird for the index; Samantha J. Elmhurst and Debbie Maizels for artworks; and John and Fiona Martin for allowing us to photograph Gromit the cat. A special thanks also goes to Bruce Fogle for always being graciously available despite being busy at his practice, and for enlivening meetings with tales of his four-legged friends.

## Picture credits

The publisher would like to thank the following for their kind permission to reproduce their photographs:
(**Key:** t=top, b=bottom, r=right, l=left, c=center)

1 Getty Images/Martin Rogers; 2–3 Bruce Coleman Ltd/Kim Taylor; 3 Corbis/Julie Habel (bl); 4–5 Getty Images/Desmond Burdon; 6–7 Getty Images/Arthur Tilley; 7 Corbis/Peter Johnson (bl); 8–9 Getty Images/G.K. & Vikki Hart; 10–11 Getty Images; 12 Getty Images/Bill Ling (tl); 12–13 Getty Images/Malcolm Piers; 14 Corbis Stock Market/Lester Lefkowitz; 21 Getty Images/Alan & Sandy Carey; 22 The Art Archive/Eileen Tweedy; 23 Bruce Coleman Ltd/Rita Meyer (t); 39 Science Photo Library/National Cancer Institute; 44 Bruce Coleman Ltd/Jane Burton; 45 Science Photo Library/NIBSC (tl); 49 Getty Images/G.K. & Vikki Hart; 53 Tetsu Yamazaki (t); 64 Chanan Photography (cl), (cr), (bl); 65 Chanan Photography (br), Tetsu Yamazaki (bl); 70 Chanan Photography (c); 74 Tetsu Yamazaki (b); 78 Tetsu Yamazaki (cr), (bl); 80 Tetsu Yamazaki (cr), (bl); 83 Chanan Photography (cr), (bl); 84 Tetsu Yamazaki (c), (bl); 85 Tetsu Yamazaki (c), (bl); 87 Chanan Photography (cr), Tetsu Yamazaki (bl); 88 Tetsu Yamazaki (c), (bl); 93 Chanan Photography (cr), (bl); 98 Tetsu Yamazaki (cr), (bl); 111 Tetsu Yamazaki (cl), (cr), (bl); 112 Tetsu Yamazaki (cr), (bl); 114 Chanan Photography (cr), (bl); 115 Tetsu Yamazaki (cr), (bl); 118 Tetsu Yamazaki (cr), (bl); 125 Chanan Photography (cr), (bl); 127 Chanan Photography (bl), Tetsu Yamazaki (cr); 131 Getty Images/Steven W Jones; 132 FLPA /Gerard Lacz; 134 FLPA/Martin Withers; 137 Bruce Coleman Ltd/Robert Maier (t), Barrie Watts (b); 152 Ardea London Ltd/John Daniels (bl); 157 Ardea London Ltd/John Daniels (t); 161 Warren Photographic (t); 163 Corbis Stock Market/David Woods; 166 Ardea London Ltd/John Daniels; 167 NHPA/Jane Knight; 171 Ardea London Ltd/John Daniels; 176 Getty Images/Stacey Green (tr); 182 Animal Photography/Sally Anne Thompson; 183 Bruce Coleman Ltd/Hans Reinhard (br); 191 Ardea London Ltd/John Daniels; 193 Ardea London Ltd/Johan de Meester (br); 209 Corbis Stock Market/Roy Morsch; 211 RSPCA/Angela Hampton; 230 Sands Publishing Solutions/Simon Murrell; 235 Science Photo Library/K.H. Kjeldsen; 237 Sylvia Cordaiy Photo Library Ltd/Mary Heys; 238 RSPCA; 239 RSPCA; 245 FLPA/Panda Photo bl; 230 Sands Publishing Solutions/Simon Murrell; 250 Sylvia Cordaiy Photo Library Ltd; 252 www.ThePetCentre.com (cl); 257 www.ThePetCentre.com (br); 257 RSPCA/Angela Hampton (tl); 259 Bruce Coleman Ltd/Hans Reinhard; 260 Sylvia Cordaiy Photo Library Ltd/James de Bouneviale; 262 Bruce Coleman Ltd/Harald Lange; 263 www.ThePetCentre.com (tl), (tr); 265 Bruce Coleman Ltd/Jane Burton; 266 RSPCA/Andrew Forsyth; 272 Science Photo Library/J.C. Revy; 274 Oxford Scientific Films/Sydney Thompson/AA; 277 RSPCA/Angela Hampton; 278 Sylvia Cordaiy Photo Library Ltd/Monika Smith.

All other images © Dorling Kindersley; for further information see www.dkimages.com